The Prevention
of Youthful Crime:
**The Great Stumble
Forward**

Methuen: Canadian Sociology

The Other Canadians: Profiles of Six Minorities
Morris Davis, Joseph F. Krauter

Violence in Canada
Mary Alice Beyer Gammon

The Prevention of Youthful Crime:
The Great Stumble Forward
James C. Hackler

Minority Canadians: Ethnic Groups
Joseph F. Krauter, Morris Davis

An Introduction to Criminal Law
Graham Parker

The Prevention of Youthful Crime: The Great Stumble Forward

James C. Hackler
University of Alberta

Methuen
Toronto London New York Sydney

Canadian Cataloguing in Publication Data

Hackler, James C., 1930-
The prevention of youthful crime

Bibliography: p.
Includes index.
ISBN 0-458-93180-2

1. Juvenile delinquency—Canada—Prevention.
I. Title.

HV9108.H32 364.36′0971 C78-001077-9

1 2 3 4 5 82 81 80 79 78

Printed and bound in Canada

Contents

Acknowledgements

Many people influenced and assisted me during the writing of this book. Particular appreciation goes to Joan Brockman, who read and commented on several versions of the manuscript. Hans Mohr and John Klein provided particularly helpful comments. Karol Krotki, Leah Lambert, Tony Parlett, Brian Murphy, Paul Gendreau, Irvin Waller and helpful criticisms by reviewers broadened my horizons considerably, though I neglected to follow many of their suggestions.

Students pointed out flaws in earlier versions of the manuscript, including Roy Hagen, Neil Warner, Sandie Allen, Lorne Gibson, Dave McGuire, and Dennis Ternes. The editorial staff of Methuen and my wife Bunny Hackler helped me to resist those tedious phrases academics like to employ. Ilze Hobin and Beverly Whiting put considerable work into the charts and typing.

Some authors give credit to many others while taking any blame for faults that appear in their work. I am of a less magnanimous nature, but I would have difficulty distributing the blame among all those who have influenced my thinking and helped with this enterprise. Therefore, I have no choice but to accept the responsibility for the deficiencies in this work.

Foreword

Originally, the goal of this book was to discuss an issue that has been neglected in Canada. It soon became clear, however, that the problems of developing meaningful strategies in response to youthful crime cuts across national borders. While there are some differences between the Canadian and the American scene, almost all of the issues discussed here apply to both countries. It is to be hoped that the person reading this book in the United States or England will appreciate the references to Canadian sources. At times an American reference would be more appropriate, but the goal here is not to use big name authorities to convince the reader that a particular argument is correct. In fact, I am skeptical about the correctness of most arguments. Instead, I strive to provide a variety of perspectives. Hence, bringing less known Canadian studies to the attention of the public seems to be a justifiable bias.

This book is also a reaction against some of the general anthologies on criminology that have appeared in Canada. Since there is a shortage of scholars in criminology in Canada, books on specific topics within criminology might utilize their talents more effectively than do the wider ranging anthologies. It is difficult to prepare a balanced text on Canadian crime or delinquency because of the unevenness of Canadian scholarship in these areas. Some pioneer work on sex offenses has been done by Hans Mohr, Alex Gigeroff and others at the Clarke Institute of Psychiatry in Toronto. The drug research done by Reginald Smart and Paul Whitehead is an example of a significant contribution by an interdisciplinary team. Psychiatrist Bruno Cormier and sociologists Denis Szabo and André Normandeau of Montreal have frequently cooperated in projects that cut across disciplines and cultures. John Hogarth and John Hagan have made unique contributions to our understanding of criminal justice systems, but there are many specialties within criminology where Canadian contributions are negligible. Hence, collections of

Canadian articles, particularly those that make extensive efforts to avoid using American sources, are frequently limited.

This book does not attempt to deal with all aspects of delinquency. For example, it deliberately neglects theories of delinquency causation. These are well covered in the American and English literature, and there is little reason to believe that there is a theory of delinquency unique to Canada. Instead, I focus on policy questions. Many of us want to know, "What can we do?" The approach offered here is admittedly modest and cautious but, I hope, realistic. The book tries to encourage Canadian policy makers, and those in other parts of the world, to avoid some of the less profitable activities connected with the operation and evaluation of delinquency prevention programs and to avoid repeating mistakes already made elsewhere.

James C. Hackler
Edmonton, Alberta.

Chapter 1

Setting the Stage

A man should never put on his best trousers when he goes out to battle for freedom and truth.

—HENRIK IBSEN

The Prevention of Youthful Crime: Progress or Confusion

The reader of this book may wonder at times whether it is about: 1) the prevention of delinquency, 2) the evaluation of delinquency prevention programs, or 3) why it is so difficult both to evaluate programs and to launch them. The first topic makes little sense without the second, and the second cannot be appreciated without the third. My goal is to discuss the prevention of youthful crime, but I believe a more meaningful discussion will result if the problem is approached in a somewhat indirect manner. One reason for this approach is that there has been an increased interest in the evaluation of programs that attempt to change people. This interest in evaluation influences the programs themselves.

The evaluation boom

In addition to the increased demand on the part of various agencies that delinquency prevention programs be evaluated, there have been a number of books and articles in the past ten years on techniques for doing evaluation research. These range from encyclopedic works such as the two-volume *Handbook of Evaluation Research* (Struening and Guttentag, 1975) to smaller guidebooks (Weidman *et al.*, 1975). This book is not primarily concerned with advising researchers on how to conduct evaluations. True, it describes pitfalls and indirectly suggests some ways to avoid them, but the goal is to cast doubt on some of our evaluation strategies rather than to improve techniques.

Others share my skepticism about traditional evaluation procedures and have been offering alternate strategies for assessing the impact of various programs (Weiss, 1970; Deutscher, 1974). I touch on alternate evaluation strategies, but my major point is that it might be wiser *not* to conduct evaluations except under special circumstances. This stand has brought shrieks of horror from scholars who specialize in evaluating programs and from policy makers who feel they need to know which programs work. However, it is important to ask if we do not actually create additional problems by launching certain types of programs and then make things even worse by evaluating them. There is a growing literature suggesting different ways of doing evaluations, but it is rare to focus on the negative aspects of evaluation and conclude that they might outweigh any advantages.

In a discussion of some of the contradictions involved in the evaluation of volunteer court counselors and volunteers in probation, Hans Mattick and Broderick Reischl (1975) point out that the basic conditions for evaluative research did not exist in the various courts and volunteer programs they visited. Even if evaluation were possible, it would lead to a situation where one program would likely suffer at the expense of another. Theoretically, this would be fine; one simply eliminates the less effective program. But let us assume that a volunteer probation officer program demonstrates greater success than regular probation practices. Would this damage relationships within the justice system? If these programs are to survive, it may not be efficiency nor effectiveness that is important, but acceptance by the administrators and personnel of the court. Mattick and Reischl conclude that evaluation is largely superfluous, and possibly disturbing, to these relationships.

A major theme in this book simply extends their reasoning. In most deliquency prevention programs, evaluation probably adds little useful knowledge while posing threats to the organizational relationships necessary for innovative programming.

Some Negative Aspects of Intellectual Debate

Most people would agree that constant debate on social issues is desirable. However, certain features of this debate may be counterproductive. Supposedly debate leads to an exchange of ideas, but frequently the result is a drawing of battle lines on the basis of ideology. Merton (1972) describes a typical situation:

> Under conditions of acute conflict, each hostile camp develops highly selective perceptions of what is going on in the other. . . . Each group becomes less and less motivated to examine the ideas of the other. . . . The members of each group then scan the outgroup's writings just enough to find ammunition for new fusillades.
>
> The process of increased selective inattention to ideas of the other produces rigidified all-or-none doctrines. . . . In the midst of such polarized social conflict, there is little room for the third party [who is] uncommitted in the domain of knowledge to, for them, situationally irrelevant group loyalties, who try to convert that conflict into intellectual criticism (1972: 40).

Under these conditions the goal is not the search for knowledge but winning the debate. This characteristic is not limited to fringe groups in criminology, but also influences the thinking of many otherwise reasonable scholars. For example, some criminologists automatically react emotionally to any mention of radical ideas that call for a complete restructuring of society. Similarly, other criminologists cannot bring themselves to share in a discussion of biological variables. This infighting leads to a parochialism that has limited the contribution of many fine minds. In addition, identification with certain ideological perspectives has influenced career opportunities. Whether this has been advantageous or disadvantageous for the individuals concerned is difficult to say, but the flow of information between academics and policy makers has probably been hindered by this polarization.

This tendency to become committed to an ideology influences delinquency prevention programs by making it difficult for agencies to consider possibilities that do not conform to specific ideological preconceptions. The camps and ideologies that develop at the academic level also exist at the agency level, even though the battle lines are drawn at different points on various spectrums. If one is ideologically committed to either the right or left, one is careful to present ideas from only one position and a simplistic schematization of the issue results.

Unfortunately, however, in the area of delinquency prevention, the facts are fuzzy. Imposing an artificial order on a confused reality is dangerous. The scholar who presents arguments in a clear and forceful manner is rewarded by his university and his colleagues. His name "stands" for a certain perspective. Unfortunately there are opposing sets of ideas that are equally clear and forceful. The stand taken in this book is that the truth about delinquency is complex, and the facts concerning delinquency prevention programs are not known. My goal is to reflect that confusion rather than dispel it. There *are* inconsistencies between facts, theories, and policies; and the tendency of some authors to comfort the public with seemingly reasonable formulas may in fact be harmfully misleading.

While there may be a need for formulas and theoretical frameworks, the reader should not assume that an answer to the delinquency problem exists. It might be wiser to live with many different sets of ideas that try to explain delinquency and offer solutions. As long as we are not convinced that one of these frameworks is truly accurate, we are more likely to retain the flexibility needed to absorb new knowledge as it appears. I will illustrate this approach with some specific examples.

Perspectives on Delinquency Prevention

Regrettably, delinquency prevention programs tend to adhere to one perspective or another. Although it may not be possible to combine different perspectives into a single program, a coordinated approach may not be necessary. It may be wiser to accept the patchwork of activities presently being administered as a patchwork rather than to pretend it represents a coordinated effort to deal with youthful crime. Furthermore, there is a need to distinguish between the way people have analyzed society and the way they have attempted to change it. The radical criminologists provide a good illustration of this point.

In their analyses of society, radical criminologists have questioned certain assumptions. They call attention to the harmful acts of powerful people, systematic biases in social welfare agencies, the role of conflict and power in determining what is deviant, and the needs of agencies (which frequently take precedence over the needs of clients) (Taylor, Walton and Young, 1973; Quinney, 1970; Chambliss and Seidman, 1971; Krisberg, 1975). This book will frequently draw on insights from radical writers even though I generally favour middle-of-the-road policies. Revolutionary changes have frequently created as much harm as good in the past, and I suspect that this would be true for dramatic changes in dealing with youthful crime. My point is not to discuss actual proposals at this time, but to emphasize that consistency between *explaining* crime and *responding* to it is not mandatory.

On the other side of the coin, conservative writers frequently base their arguments on assumptions that make me uncomfortable; but when their policy recommendations are divorced from their philosophy, the former occasionally have merit. It would be healthier if conservative thinkers would consider radical proposals for change, and if radicals weighed conservative solutions more carefully.

At present the dynamics of making changes in the criminal justice system are poorly understood, and therefore it is important to think through the possible consequences of any type of change regardless of its ideological source. By rejecting certain types of suggestions on ideological grounds we limit both our imagination and our flexibility. We must not confuse ideological purity with wisdom.

My plea is not simply for eclectic thinking and broadmindedness. Biases and selective perception are clearly reflected in this book. Rather, I am committed to weak convictions rather than strong ones. No one has provided ideas and recommendations concerning delinquency that are clearly superior to all others. It is somewhat easier to reject weak ideas, but the major theme of this book is that progress in delinquency research will at best be very slow and we should be wary of all panaceas. This aspect of human behaviour *is* confusing and recognition of this fact calls for a cautious and probing strategy. Perhaps other world problems are clearer, and dramatic action may be called for in many spheres of human concern, but delinquency prevention is not such an area. The delinquency issue is complicated not only by the complex mixture of morality and underlying assumptions, but also by the poorly understood dynamics of a society that encourages personal freedom on the one hand and demands conformity on the other.

Understandably, then, I am inclined to favour gradual change. I fear dramatic leaps and believe that slow gains may have a more positive effect in the long run. Many reject this gradualist approach. The serious student of delinquency prevention should read Thomas Mathiesen's review of penal reform organizations in Scandinavia (1974). He definitely favours permanent revolutionary change and warns against those reform movements that are integrative and accommodating. Thomas Murton argues against gradualism and the dangers of cooperating with a system that is and always will be repressive unless dramatic changes are made (1976). One should also read James Wilson's *Thinking About Crime* (1975). Wilson argues for the increased certainty of punishment, among other things. While admittedly not enthusiastic about most conservative recommendations, I try to consider and assess programs advocated by the conservative element.

The strong commitment to ideological perspectives is not the only distortion that develops in the study of delinquency prevention. Another is the arbitrary distinction we make between juveniles and young adults.

The Arbitrary Border Between Delinquents and Adults

It is necessary for us to think in categorical terms, but frequently these categories create a false image of reality. This is particularly true when studying delinquents and young adult criminals. A seventeen-year-old boy who steals is an adult in Nova Scotia, New Brunswick, Ontario, Saskatchewan and Alberta, but he is a child in Quebec, Manitoba and British Columbia. The problems that arise out of this differnce can be illustrated by a seventeen-year-old couple who were living together in Ontario and decided to visit the Calgary Stampede. On their westward trip they ran into several inconsistencies. While consenting adults might live together in Ontario, the Manitoba authorities frowned on two "children" sharing a motel room. But in Saskatchewan they became adults again. Once in Alberta, the situation became even more awkward. Since the legal age is sixteen for boys and eighteen for girls, this seventeen-year-old male adult was contributing to the delinquency of a seventeen-year-old female child. In fact, he was committing statutory rape.

These differences in age limits from province to province are no more ridiculous than many other features of bureaucracy. If this book is to discuss delinquency prevention sensibly, it must take such factors into account. Surely it is illogical to argue that a seventeen and a half year old should be treated as a misguided child while an eighteen and a half year old is an adult menace. The fact that young people are being processed by both a juvenile and an adult system is part of the Canadian reality. This is not necessarily bad or good, but meaningful programs for the prevention of youthful crime must somehow bridge the gap across this arbitrary age line.

More extensive research has been done on programs for young adults in prisons than on programs for juveniles in training shcools, and I use both sources in this book. I am aware that many scholars and practitioners are willing to combine juveniles and adults when they discuss causes of crime and delinquency, but tend to keep them separate when they discuss prevention. On the one hand we help, treat, and rehabilitate misguided youngsters; on the other hand, we punish, restrain, and occasionally try to rehabilitate adults who should know better. Although various bureaucratic units must make this distinction, it is a handicap to a reasonable analysis of the problem. Therefore, the reader should be aware that I will be drawing illustrations from both adult and juvenile programs.

Revolutionary versus Modest Changes

It has often been said that the prevention of juvenile delinquency would require basic changes in society. Those changes could be radical and revolutionary. But are such dramatic changes likely? An alternate perspective would argue that major changes are not possible in a society that is stable and relatively content. Therefore, only modest changes within this somewhat fluid structure are possible. Delinquency prevention programs must fit into the present scheme of things. These two approaches are not necessarily mutually exclusive, although some scholars believe they are. Dramatic changes might take place in some areas while others remain relatively stable. In this book I wish to consider options reflecting both orientations.

If we consider major changes as a basis for delinquency prevention programs, we must consider a number of crucial questions. For example, why is delinquency and youthful crime selected as an area of concern while more damaging elements of society are ignored? Why are measures which seem obviously beneficial for society resisted by professionals in the field?

If, on the other hand, we orient ourselves toward modest changes, usually within ongoing agencies dealing with the prevention of crime, other more specific questions must be considered. When carefully considered programs are launched, why is it so difficult to evaluate the results? To what extent can we place confidence in the recommendations of those who give advice in the delinquency prevention field? Are certain practices clearly counterproductive? Until these questions are answered, it is difficult to discuss actual programs. The programs themselves must be viewed as part of a dynamic process—a process that concerns the interests of the professionals and agencies involved as well as the interests of the juveniles themselves.

Perhaps the major change and minor change approaches are incompatible. Those who argue forcefully for the revolutionary model often vehemently reject the possibility of meaningful gradual change. Others strongly advocate stability, favouring changes that permit continuity in the social order. Determining which perspective is correct is difficult, because facts, theories and passion do not clearly support one side over the other. I deliberately favour standing in the middle, leaning one way at times and then the other as circumstances change and ideas evolve. This is not a careless way to approach delinquency prevention. Nor is it necessarily objective or superior. Rather, it assumes that the present state of the discipline is feeble.

While some major reorientations would be needed to change the delinquency picture significantly, it is doubtful that society will move in these directions. Therefore, patchwork changes within existing programs and an occasional stumble forward may be the realistic alternative.

Chapter 2

The Need To Do Something

It is time you knew of Tagoona, the Eskimo. Last year one of our white men said to him. "We are glad you have been ordained as the first priest of your people. Now you can help us with their problem." Tagoona asked, "What is a problem?" and the white man said, "Tagoona, if I held you by your heels from a third story window, you would have a problem." Tagoona considered this long and carefully. Then he said, "I do not think so. If you saved me, all would be well. If you dropped me, nothing would matter. It is you who would have the problem."

—MARGARET CRAVEN

Responding to Delinquency

It is appropriate to ask how society selects and responds to those features that are seen as troublesome. Social problems change from time to time. Frequently these changes reflect the current concerns of the public as much as the "problem" itself. For example, the Ruhr Valley in Germany has suffered from pollution for many years, but the workers at the Krupp factories and other heavy industries in that area have not complained about the "pollution" problem. Those most concerned with pollution do not necessarily live in areas where this problem is the most threatening. Similarly, these concerns change with time. At an earlier period in this century, pollution was viewed as a major concern. Then interest faded. In the 1960's interest was revived. Now it seems that this particular "social concern" is again losing its grip on the public imagination.

Although there is always much public interest in delinquency, different aspects attract attention at different times. In the late 1950's gang wars received much publicity. In the 1960's drug use attracted great attention. In the late 1970's these aspects have been the focus of less public interest, even though these activities have probably continued with only modest changes. In other words, delinquency, or any other social problem, cannot be isolated and studied outside of its social context. Since we cannot study everything at once, we have to focus on different aspects of the delinquency problem, viewing the situation from one perspective and then another. Our first task is to note how society responds to delinquency and distinguish which responses are temporary and which are enduring. This may help us to understand the dynamics of societal responses to juvenile delinquency.

Even though the definition of a social problem varies from time to time and place to place, we should not treat all social ills as simply being "in the eye of the beholder." Rather, social problems are deeply woven into the fabric of society and cannot be understood without taking into account the reaction of the public, the social structure of the society, the relations between various elements in the society, and the social characteristics of human beings. It is difficult to recognize many aspects of this complex pattern and to discern which behaviour patterns are the most important. The actors who "cause" the problems or who initiate action are not always easy to identify. Those who stand at centre stage may actually be less important than those in supporting roles or those who operate the lights, write the scripts, or prepare the make-up. However, we have a tendency to provide simplistic answers to most questions concerning social problems. This is also understandable. The news media want to cover a topic in a few minutes; policital leaders need to present issues in clear, unambiguous terms. One characteristic of society which influences social problems is that the public demands straightforward answers to questions concerning topics such as delinquency and crime. Before attempting to recommend some reasonable responses to delinquency and crime, we need to review the dynamics of societal responses and the settings in which these responses take place.

Of course, the behaviour of individual delinquents is not irrelevant. However, discussions of delinquent behaviour appear extensively elsewhere. Certain aspects of the agencies concerned with delinquency have also been reviewed extensively in the last decade, the juvenile court, for example. This book will concentrate on the activities surrounding delinquency prevention, the demands society puts on those who work in this field, and the attempts to assess the effectiveness of these activities.

The "We've Got to Do Something" Syndrome

After an outbreak of vandalism, purse snatching, or other malicious behaviour by local juveniles, there is usually a public demand for action. Under such circumstances it is unwise for some academic to point out that the harm done to life and limb by juveniles is a tiny fraction of the injuries caused by the automobile or that the economic losses are trivial compared with those resulting from cheating on income tax, and the variety of crimes committed by more affluent members of society. Enduring certain nuisances while concentrating on vital problems has never characterized human society. Down through the ages our literature is filled with comments of how the younger generation is going to hell. While other social problems come and go, attempts to "reform" the young continue. Although juvenile delinquency may be receiving more attention that it deserves, in terms of its danger to society, it is clearly a legitimate social problem. Yet we should keep in mind that this concern is heavily tempered with emotionalism and confusion, which in turn influence the problem itself. Individuals and agencies working in the delinquency field are a product of these factors and their responses are conditioned by them.

Like others who respond to social problems, these individuals and agencies are part of a dense social web. Trying to understand that social web, including some of its inconsistencies, is different from condemning or praising everyone connected with crime and delinquency control business, even though some scholars prefer condemnation to understanding. However, we must recognize that this chronic, emotional concern with the "delinquency problem" creates a situation that must be analyzed as part of the problem.

Clearly, then, we've got to do something—not because delinquency is objectively a tremendous threat to society, but because the demands for action are always there. Since we must act, it is normal to ask the "experts" to research the problem, analyze the causes, generate reasonable proposals, launch programs based on these proposals, evaluate these programs and rationally select the programs that "cure" delinquency. Many believe that this scientific approach will lead to the "solution" of the problem. Although a scientific perspective on understanding human behaviour is valid to a degree, there is a growing belief that this "rational" approach to problem solving is oversimplified and not as revealing as was initially hoped. Therefore, I will devote considerable attention to such factors as the problems connected with the launching of delinquency prevention programs and their evaluation. Some of these activities, I will argue, are self-defeating.

Hans Mohr, a sociologist at York University who was with the Law Reform Commission of Canada for three years, argues that the logic of social science practices and the logic of social practices are not the same and therefore should not be used interchangeably. The strategy for dealing with a scientific problem is not the same as that directed toward a social concern. The response of a community to delinquency will not be "rational" in terms of "curing delinquency" if we judge it by scientific standards. However, community behaviour makes more sense when one understands that there are many different forces pulling in different directions. Community action will be a compromise response to these pressures. The public response will "make sense" even though it ignores relevant scientific knowledge. Similarly, the activities of those doing research on delinquency, launching programs, conducting evaluations, or drafting legislation will have their own dynamics. It is erroneous to believe that deductions that arise out of social science research will or should automatically be transformed into social policy. Nor should we assume that a supposedly reasonable social policy will automatically influence delinquent behaviour. Many researchers in delinquency continually complain that social policy fails to incorporate social science findings. Actually, social policy does utilize social science research, but how and when this occurs is contingent on a number of other factors.

This does not mean that social science research is unimportant. Rather, it might be wiser to see the social scientist as a person who provides a smorgasbord of facts and ideas. The policy maker must choose from this selection to put together a reasonable meal. The scientist may recommend spinach because it has lots of vitamins, but if people hate spinach, they will overlook its benefits. In other words, as a strategy to obtain social action researchers should generate many alternatives. What is finally selected for public policy is based not just on what is "correct" but also on what will be acceptable to a wide portion of the public. It is clear that when the government official expects the scientist to draft legislation or when the scientist expects the public official to enshrine research findings in legislation, both of them will be disappointed.

The ineffectiveness of men of goodwill

The confusion which exists in our attempts to develop a clear social policy regarding delinquency prevention is the product of neither a deliberate strategy nor ignorance. True, these two components may contribute, but the facts of delinquency are difficult to distinguish from plausible hypotheses and myths. One of the major stumbling blocks to effective social policy is the persistent belief that the intentions of "men of good will" surely result in progress.

This faith in the power of good intentions is a common response to the "we've got to do something" syndrome. However, developing courses of action on the basis of good intentions does not automatically lead to effective social policy. Just as the best will in the world, combined with the best existing knowledge, has failed to cure cancer, so the best intentions and the best existing knowledge have failed to rid the world of delinquency.

An appropriate first step, then, to a discussion of policies related to delinquency, may be to examine the various perspectives and orientations which people have toward the problem of correcting or treating people who are considered deviant. Different orientations will naturally advocate different courses of action. These orientations and recommended courses of action are a product of prevalent ideologies and beliefs. Any action program should be viewed within the context of the larger social milieu.

Societal Attitudes Toward Treatment

During the nineteenth century in Italy, public officials were concerned because people kept urinating in the street. Public urination was illegal and people guilty of it were punished. A famous criminologist of that period, Cesare Lombroso, suggested that such criminals be confined for their actions. Reflecting his own conclusions about crime, Lombroso logically argued that people who commit crimes are inherently different from others and there is little that one can do to change these innate characteristics. Therefore, society should simply confine those who commit criminal acts. However, a young student of Lombroso, Enrico Ferri, who was to become a famous criminologist in his own right, suggested an alternative: public urinals.

The point is, it is possible that no action program is needed, at least in terms of correcting deviants. Changes made elsewhere in the social milieu may be more meaningful. The need for action and the nature of both prevention and treatment programs come out of our image of man and society. For Lombroso the problem lay in the make-up of human beings. Ferri saw it as the result of a specific deficiency in society. Regardless of the correctness of any social perspective, its simple existence is a social fact. We must maintain a critical attitude toward our images of man and constantly reevaluate any policy proposals in this light.

The resistance to the acceptance of new knowledge

Let us begin with two questions: does knowledge have any impact on social policy and would we recognize a solution if it was in fact discovered?

The story of Ignaz Semmelweis, a Hungarian physician working in Vienna in the nineteenth century, is revealing. This young doctor noted that women who gave birth to children in hospitals died more frequently than those who gave birth in rural areas or even in the streets next to the hosptial. He performed many autopsies on victims of "childbed" fever and observed the practices of his colleagues with the hope of finding an answer to this problem. He noted that doctors examined cadavers, wiped the blood and pus on the lapels of their coats, then without washing their hands, proceeded to probe the vaginas of pregnant women.

It dawned on Semmelweis that doctors were somehow transferring the infection which they contacted in their surgical activities to healthy patients. His conclusion was that it would be wise if the doctors washed their hands before examining pregnant women. It seemed like an obvious solution, but the medical profession at that time showed little inclination to change its habits. It is difficult for us to imagine how a professional mentality could be so obtuse. In spite of remarkable declines in the death rate of pregnant women in Semmelweis' care, other doctors refused to acknowledge the demonstrated connection between dirty hands and infection. They clung to their filthy coats as status symbols in a professional hierarchy, and it was some time before they adopted Semmelweis' suggestions.

Likewise our programs dealing with juvenile delinquents frequently ignore vitally relevant knowledge. Social change takes place for a variety of reasons, and the discovery of new knowledge may be only *one* of the less important contributors. For those who set great store in public education this is an uncomfortable thought. Although we must not abandon our pursuit of knowledge, perhaps we should not be surprised when society does not utilize what we consider relevant knowledge until *other* dynamic processes have come into play.

Just as the customs and status-determining characteristics of medicine were more crucial than knowledge in Vienna in the middle of the nineteenth century, the benefits derived by those who administer the criminal justice system may outweigh academic knowledge. For example, certain ideas about "law and order," although based upon acknowledged ignorance and half truths, may form an enduring psychological base for the majority of the population.

When a policeman is killed in a shootout with a criminal, there is usually increased public demand for the death penalty. However, capital punishment may be irrelevant to the problem of protecting policemen. Most policemen, like the rest of us, risk their lives in auto accidents much more often than they do on the job. Also, intervention in family arguments is more frequently the cause of police injuries than confrontation with criminals. But the public is not always interested in objective knowledge. Justice, revenge and many other concepts may be more important. We must accept the reality that the application of knowledge plays a minor role in influencing social policy when emotions are involved and other social processes are operating.

Our mistake is in assuming that the knowledge *should* be applicable to such policy decisions, or that it should be more relevant than other factors, such as the needs and biases of those who administer a system. For example, the evidence that counseling or psychiatric treatment are irrelevant to the success or failure of delinquent rehabilitation programs is unlikely to influence the behaviour of those who are in charge of delivering the services. Unless those in authority are satisfied that their needs for security, power and prestige can continue to be met under the proposed policy change, they will resist such changes. The actual effectiveness of counseling is but one of many factors that will influence the persistence or change in delinquency prevention practices.

In addition to arguing that knowledge influences social policy only when certain conditions exist, we might well be cautious about applying new knowledge immediately. Let us speculate on the long-term consequences of any obviously sensible recommendation. Let us assume that Semmelweis had been successful early in convincing his colleagues to wash their hands. Let us further assume that the five million or so mothers who died of child-bed fever survived instead. Would Europe have had a population explosion which would have depleted its resources, led to starvation, etc.? Of course, one could speculate in the other direction. The increase in fertility could have led to the discovery of reliable birth control methods sooner and a response to population pressures at an earlier level in our technology. This in turn might have influenced the rest of the world and led to the stabilization of world population early in the twentieth century. Today's wisdom may be tomorrow's folly.

Is knowledge always useful?

Let us provide another illustration. When juvenile corrections in Alberta were transferred from the Attorney General's Department to the Department of Health and Social Development, changes were made in one of the training institutions. A high wire fence topped by barbed wire which circled the perimeter of the grounds was removed in an attempt to create a new image for the training school as a place conducive to rehabilitation. Soon the rate of escapes soared. The police were annoyed. The staff had to pay more attention to locking outside doors. Conducting activities out in the yard became a problem. After a few years many people wondered whether removing the fence actually restricted the freedom of the juveniles because of the need for compensating measures.

Obviously, hindsight is more accurate than foresight. Applying current knowledge is not always the "wisest" choice. For example, it would now be difficult to rebuild the wire fence around that institution even if new knowledge suggested that its advantages outweighed its disadvantages. The point is that the conservative manner in which knowledge works its way into policy decisions may have certain positive attributes, even though this delay causes frustration and arouses charges of incompetence.

True, humility should not paralyze us. Many reforms make sense. Unforeseen negative consequences may occur, but such risks should not be used as a reason for opposing all change. On the other hand, since the consequences of reforms may be negative, change should be approached cautiously.

We might benefit from looking carefully at research and ideas which try to trace the consequences of programs that have been launched. Instead of asking, "How does one prevent delinquency?", we should be asking, "What have been the unanticipated consequences when carefully reasoned delinquency prevention programs have been introduced?"

Treatment versus justice

In the above section I have tried to show that delinquency prevention programs will be influenced by the social milieu. Current beliefs, which may be considered "knowledge" by some but not by others, will play a role, but not necessarily a direct one. A number of factors will influence the way knowledge is used or ignored. Let us now turn to the question of what might happen when certain ideas are polarized. For several decades North America has favoured a philosophy advocating help or treatment rather than punishment as a means for changing delinquent behaviour in juveniles. At the same time counter pressures to the treatment approach have been growing. These criticisms have arisen from disappointment with the effectiveness of treatment programs. Another source of pressure against the treatment approach is generated by some of the questions raised by the neo-Marxists. Some argue that the institutions generated by the "child-saving movement" were created to meet the needs of those who wanted to do the saving rather than those to be saved (Platt, 1969; Dahl, 1974). There is a further suspicion that juveniles may not have benefited from a juvenile court philosophy that pays little attention to legal safeguards in its efforts to help rather than punish the child. Some scholars argue that the child is presently getting the worst of both worlds (Lemert, 1971).

While some are expressing concern for justice, others are advocating more comprehensive treatment programs. Here in Canada we tend to import many treatment programs from the U.S., and frequently this has certain advantages. However, programs are not selected on the basis of empirical evidence demonstrating their success. Such evidence is sadly lacking. Instead our actions have been based largely on faith, faddism and the opinions of administrators on whether an imported program will "fit" the Canadian scene.

> To the extent to which public policies are ambiguously derived out of conflict, programs cannot be rationally designed. Programs so generated become compromises, efforts to contain conflict. They are thereby intelligent, but they remain less than rational (Nettler, 1972: 5).

Let us assume, however, that society has resolved some of the issues raised above and government programs are moving forward in a coordinated manner. Are there other pitfalls and unanticipated consequences that require our vigilance?

The Dangers of Doing Something

When delinquency prevention programs are launched and researchers are asked to make an evaluation they should be prepared for certain unpleasant results: (1) strains will occur between researchers and action workers; (2) experiments with groups of delinquents can easily backfire; (3) some programs might produce more sophisticated criminals, and former delinquents who seem reformed may in fact have become more skilled delinquents; (4) pressures to demonstrate success may increase the likelihood of doing harm; and (5) some projects may disregard knowledge that might be helpful.

Strains between researchers and action workers

Normally, one might assume that researchers and directors of delinquency prevention programs would agree on common goals, but it is worth noting that some researchers may have different interests. While community leaders and those administering social policy painfully develop what appear to be sensible programs, social scientists are frequently happy to produce findings that are contrary to hopeful expectations. In fact there seems to be more reward for scholars if they find something "surprising" or at least "interesting" (Hagan, 1973). Since these "interesting" findings frequently reflect negatively on the effectiveness of a given program, they can be a source of strain between researchers and program directors. Clearly, those launching delinquency prevention programs should be prepared for a series of deflating experiences whether it be from the findings themselves, the sponsoring agencies, or from the slings and arrows of academic critics or literate journalists.

Experiments with gang workers: changing the situation

An excellent illustration of unanticipated consequences is provided by some of the attempts to use street workers to modify the behaviour of warring juvenile gangs. A strategy for dealing with delinquent gangs was pioneered in New York City in the 1950's which used street workers who got involved with delinquent boys in their own settings. These detached worker programs were later launched in Syracuse, New York, and this project eventually influenced the establishment of the Youth Service Bureau in Ottawa. The activities in Ottawa in turn had an impact in Vancouver and influenced the Spring Street Project (Keech, 1962; Ratner, 1974). In the United States this approach was heralded in the 1960's as one of the most important strategies for combating juvenile delinquency. It was clear at that time that a street gang worker was seen as a means of preventing delinquency.

While I shall discuss gang workers in more detail in Chapter 9, of interest here is the fact that the street worker was the main method for dealing with gang delinquency in the early 1960's. Naturally, policy makers need to know if such a strategy is effective. Let us assume that we have adequate funds and skills to test the effectiveness of gang workers. We might select twenty gangs in a large city for study. We would randomly assign detached workers to ten of these gangs, being sure that the gangs receiving the detached worker are similar in composition and locale to the ten gangs in the control group. By comparing the two groups of ten gangs over time, we could then judge the effectiveness of the detached worker in reducing delinquency.

The design is quite logical, but could unanticipated problems arise? Let us assume that one gang, the Dragons, has just received a gang worker. A gang member says to his friends:

> Now that the city has recognized that we Dragons are really a very tough gang by giving us a gang worker, we do not have to establish our reputation any further by going out and getting our heads broken open in those gang wars.

As a result, the Dragons seem to quiet down. In the meantime, another gang, the Kings, which did not receive a detached worker, feels slighted.

> We Kings are just as tough as the Dragons. Our reputation is just as bad. What do we have to do to get a gang worker? Do we have to kill somebody?

Therefore, the Kings increase their violent activities to compensate for the fact that their tough reputation has been insulted.

As the reader can readily see, launching an action program with a careful research design which would permit an evaluation could in fact change the situation so that the "control group" has been influenced more than the experimental group. One could argue that the use of the gang worker helped. It was not the "treatment" that caused the problem. Rather, establishing a scientifically designed control group created the difficulties.

Let us describe another situation. A detached worker is sent out to a delinquency-prone area to work with a gang identified by the police. As he hangs around street corners, he has trouble locating the gang. He reports back to headquarters and is told that the police are convinced that there is a gang operating in the area. Returning to his search, the gang worker does manage to find a few of the members of the gang, but he is told that the gang has broken up. The former gang members begin to feel sorry for this detached worker, who is under pressure to find this gang, so the boys offer to reorganize. Some skeptics might argue that such an occurrence is very unlikely. In fact, the pressures which can develop within programs could lead to even more unusual occurrences.

Improving illegal skills

One of the most carefully evaluated programs in Canada was a treatment program at Matsqui Institution, a federal medium-security prison for delinquent drug addicts, located at Abbotsford, British Columbia. The treatment involved a therapeutic community setting, daily group therapy, and an academic upgrading program to grade 10 (Murphy,

1972). Surprisingly, the control group did better than the group receiving the sophisticated treatment. The findings indicate that the treatment made no difference in terms of changing the amount of time legally employed or the dollar value of legal earnings; however, compared with the control group, the treated group spent more time illegally employed, had more illegal earnings, and used more drugs after completion of the program.

It seems that treatment group members learned to express themselves in ways more likely to be pleasant to others. This social ability combined with academic skills learned by the treatment group made little difference in the legal employment sphere but gave them an edge over other delinquent addicts in the competition for scarce illegal opportunities and drug supplies.

Sophisticated crime disguised as success

Another study in British Columbia by Tony Parlett and Eric Linden focused heavily on upgrading education (Parlett, 1974). While it may have been effective in terms of achieving higher levels of educational skills, Parlett notes that there could have been some unanticipated consequences.

> One of our most successful graduates from the programme has now spent more time on the street, i.e., less time in jail, than at any time in his adult life. If we did not know his background quite intimately we would consider him a successful citizen. However, the amount of money which we know he spends is very much greater than he earns. (8 or 9 times greater). Thus we are aware that he is successfully dealing in the heroin trade. He was, before we educated him, a minor, unsuccessful trafficker. Now he is a major, successful dealer. (Parlett, 1975)

This last study is particularly relevant because it illustrates how some subjects would normally be rated "successful" if the researcher did not know the truth of the situation. It is important to realize that we can get into various kinds of trouble when reacting to the demand to "do something." First, the program itself can have a negative impact on the clients; second, skilled researchers can be led astray; and third, attempts to evaluate a program, instead of simply observing it, can create a distorted picture of the program's success.

The impact of pressures to demonstrate success

Even with the best of intentions, it is very difficult to guarantee that "doing something" will not cause harm. As argued earlier, there is some doubt that we can rely on good intentions in the first place. When there is pressure on a program to succeed, it is quite common for such programs to serve those clients who will increase the likelihood of a successful result for the agency instead of serving clients most in need of the service (Krause, 1966; Scott, 1967); i.e., delinquents who show promise are recruited over those who seem more likely to get in trouble. Assuming that the service is a beneficial one, it might be denied certain portions of the population. This could increase the problem because higher officials insist upon an evaluation which will help them decide on the future of such a project on the basis of proven success or failure. In other words, the compulsion to "do something" combined with the need to provide evidence of accomplishment can increase the likelihood of doing harm.

More frequently, attempts to launch small projects arise out of common sense and enthusiastic humanitarianism. At times knowledge is available that is contrary to the common sense ideas expressed by well meaning individuals.

Ignoring relevant knowledge

Do action programs launch activities which are contrary to present knowledge? The desire to do good is often so overwhelming that it is easy to ignore present knowledge. For example, a sociologist was invited to advise a project which was designed to motivate underprivileged students to want to go to college. The consulting sociologist noted that one of the popular theories of deviance emphasized the discrepancy between desire to have certain things and the actual means available to reach these goals. When the gap between the aspirations and the means to achieve those goals is large, it is claimed that there would an inclination toward deviant behaviour to achieve those goals (Merton, 1938). Therefore, the visiting sociologist asked if the program would also provide the means to achieve the new goals; that is, would it provide scholarships so the increased aspirations would be realized.

No, he was informed that the project was not designed to provide scholarships; it was designed to motivate underprivileged students. The sociologist argued that increasing aspirations without increasing means could lead to a rise in frustration and delinquency. Perhaps it would be better to lower aspirations and decrease frustration. The sociologist was not invited back.

In fairness to the above project, the evidence supporting the "stress and structure" theories of delinquency is not strong, but the point is clear. If facts or knowledge contradict our view of certain activities as inherently "good", there is reason to believe that people will prefer to be "good" even though wrong.

Knowing the cause, of course, will not necessarily provide a cure (Nettler, 1970: 168). Some causes might not be alterable. If low I.Q. led to delinquency, there might be little we could do. If in fact the "causes" of delinquency are largely unalterable, our tendency to "do something" should be examined even more carefully.

In their study of delinquency in a birth cohort, Wolfgang, Figlio and Sellin (1972) have noted that many offenders tend not to repeat their delinquency. In fact, their data suggest that there is little to gain by treating first, second or even third offenders. Those with a fourth offence or more might profitably be the target of intervention. This recommendation differs markedly from the more frequent comment, "We must intervene earlier, so we can help." The same study also notes that offenders who were punished severely had worse subsequent delinquent careers than those who were punished mildly, even after controlling for the category of offences.

True, there may be situations where only dramatic changes can bring about any changes, and this may apply to some aspects of juvenile programs in some parts of North America. It is also possible that loud voices crying for drastic changes will help set the stage for more cautious reforms; but despite the criticism from the Left that a policy of gradualism will automatically be ineffective, I would argue that none of the advocates of revolutionary changes has demonstrated the superiority of their recommendations. The same judgement applies to law and order advocates on the other end of the political spectrum. There may be times when a situation is considered so serious that we are willing to accept the gamble of an extreme policy, but we should be acutely aware that it is a gamble. An alternative strategy is to see delinquency as a trade-off for other features in our society. How much are we willing to pay for a highly individualistic society?

Delinquency: The Price We Must Pay for Individualism?

That delinquency is a social evil is a point of view most people would accept; that it may be a necessary one is an opinion many would find abhorrent. In this context the analogy of delinquency and disease can prove useful.

I personally find that treating delinquency as if it were a sickness is a dubious strategy, but let us ask if certain sicknesses are not useful to society. In Africa, sickle-cell anemia is common in certain areas. It is inherited through a recessive gene; that is, some people in the population carry the disease in their genes but show no symptoms of the disease themselves. Africans with recessive genes for sickle-cell anemia have a greater resistance to malaria and are, therefore, able to live in areas where that disease is common.

A second category includes those individuals who inherit genes for sickle-cell anemia from both the father and mother. Under these conditions the recessive trait becomes dominant. These people will be anemic and it is likely that they will not live very long.

A third group of individuals will not inherit genes for sickle-cell anemia from either the father or mother and will be incapable of producing offspring who have the disease or passing on the characteristics. However, such individuals will have a relatively low tolerance to malaria and will die more easily in infested areas.

As we can see, this particular disease has certain positive effects. It enables some persons to live in malaria-infested areas. On the other hand, approximately one-quarter of the children born to a population where this gene is widespread will be anemic and will die young. A primitive society without the technology to eliminate malaria might look upon sickle-cell anemia as a "price" paid for protection against malaria.

Can juvenile delinquency be seen in a similar manner? Is it the price we pay for a creative and individualistic society? Those who are treatment-oriented will resist such a philosophy. Perhaps it is necessary to accept that random delinquency is preferable to organizing these deviants for the purpose of social improvement. After all, Hitler was successful in turning hoodlums into soldiers by giving them uniforms and letting them go around assaulting citizens and breaking up printing presses. Drastic and over-simplified cures have failed to work in the past, yet they continue to attract supporters. Even a past president of the Canadian Psychiatric Association, Keith Yonge, has suggested that special work camps be established for young people who use drugs and refuse to take advantage of the educational opportunities in our society (Edmonton *Journal*, November 21, 1969). The possibility that the cure could be worse than the disease is relevant to a balanced perspective on delinquency. A little delinquency may be essential to a healthy society.

It is tempting to advocate complacency, but instead I will return to my earlier statement that youthful criminal behaviour will continue to be an ongoing social concern. The public will be prodding various authorities to respond. There are valid humanitarian reasons for responding to that prodding. The victims of juvenile crime are not the only ones to lose. Most juveniles who engage in delinquency are not reaping any benefits from it. Despite the difficulties of formulating intelligent responses, this book will argue that there are some activities that increase the odds of achieving a small, but positive, gain. Thinking of delinquency as a disease that can be eradicated or a war that can be won is nice-sounding rhetoric for politicians; however, it is unlikely that delinquency will be cured, solved, or conquered in battle.

The Great Stumble Forward

Given the debate between those who wish to "treat" and those who wish to return to a more legalistic approach, we can anticipate a greater demand for evidence that a specific program works or does not work. Hence, there will be an increasing demand for the evaluation of programs. Those of us in the research business should welcome this increased interest in evaluation. However, it is possible that some of these efforts could consume vast amounts of scarce resources and have a variety of negative side effects.

We can accept programs as reflecting the needs of the public, but to evaluate them with the hope that they will enable us to achieve logically formulated goals implies a rationality they do not possess. If we were allowed to conduct an evaluation to question assumptions and understand processes, perhaps we could make more progress; but the mandate of an evaluation is frequently given in the following manner: Did those who were treated with procedure A commit fewer crimes than those who were treated with procedure B? Or those who were not treated at all? Such a mandate automatically provides us with intellectual blinkers.

In the following two chapters we will argue that it is extremely difficult to conduct an objective evaluation, that attempts to do so may actually defeat other important purposes, and the pressure from political and other forces to conduct evaluations can in fact make the situation even worse.

Yet stumble forward we must. Society demands it and the reasons for proceeding outweigh those for doing nothing. Our rather trivial accomplishments should make us hesitant, but the momentum is great. Despite loud and seemingly confident voices, the direction is not clear. There is good reason to believe that some of the seemingly promising routes will in fact be long detours. Even if we correctly identify some of the routes which will bring us closer to the goal, the path will probably be bumpy. There may be tremendous forces dragging us down certain roads, and usually it will be difficult to distinguish the cries of those who are wise and courageous from those who are simply frightened and confused. A reasonable strategy suggests that we should study the experiences of those who have stumbled on ahead of us. Therefore, let us look carefully at some of the more sophisticated delinquency prevention programs and their evaluations to see if we can chart a reasonable course.

Chapter 3

The Value of Evaluation

Turning back, he asked the pundits about the method they followed in instructing the bird. It was shown to him. He was immensely impressed. The method was so stupendous that the bird looked ridiculously unimportant in comparison. The Raja was satisfied that there was no flaw in the arrangements. As for any complaints from the bird itself, that simply could not be expected. Its throat was so completely choked with the leaves from the books that it could neither whistle nor whisper. It sent a thrill through one's body to watch the process.

—RABINDRANATH TAGORE

Program Assessment and Its Problems

If delinquency prevention programs could be accurately assessed without consuming vast amounts of scarce resources, and without having a variety of negative side effects, I would certainly favour the evaluation of such programs. My skepticism about the feasibility of evaluating delinquency prevention programs is based on three factors: (1) it is extremely difficult to conduct an objective evaluation, (2) attempts to do so may actually defeat other important purposes, and (3) the pressure to evaluate coming from political and other forces can in fact make the situation even worse.

In other words, launching delinquency prevention programs is a hazardous task. Trying to evaluate them, to assess whether they did decrease delinquency, may be even more hazardous. Common sense leads us to think we ought to attempt to evaluate our efforts to reform delinquent youngsters, but common sense could be wrong.

My discussion will start with some of the assumptions underlying evaluation research and those features which are necessary to make such research meaningful. At the end of this chapter I will describe how some of these features were applied in a specific program and argue that it would be unwise to launch such an activity in Canada. In the next chapter a few carefully conceived and executed programs will be reviewed. The findings from these programs and a brief assessment of similar Canadian endeavours further support an extremely cautious approach to evaluation research. Finally, in Chapter 5, I try to offer some constructive alternatives. I believe it is possible to develop an evaluation strategy which would avoid some of the problems discussed below while providing answers to similar questions.

It is important to realize that society may be asking the wrong questions. In general, delinquency prevention programs are designed to "cure" delinquents. The goal is to change "them" so they fit better into the larger society. One does not have to be a flaming radical or argue that it is the society that criminalizes individuals to realize that we may be asking questions that miss the point. As I discuss various attempts to evaluate delinquency prevention programs, it must be kept in mind that the important actors on this stage are not the juveniles alone, but include those who are trying to change them and those who are in a position to influence in a variety of ways a specific delinquency prevention program.

For the moment, however, I will concentrate on the more traditional perspective of correcting youth who have gone astray. The reader should not assume that this conventional perspective is outmoded as some scholars have argued. An orientation toward rehabilitating or "correcting" youth may be oversimplified and may make some erroneous assumptions, but to take the opposite view, that all the problems lie in the nature of society, is equally oversimplified. Regardless of what brings juveniles into conflict with society, attempts to reduce that conflict and modify behaviour can be meaningful and should not automatically be seen as the tactics of powerful people imposing their will on lower class and powerless youth.

The Meaning of Evaluation

What do we really mean by evaluation? It is normal for a government, a minister, or civil servant to say that if we are going to spend a great deal of money on a particular program, it should be "evaluated" so that we can decide whether it has been effective and should be continued. The implication is that if the evaluation proves that the program was effective, it will be supported in the future. If not, it will be dropped. It sounds perfectly logical, but it is in fact simplistic. Before going into this issue in detail, let us look at the formal requirements of a test of the effectiveness of a delinquency prevention program.

1. There should be a clear set of program procedures which could be repeated at different times with different subjects and by different administrators. In other words, the program should not be dependent on the unique personality of a person involved in the program.
2. There must be some division, preferably random, into treatment and control groups with the two groups differing as little as possible.

3. There must be a measure of the behaviour that is to be changed before and after the program for both the treatment and control groups.
4. "Success" must be definable and compatible with reasonable expectations as to what success should be; that is, "success" should reflect not just happiness, personal adjustment, or faith in the program, or the opinion of observers: it should refer to criminal behaviour.
5. There should be a follow-up in the community for both the treatment and control groups some time after the program has ended.

Charles Logan (1972) applied these criteria to practically all of the experimental studies which have been conducted in the United States up until that time. After examining approximately one hundred studies, he came to the conclusion that none could be described as adequate. When the two criteria of a proper control group and at least a reasonably well-defined program are combined, only four studies survive. However, Logan argued that none of these studies had a follow-up and hence did not satisfy the fifth requirement. Since Logan's article appeared, follow-up studies have been completed in two of those four studies (Empey and Erickson, 1972; Hackler and Hagan, 1975). These two studies will be discussed in more detail below, because their experiences and difficulties should help us to assess the likelihood of similar attempts succeeding in Canada.

This review of evaluation programs will help explain why the normal logic that is applied to evaluation is simplistic. For reasons that are not obvious to the casual observer, successful evaluation has been extremely difficult to conduct. Despite the resources, interest, and expertise available in the United States, very few crime and delinquency prevention programs have met the minimum criteria for a genuine evaluation.*

Tests of correctional or preventive effectiveness which meet the required standards stated above are rare in Canada. The best illustrations of such rigorous evaluations tend to come from psychologists working in correctional settings. The evaluation of the project with drug users in British Columbia (Murphy, 1972), mentioned in the last chapter, the work done by Paul Gendreau and Don Andrews at the Rideau Correctional Centre in Ontario, and the attempts to modify social attitudes and moral judgment in a maximum security penitentiary in British Columbia (Parlett, 1974) were experiments using control groups and meeting requirements 1 through 4 as stated above. Requirement 5, a

*Recently, many programs have been appearing in the U.S. that have apparently been rigorously evaluated with funds from the Law Enforcement Assistance Administration and other well-funded agencies. Despite the many "exemplary projects" now published by the LEAA, I believe the generalizations made here are valid.

follow-up in the community for both the treatment and control group some time after the treatment has ended, is more difficult to assess. The question is really, "How long?" Ideally, we should follow such cases for many years, but there are practical limitations.

At the present time, then, Canada has only a few specialists who have conducted rigorous evaluations. Since the review of research by Logan in 1972, the United States has seen many more evaluations. Some of these could be considered "rigorous." However, very few of these rigorous projects also included a long term follow-up. The important question is: are these evaluations worth the effort, the time, and the strain? Or stated differently: are there other ways of studying delinquency prevention programs that would be more profitable?

Before debating this question, we need to be clear on what we mean by evaluation. Normally, we think of the traditional experimental design, which consists of experimental and control groups. The experimental group receives some sort of treatment, such as counseling, while the control group gets none. Naturally, the control group must resemble the experimental group as much as possible, and all other experiences except for the experimental variable must be the same for both groups. The goal is to assess the impact of one or more experimental variables. Such a strategy theoretically should answer the question "Does it work?"

A second strategy attempts to approximate the experimental design by using "comparison" groups. While not as ideal as true control groups, these can yield useful information. The work done by Robert Ratner with the Spring Street Project in Vancouver is such a study (1974). It will be discussed in more detail later. Ratner attempted to apply experimental criteria to evaluate the impact of an intervention program. As in so many projects of this sort, the difficulties of obtaining a true control group proved insurmountable. The Spring Street Project illustrates some of the compromises which often must be made between the scientific model and reality.

In Ontario, some sophisticated attempts have been made by Leah Lambert and her colleagues at the Ministry of Correctional Services to launch rigorous evaluations, but each attempt has been forced to compromise with the ideal criteria for a true evaluation. Several findings from these Ontario studies will be discussed in later chapters, but for now it is important to note that by shifting away from the "ideal" evaluation model, the experimental design, the Ministry of Correctional Services in Ontario may have gained meaningful knowledge without creating some of the strains inherent in the experimental design. Those studies that emphasize comparisons among groups that differ on known characteristics may not yield as clear answers as the true experimental design, but they may be a reasonable compromise.

In addition, they may be more flexible in dealing with other questions besides "Did it work?"

A third strategy focuses on the process and dynamics of a given project. It does not ask "Does it work?" but rather "What happened?" The emphasis is on the ongoing dynamics of a program. Unfortunately, most policy makers insist on clear goals and information which relates directly to the achievement of those goals. Hence, "process analysis" does not usually satisfy officialdom as much as "outcome analysis." Irwin Deutscher argues that one must be careful to avoid this "goal-trap" in doing evaluation research (1974). A number of other scholars in the United States are focusing on this type of assessment for programs that will influence human beings (Weiss and Rein, 1969; Weiss, 1970; Salasin, 1973). In Canada, Brown, Zelhart, and Schurr refer to summative and informative evaluation (1975), the former seeking to "prove" something while the latter is directed toward "improving" an ongoing project. In Canada this movement to consider various ways of evaluating programs is only beginning.

A fourth strategy is to concentrate on the masses of data already gathered by official agencies. There are several limitations to this alternative, but one clear advantage is that it would create minimal disruption for ongoing programs. We will concentrate on this fourth strategy in Chapter 5.

I will not discuss the second and third strategies in detail, although I definitely favour them. Both of these strategies are promising for the Canadian scene. Instead, I will spend the next two chapters arguing against the use of the experimental design; that is, the first strategy which attempts to answer the questions, "Did it work?" and "Is it good?" It should be noted that most researchers in Canada who have been quoted above do not share this view. Although they are aware of the difficulties in evaluation research, they feel that rigorous evaluation is necessary to guide policy. The difference in my perspective is largely a matter of degree. I agree that as programs are launched we need to understand them better. However, understanding if the program works may be a question that is too narrow. Trying to understand what is happening among the staff and among the community, as well as among the juveniles, may be equally important.

The goal of this chapter is to call attention to the fact that assessing delinquency prevention programs involves risks and such risks should be weighed carefully before we apply the most rigorous scientific model. The experimental model has been placed on a pedestal and possibly it should only be used when certain conditions are present.

It is important to note that other less rigorous "evaluations" have been made in Canada. There have been intervention programs conducted in Ottawa, attempts to provide work opportunities in Manitoba, and college students have worked as volunteer probation officers on a one-to-one basis with juveniles in Edmonton. Many programs have been launched across Canada, and almost always there is an attempt to assess their effectiveness. Unfortunately, there tends to be an almost universal correlation between the results found by "non-rigorous" evaluations and those which apply the requirements described above. The "soft" studies are almost universally successful. The "hard" studies are almost universally unsuccessful or reflect no change. "This conclusion is supported by the most sophisticated research studies: generally, the more rigorously scientific the methodology the less likely is success to be reported" (Doleschal and Klapmuts, 1973: 610). After looking at some of the pressures which are brought to bear on those who conduct projects, it is not surprising that the soft evaluations lead to conclusions of success, but it is necessary to view such findings with caution.

Later I shall examine a few of these Canadian programs because they do provide insight, but truly rigorous evaluations which meet scientific standards are rare in Canada. I hope to explain why this is true and why it is undesirable to strive for this unrealistic goal by examining a few illustrations from the U.S. We do not have to repeat the same mistakes in Canada.

With the possible exception of England, the European scene has probably been much less promising than the U.S. A 1963 survey conducted by the Council of Europe found that no rigorously scientific evaluative research had been undertaken regarding the effectiveness of delinquency prevention programs (Doleschal and Antilla, 1971). It is, of course, possible that careful evaluations have been made since then. Rigorous evaluation has not provided the information which we need. It will be instructive to examine some of the more sophisticated attempts in the U.S. to see why I argue that the rigorous experimental design is a poor investment of time and resources in Canada, and possibly in all but a few select situations in the world.

Features of Effective Evaluations

I have already discussed the basic requirements of an evaluation that would properly determine the effectiveness of specific activities. I will now discuss those features of effective evaluations which could be utilized in less rigorous evaluation designs as suggested later in Chapter 5. I will illustrate these features using a few sophisticated programs launched in the United States. Unfortunately (or perhaps fortunately), we do not have comparable experiments in Canada, although an extensive evaluation is underway at the Boscoville Institution in Quebec (Le Blanc, 1977). There is the danger, however, that Canada will follow its traditional pattern of committing the same blunders made by the

United States ten years ago. The main purpose of this section is to convince a few people that we should skip this stage and make newer and more innovative mistakes.

The need for a theoretical rationale

When launching a delinquency prevention program, most people who design such projects have "reasons." Usually these reasons could be stated in a fairly explicit manner. If one lays out a clear, explanatory model as to why the actions taken in a particular program will lead to a decrease in delinquency, it might lead to gathering information which would be overlooked if a clear theoretical rationale were not used. We shall illustrate our argument with the Cambridge-Somerville Youth Study which began in 1936.

Dr. Richard Cabot of Harvard felt that many delinquents and potentially delinquent boys would develop into upright adults if they were provided with intensive and long-term counseling. Two carefully matched groups of boys of 325 each formed the experimental and control groups. Boys from nine to eleven years of age were given intensive counseling for approximately seven years. Intervention techniques were not limited to counseling alone. For example, one boy suffered from an ear infection which made him smell badly. Medical treatment was obtained, the ear infection was cured, and the child was more appreciated by those around him.

The extensive data gathered by this project have been carefully analyzed (Powers and Witmer, 1951; McCord and McCord, 1959), but I shall simply note that the final findings were disappointing. Those who received intensive counseling and related intervention ended up in court and in jail just as frequently as those who received no treatment. Unlike many projects, this classic study followed the boys later in life and still found no discernible impact from the treatment program.* Although future counseling projects have followed, those which have been carefully evaluated have led to the same conclusion.

My interest in this project, however, is to illustrate the possible use of a theoretical rationale. Ask yourself just how counseling might affect a delinquency rate. With a little thought, it seems obvious that counseling, if successful, would influence court appearances through a series of other variables. Figure 3.1 offers a plausible model. It states that counseling leads to a better self image, which in turn leads to greater success socially, which leads to a decrease in delinquency, and finally to fewer arrests. Others could come up with a more elaborate model. In fact, one could utilize several different models for the same program. This might

---

*A thirty-year follow-up suggests that those who received more intensive service did even worse than those who received less (McCord, 1977).

Figure 3.1
A Possible Theoretical Rational
for a Counseling Program

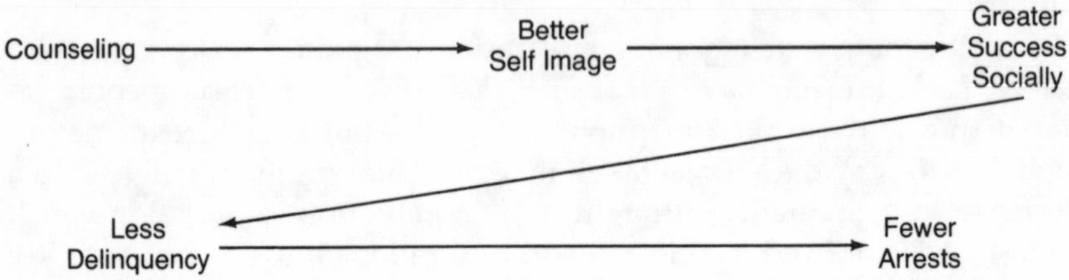

lead to the gathering of additional data which would permit the testing of contrasting theoretical rationales. Note that in Figure 3.1 the rationale is based upon causal sequences from one step to the next. This is only one way to proceed. Different assumptions and a different rationale could link concepts together in a different way. The point is that systematically linking the concepts together and spelling out the reasoning may lead to gathering more appropriate data.

It is possible that counseling could be successful in changing the self image. In addition, it might lead to greater success socially and a decrease in delinquency. Nonetheless, the school, the police and other agents of social control might not recognize that decrease in delinquency and continue to arrest boys at the same rate as they did before counseling was introduced. In other words, it is possible that a program could be partially successful, but because official delinquency did not change, that partial success was not apparent. A carefully stated theoretical rationale simply leads to asking more questions. This increases the likelihood of finding reasonable answers. Without an explicit rationale, data are often gathered haphazardly and those variables crucial to a more meaningful explanation can easily be neglected.

Success for delinquency prevention programs is usually judged only in terms of formal contact with the police. Perhaps this is an unreasonable criterion. There are many factors that influence the amount of contact with police aside from delinquent behaviour itself; for example, the tendency of adults to report juveniles (Black and Reiss, 1970). Similarly, meaningful changes could take place without modifying police contact. Since changes in arrest rates are rarely influenced by prevention programs, selecting other criteria may be wise. A clear rationale might suggest changes in attitude, employment, success in school, etc. as possible alternatives to contact with the police.

The New York City Youth Board prediction study in the late 1940's illustrates the need for a clear theoretical rationale. The study focused on the question of how "bad" family situations lead to delinquency in high delinquency neighbourhoods. Jackson Toby suggests that there are two quite different mechanisms by which a bad family situation might lead to delinquency:

1. Parental rejection and neglect damage the personality of the developing child. Lack of impulse control results from pathological socialization. The psychopathic or neurotic boy reacts with violence to trivial provocations, sets fires, and steals purposefully.
2. Parental inadequacy and neglect by reducing family control thereby orient the boy toward his age mates in the neighbourhood. (The family and the peer group are in a sense competing for the allegiance of boys in the high delinquency neighbourhoods.) If the peer group is delinquent, a boy's desire for acceptance by his peers tempts him to participate in delinquent activities (Toby, 1965: 168).

A program might favour one rationale over another, but *both* rationales might be tested by a program if more care were taken to gather the appropriate data. In addition, a clear rationale might lead to a more careful consideration of intervention techniques. Clearly, then, an action program should state one rationale explicitly, but I would argue that it would be advantageous to state others as well and test alternatives.

It is interesting to note that the two mechanisms suggested by Toby by which a bad family situation might lead to delinquency are still postulated, and each side has its adherents; but we still don't know which is the better explanation or whether they both should be discarded.

Incidentally, in this New York City Program which dealt with "bad" family situations, the treatment focused primarily on a psychological approach. After the four-year experiment, members of the treatment group were just as likely to become delinquent as members of the control group.

The search for interaction

Even though one youth might respond favourably to a given program, another might respond quite differently. Therefore, it is important for us to determine if there is an *interaction* effect between the type of clients and the type of program. The Pilot Intensive Counseling Organization (called the PICO Project for short) took this factor into account (Adams, 1961). Again, I shall simplify the study to illustrate my point. The treatment in this study consisted of once or twice weekly individual counseling sessions with trained counselors. The treatment group and the control group were divided into amenable youths (aged seventeen to twenty-three years) and non-amenable youths. An amenable youth was one who was bright, verbal and anxious. In addition there was evidence of an awareness of problems, insight, desire to change, and acceptance of treatment. Figure 3.2 illustrates the research design. Approximately one hundred youths fell into each of the four groups. The two hundred amenable youths were divided into experimental and control groups as were the two hundred non-amenables.

Figure 3.2
The Experimental Design of the Pilot Intensive Counseling Organization (PICO)

	Amenables	Non-amenables
Experimental Group	100	100
Control Group	100	100

Source: Chart from Stuart Adams, "The PICO Project." Pp. 213-224 in Johnston, Norman, Leonard Savitz, and Marvin E. Wolfgang (eds.), The Sociology of Punishment and Correction. *New York: Wiley, 1962.*

After being released from treatment, records were kept on the four groups to see which were more successful. Figure 3.3 shows the success rate for each group. As one can see, the success rate for the two control groups is practically the same—it made no difference whether or not the youth was amenable or non-amenable. When the treated amenables are compared with the control amenables, those receiving treatment did better than their controls. However, the opposite seemed to happen when the treated non-amenables are compared with control non-amenables. That is, those who received treatment among the non-amenables did *worse* than their control group.

It is tempting to provide an *ex post facto* explanation at this time. Although *ex post facto* explanations must be treated with caution, perhaps they can illustrate another hazard of doing evaluation research in this regard. Let us assume that the amenable youth attempts to make a good impression on his counselor. The treatment experience could be a rewarding one for the counselor as well. He might feel that he has successfully "exorcized" the devils out of the youth. At the end of the treatment program, he might tell the probation officer that this case is "cured." The probation officer might pass the same information on to the police. A month later the youth steals a car and a policeman has another talk with the probation officer. But the probation officer assures the policeman that the boy is cured; therefore, it might be worthwhile giving him another chance.

Let us follow the same process with a "non-amenable" youth. The counseling experience is *not* seen as successful by either the client or the counselor. The youth resents talking with the "shrink." The counselor feels the devils have not been successfully "exorcized." He tells the pro-

Figure 3.3
Cumulative Percentage of Past-Release Time Spent in Return to Custody in California State Facilities, by Amiability and Treatment Status

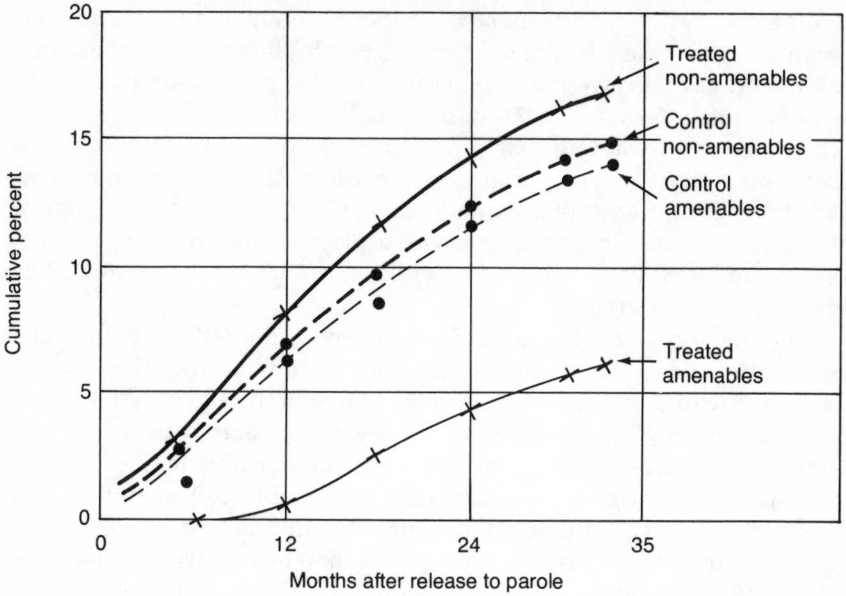

bation officer that this youth is going to get into trouble. The probation officer warns the police. A month later the youth steals a car and the police say, "I told you so." The probation officer says, "I knew it would happen." The boy is sent back to the institution. He is recorded as a "failure" by the program. Both boys stole cars, but their actions were defined differently in terms of the success of the program. In fact, the program might have *increased* differential identification.

Admittedly, this illustration is a bit far-fetched, but it illustrates the possibility that a classification system and definition of certain experimental groups could have ramifications for final outcomes. Incidentally, later stages of this program seem to give rise to different results. This study and other sophisticated projects conducted in California warn us that inconsistency of findings is typical rather than atypical. How much faith should we place in smaller, less sophisticated projects conducted in Canada?

Interaction effects lead to some interesting speculation. In another California study it was learned that when therapy was administered by a specialized psychiatrist or a psychologist, the failure rate on parole was almost two and a half times *higher* than if the therapy was provided by a social worker without specialized training (Adams, 1959). The fairly common finding that highly "qualified" treatment personnel are frequently less effective than their less well-trained counterparts has not endeared some evaluations to those who advocate higher professional standards. This is particularly true of the Canadian scene. The claim is continually made that we must raise the requirements for those who perform certain roles. It is not surprising that findings such as these just mentioned have received little publicity—in fact, publication has probably deliberately been suppressed in a few cases.

It is also worth noting that programs for adults do not necessarily operate the same way for youth or vice versa. In Israel, Shoham and Sandberg (1964) found that when one compared a suspended sentence plus probation for first offenders with a prison sentence, only first offenders under 20 years of age did better on probation; those from 21 to 45 actually did worse.

While it is not very difficult to look for interaction effects within different categories of a single variable, for example, amenable youths compared with non-amenables, a more elaborate research design is required to see how the combination of several variables operates at the same time. I turn now to a project which had an elaborate design with the hope of studying many of these interaction effects. This project also illustrates the sort of impractical designs a theoretically oriented sociologist may attempt to impose on a program when he is naive and unaware of the difficulties inherent in carrying out action programs.

The Opportunities for Youth Project

It takes a real innocent to conduct an experimental program in delinquency prevention following the textbook. However, inexperience leads one to attempt things which more experienced people know are impossible. The Opportunities for Youth Project in Seattle (Hackler, 1966) was one of those few studies which met most of the requirements for an adequate research design (Logan, 1972).

The theoretical rationale for the Seattle Opportunities for Youth Project (the name was used there approximately eight years before it was introduced to Canada) is illustrated in Figure 3.4. The developmental sequence systematically links specific variables in a causal chain as follows:

(1) Having low esteem leads to (2) the anticipation on the part of others that ego will act badly or at least not be able to act properly; this leads to (3) ego's perception that others anticipate improper behaviour if (a) opportunities to play conforming roles are perceived as blocked by those in dominant positions, such as teachers, and if (b) ego views the self relevant responses from primary and non-primary significant others as valid; this would lead to (4) the development of a delinquent self concept; which leads to (5) the search for roles compatible with the delinquent self concept; this leads to (6) delinquent behaviour; and finally

Figure 3.4
The Theoretical Rationale for the Opportunities for Youth Project

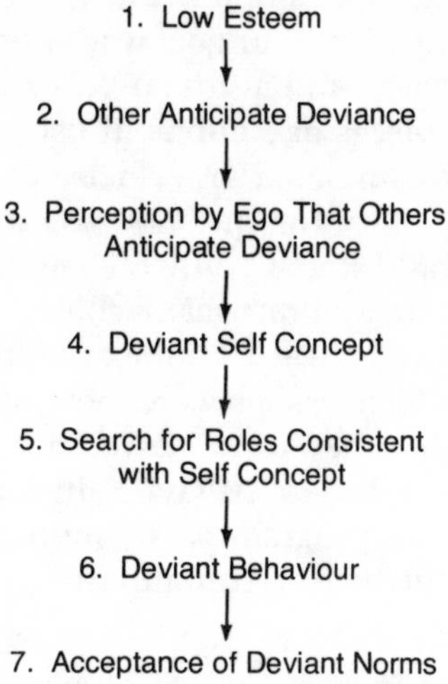

leads to (7) the selective endorsement of delinquent norms through dissonance reducing mechanisms (Hackler, 1971: 64).

This attempted explanation of delinquency has certain implications for intervention. For example, it states that the formation of deviant norms would come *after* deviant behaviour. Therefore, one would not attempt to change delinquency by changing the attitudes or norms of youth. To be effective, one should start at the beginning of the causal chain. It is difficult, however, to change the esteem of a child or his family. Certain racial and ethnic groups will be held in lower esteem in certain communities and changing that status would be far beyond most delinquency prevention programs. Step 2 is also difficult to alter. Teachers and others who are in contact with children frequently anticipate that children from "the wrong side of the tracks" will be more delinquent than those from higher status families. Ideally, it would be beneficial to change teachers and others so that they would not anticipate deviance from low status groups, but in the Opportunities for Youth Project, we felt it was more realistic to focus on step 3. Could we change the perception on the part of the boys that other people thought they were delinquency prone? The experimental program focused on this particular variable. The main experimental techniques were teaching machines and a supervised work program.

The setting for this program was four public housing projects in the city of Seattle. We included some nearby neighbourhoods with one of the housing projects in order to provide us with an adequate number of thirteen- and fourteen-year-old boys who were the target of the project.

Figure 3.5 shows the strategy which was used in the four communities. In communities A and B we conducted a teaching machine testing program. Note, this was not a remedial education program even though many people were under that impression. Remedial education implies that a student is not adequate. Our goal was to emphasize the opposite. Instead, we asked thirteen- and fourteen-year-old boys to test teaching machines. Were these pieces of equipment useful for teaching younger children? When a boy completed an exercise and came to the teacher saying that he had got all of the questions right, the teacher was supposed to respond with, "I knew you were capable of getting the right answers. Now tell me if it is a practical machine." Finally the boys began to point out how one could cheat with the machines, how they might be helpful or unhelpful, which lessons were more useful, etc. The idea was to convince the boys that they were viewed as capable and that adults anticipate adequate, non-deviant behavior. In communities C and D no teaching machine testing program was conducted so that they could provide a contrast for the boys in communities A and B.

Figure 3.5
The Experimental Design of Seattle Opportunities for Youth Project

	Attempt to Create Positive Community Attitude Toward Youth	No Attempt to Modify Attitudes
Teaching-Machine Testing Program	Community A	Community B
No Teaching-Machine Testing Program	Community C	Community D

Originally, we planned to make communities A and C the focus of another experimental variable and make comparisons with communities B and D. We felt we could create a positive community attitude toward youth by utilizing a variety of techniques. One way would have been to use a fake questionnaire. Instead of asking people their opinions, we used leading questions such as, "Don't you think the boys are doing a good job working around this community?" We also planned to have evening gatherings which might develop some appreciation for what the boys were doing.

In Figure 3.5 one can see the possibility of studying interaction. We have four possible combinations. (1) Community A would receive *both* the teaching-machine testing program *and* attempts to change the community. (2) Community B was to receive the teaching-machine testing program but no attempts to change attitudes. (3) Community C was to get no teaching-machine testing program but was to receive attempts to create a better attitude, and (4) community D would receive nothing. When we conducted our initial surveys to study the attitudes of the adults in the various communities, we found that there were wide discrepancies at the beginning. This placed us in a dilemma. Should we attempt to change attitudes or should we simply treat the two communities with the most positive attitude as communities A and C? Since the project was already complicated enough, we decided to use attitudes toward the youth as a background variable instead of as an experimental variable. No attempts were made to modify attitudes. Communities B and D were simply less positive in their attitudes toward youth than communities A and C.

Within each community we attempted to conduct various employment programs. The basic idea was to give boys a successful work experience. In Figure 3.6 one can see that there were five different groups in each community. Approximately sixty boys were recruited in each of the four communities and randomly assigned to these various groups. The first group was to consist of ten boys working with an "informal" supervisor. By informal we meant that the supervisor was to display confidence in the boys and anticipate non-deviant behaviour. They would be given the keys to the tool shed, and their pay cheques would be passed out at the beginning of the work period. Naturally, fourteen-year-old boys would rake up a pile of leaves and then jump in them, but since they were normal, dependable, non-deviant youngsters they would rake the leaves up afterwards. Naturally, fourteen-year-old boys would occasionally come to work late, but after losing a little pay, they would be coming on time.

Figure 3.6
The Experimental Design in Each Community

Group 1—Work as group with informal supervision	10
Group 2—Work as group with formal supervision	10
Group 3—Work individually with minimal supervision	10
Group 4—No work but teaching machine testing[1]	10
Control Group—No work—No teaching machine testing	20
	60

[1] In Communities C and D, Group 4 was part of control group.

In the second work group the supervisor was to be "formal" and anticipate deviant behaviour. Boys could not be trusted with the keys to the tool shed, and their pay cheques would be passed out after the work period. Being undependable, they would probably rake up a pile of leaves and jump in them. Since undependable boys come late to work, they need to be punished by reducing the pay cheque.

In recruiting supervisors for the various work groups in the four housing projects, we tested all applicants using the Adorno Authoritarian Scale. We were fortunate in finding two "authoritarian" types to supervise our "formal" groups and two non-authoritarian types to supervise the "informal" groups. Incidentally, one of the "formal" supervisors was black and the other white and one of the "informal" supervisors was black and the other white. Everything was working out beautifully in our textbook design.

One can see the possibility of tests for interaction. Would a black youth, working with a white supervisor, in an informal atmosphere, taking part in a teaching machine testing activity, and living in the community with a positive attitude toward youth do better than a black boy, with a black supervisor, in an informal setting, etc? The number of possible combinations which could be tested by our ingenious design was indeed formidable!

After congratulating ourselves on our cleverness for several months, certain weaknesses began to appear in the program. For example, the boys saw no difference between the "formal" and "informal" supervisors. On objective rating scales, they liked both types of supervisors very much and saw them in a very generous and supportive light. Obviously, if the boys did not view the supervisors as authoritarian, there was no point in continuing such a distinction. Another experimental variable was lost and groups 1 and 2 were analyzed together in the end as "work groups" (Figure 3.6).

Group 3 was to take part in our job placement bureau in the community. They would have practically no supervision. We were curious to see if the work opportunity by itself would have any impact. Our goal was to give all ten boys in the group equal opportunity to take on jobs in the community. Let us assume however, that you received a phone call from a very influential person in the community who wished to employ a boy to cut his lawn. The next boy on your list was undependable the last time you sent him out on a job. The person who hired him said he would not hire another boy from the project. Would you send this unreliable boy to mow the lawn of this influential person or would you be tempted to ask another boy to take on this task? The research design required that boys be sent at random. Community pressures may dictate alternate decisions. Expediency frequently won out over the ideal textbook design.

It soon became clear that not many people were interested in hiring our boys. Those with big lawns to mow lived far from the centrally located public housing projects and they usually found local boys to do these jobs. Essentially, group 3 disappeared and blended in with groups

1 and 2. Luckily, this was done early in the project so that the experimental work groups were kept reasonably intact, but another experimental variable went down the drain.

Group 4 would not be involved in any of the work groups, but in communities A and B they did take part in teaching machine testing programs along with boys who were in the work groups. In communities C and D, where there was no teaching machine testing, the boys became part of the control group.

At the beginning of the program before any of the boys were assigned to any of the work groups, each boy completed a questionnaire. We asked questions concerning attitudes, their perception of themselves, of others, their self-reported deviance, etc. Various scales were formed into 39 different variables to assess the impact of the program. We included police records, referrals to the school counselor, and ratings by teachers in addition to the questionnaire items. At the end of the year we ran approximately four thousand tables on the computer to assess the impact of the program. Rather than bore the reader with the details of the analysis, which have been reported elsewhere (Hackler, 1966), I can summarize the results rather easily. Nothing happened. True, on one variable we found that there was a rather strong relationship favouring the experimental groups over the controls; but we also found another variable which displayed just as strong a relationship in the opposite direction. In other words, we found differences, but they were random—as if the program had never taken place.

Figure 3.7
Findings Which Would Have Supported or Rejected the Theoretical Rationale

Beginning of Project

80%—believe others anticipate deviance
80%—have deviant self concept
80%—commit deviant acts
80%—endorse deviant norms

A Successful Program Supporting the Theory

30%—believe others anticipate deviance
40%—have deviant self concept
50%—commit deviant acts
60%—endorse deviant norms

A Successful Program Rejecting the Theory

60%—believe others anticipate deviance
50%—have deviant self concept
40%—commit deviant acts
30%—endorse deviant norms

We had hoped, of course, to be able to test the theoretical model even if the project did not demonstrate complete success. Figure 3.7 contains hypothetical figures which would have permitted us either to support the theory or reject it. At the beginning of the project we would establish a "baseline" percentage for each of the variables reflected in the model. For convenience, let us assume that 80 percent of the boys believe that other people anticipate deviance on their part at the beginning of the project. Similarly, let us assume that 80 percent have a deviant self-concept, and so on. If the program were even partially successful and the theory were correct, one might anticipate that the percentages would drop depending on how close the variable was to the beginning of the causal chain. For example, if the theory were correct and we were successful in manipulating the key variable (the perception by ego that others anticipate deviance), we would expect the greatest change to take place in that variable. Lesser impact would be anticipated down the causal chain (Fig. 3.7). That is, we would predict that a changed perception of others' anticipations would have more effect on the self-concept than on deviant behaviour or on attitudes. On the other hand, if the project were successful in changing behaviour, but if the theory were incorrect, the causal chain could run in the reverse direction. One would also expect the decreasing percentages to reflect that pattern. Obviously, there are many possibilities. But nothing much happened. Not only were we unable to demonstrate any impact from the program, we could not even test the theoretical model. We concluded that there was some very weak evidence that the teaching machine testing program had a slight impact, but even that may have been wishful thinking.

A separate analysis of the data to test the theoretical rationale apart from the effectiveness of the action program utilized various statistical procedures for testing causal sequences (Hackler, 1970). In the light of later criticisms (Hagan, 1973), even those arguments seem to be less convincing.

So far we had confined ourselves to "hard" objective data. However, we thought it would be prudent to ask the boys whether or not they liked the project on the final questionnaire. Admittedly, this must be considered "soft" data, but the reader can probably appreciate that the researchers were a bit anxious and quite willing to look for less stringent criteria for success. Table 3.1 shows that, by and large, the boys in both the work groups and the control groups responded favourably to the project with 76 percent of the boys in the work group being very favourable as compared to 68 percent in the control groups.

It is interesting to note that the black youths responded more favourably than the whites. In fact, we found that the black youths in the control groups were more favourable than the white youths in the work groups. These findings are consistent with some ideas suggested by

Table 3.1
Percentage of Youths Who Rated the OFY Project Very Favourably

Work Groups		
Black (59)	83%	
White (37)	65%	
Total		76%
Control Groups		
Black (43)	77%	
White (17)	47%	
Total		68%

Leroy Gould (a fellow planner of OFY now at Yale University). Black families in public housing are often upwardly mobile. When opportunities are offered that seem to be meaningful, they are optimistic. Whereas a black mother might feel that she has no opportunity of breaking out of her present situation, she is willing to make sacrifices for her children's futures. On the other hand, white families who come to the public housing projects are often downwardly mobile. They have seen better days and do not see such programs as opportunities for advancement.

It is not clear whether some of these findings have relevance for the Canadian scene. Unlike many delinquency prevention programs, the Seattle Opportunities for Youth Project received very positive support from parents, particularly black parents. I question the assumption that lower class elements in central cities are as apathetic as many social workers would have us believe. In fact, the most interesting side effect from this program was the impact of the project of adults rather than on the boys. We attempted to change children, but it seems that we had an impact on changing the attitudes of the adults instead (Hackler and Linden, 1970).

The findings of the project were reported to a large group of interested citizens in Seattle. They included our Board of Directors and other leading personages who were eager to hear the good news about how Seattle had created the first program to deal effectively with delinquency. Obviously such a clever project could not miss. My presentation, showing no impact, was not well received.

Obviously, I would have been pleased to see a successful outcome as well. When I look back on the situation, I realize that it would have been a wiser strategy to emphasize other findings in the report: the attendance rate for the work programs was over 90 percent, the boys and community responded well, etc. We were uniquely successful, compared with other projects in the United States, in terms of maintaining the integrity of the experimental design. The various stages of the project were finished on schedule. The response of the people in the community was positive. But I did not emphasize these features, assuming that they were of secondary importance. Instead, I carefully documented how nothing had happened. The Board of Directors and others who had supported the project with enthusiasm listened attentively, but for some reason they were not favourably impressed by my careful and clever research report. When I left Seattle to come to Canada, I suspect there were few people with an interest in the Opportunities for Youth Project who were sad to see me go.

Later that same year, I presented the same data to the Society for the Study of Social Problems before an audience of experienced researchers. Many had been involved in delinquency prevention programs. Here I found sympathy. Other researchers seemed to say, "So you failed too?"

The response of various audiences to such research findings should not be seen as irrelevant. They are part of the pressures which influence both evaluations and the future of action programs. Many people believe that most researchers can evaluate a project independently because they are free of pressures that would influence their decisions. I shared such a view at the beginning of the Opportunities for Youth Project. Obviously, it is naive to overlook the pressures on researchers and the pressures which their findings can create on others.

One reason why Opportunities for Youth was able to complete its evaluation was due to a unique combination of favourable factors which were not recognized as unique at the time. First, a key staff member, whose primary concern was with implementing the work program, protected the integrity of the research design by pointing out possible contamination of control groups. In other programs, control groups have frequently been contaminated by the well-meaning activities of social workers who hate to see any child "deprived" of the benefits of a program. Other programs have frequently been modified, thwarted and sabotaged. Such experiences are documented in an interesting manner elsewhere (Schwartz, 1966).

Secondly, this project had excellent cooperation from a "competing" agency. Again, that was taken for granted, but other programs have found that such competition can create severe problems (Miller, Baum and McNeil, 1966).

Despite "success" in completing a project while maintaining its integrity, findings of "no impact" can have severe political repercussions in a community unprepared for negative findings. My hard-nosed presentation of these findings may have handicapped future delinquency prevention programs in the area. As I look back on this experience, I believe it would have been wiser to present one type of report to community leaders and another to fellow researchers.

The impact of the project four years later

Logan (1972) points out that even those few projects which met certain other criteria tended to be deficient in terms of providing an adequate follow-up. Since then, we have been able to do a follow-up study of the boys in the Opportunities for Youth project (Hackler and Hagan, 1975).

In Table 3.2 we compared the experimental and control groups at the beginning of the OFY project and four years later after the project ended. We can see that at the beginning of the project 38 percent of the work group had come into contact with the police. The difference between the two was 5 percent; that is, the work group was slightly less delinquent. Four years later 33 percent of the work group had come into contact with the police as compared with 29 percent of the control group. The difference is 4 percent. The differential change between the two time periods is 9 percent. When compared with the control group, the work group seems to have done worse than those who were left alone. (Note: it is important not to try to compare the rates at the beginning of the project directly with rates four years later. Different factors are operating and they are not comparable. However, one can assume that similar biases are operating for both the work and control groups. Therefore, one can compare the differential change.)

Table 3.2
Delinquency Rates at the Beginning of Opportunities for Youth and Four Years Later

	Delinquency Rate at Beginning of Project	*Delinquency Rate Four Years Later*	*Differential Change*
Work Group (85)	38%	33%	
Control Group (70)	43%	29%	
Differences between Work and Control Group	−5%	+4%	+9%
Teaching Machines (67)	43%	25%	
No Teaching Machines (131)	38%	32%	
Differences between TM and No TM Group	+5%	−7%	−12%

The bottom portion of Table 3.2 illustrates the difference between those who worked with the teaching machines and those who did not was 5 percent (43 percent − 38 percent). At the end of the four-year period, the difference was −7 percent (25 percent − 32 percent); the differential change was −12 percent. That is, while those who were involved in the teaching machine program at the beginning of the project had greater contact with the police than their controls, after four years they tended to have less contact with the police. One could interpret these data as supporting the claim that the work experience led to an increase in delinquency, while the teaching machine program led to a decrease.

Although it is necessary to view these findings with caution, it is interesting to note that the group which took part in the teaching machine testing program had a high rate of delinquency at the beginning of the project, as did the control group for the work program. At the end of four years, the group which took part in the teaching machine testing program had the lowest rate of the four groups, while the boys involved in the work program had the highest rate four years later.

Table 3.3
Impact of Work Groups as Compared with Controls After Controlling for Race. Police Contact After Four Years

		Delinquency Rate at Beginning of Project	*Delinquency Rate Four Years Later*	*Differential Change*
White Boys (57)	Work Group	34%	23%	
	Controls	41%	35%	
	Differences Between Work and Control Group	−7%	−12%	−5%
Black Boys (90)	Work Group	46%	41%	
	Controls	47%	28%	
	Differences Between Work and Control Group	−1%	+13%	+14%

Table 3.3 follows the same strategy as Table 3.2, this time separating the boys by race. We computed the differences between the work group and the controls at the beginning of the project (34 percent − 41 percent = −7 percent), and compared them with similar differences at the end of

the project (23 percent − 35 percent = −12 percent). The differential change over time for the white boys was a −5 percent, or a "decrease" in delinquency. For the black boys the difference was +14 percent, or an "increase" in delinquency. According to these data the work program seemed to have a positive impact on the white boys, but a negative impact on the black boys.

Table 3.4
Impact of Work Groups as Compared to the Controls for Boys Having Specific Characteristics. Police Contact After Four Years

Specific Characteristic of Boy		*Differential Change—Work Group as Compared with Controls*
1. Race	White (57)	− 5%
	Black (90)	+14%
2. Referred to Counselor	Not Referred (84)	+ 6%
	Referred (70)	+ 8%
3. Intelligence Quotient	High (35)	− 1%
	Low (104)	+ 9%
4. Teacher Rating of Boy	Good (72)	−10%
	Bad (76)	+18%
5. Perception of Mother's Evaluation	Good (79)	+ 2%
	Bad (49)	+17%
6. Perception of Teacher's Evaluation	Good (70)	− 1%
	Bad (58)	+33%
7. Perception of Friend's Evaluation	Good (76)	− 1%
	Bad (51)	+48%
8. Self Evaluation	Good (86)	+14%
	Bad (43)	+23%
9. Perception of Teacher Assessment	Positive (99)	+12%
	Negative (28)	+36%
10. Alienation	Not Alienated (43)	+20%
	Alienated (85)	+ 8%
11. Attitude Toward Opportunities for Youth	Positive (71)	+12%
	Negative (19)	+41%

Table 3.4 summarizes Table 3.3 in the first line. For the remaining ten characteristics in Table 3.4, we have summarized the results of tables such as Table 3.3. We report only the differential changes when boys are

compared in terms of specific characteristics. The first characteristic is race. The others include whether or not a boy was referred to the school counselor prior to the project, I.Q., how the boy was rated by his home room teacher prior to the project, etc. Essentially, we were trying to distinguish those boys who had more "going for them" from those who faced a variety of disadvantages. Is it possible that boys who had not been in trouble in the past and who had other positive factors are in a better position to profit from programs of this sort? If we apply this logic to the data in Table 3.4, we would predict that the first row in each of these pairs of percentage changes would be negative; that is, the boys in the experimental group would do better than those in the controls. For the white and black boys represented by the first pair of percentage changes, this is what happened; the advantaged group (whites) did "better" (−5 percent) and the disadvantaged group (blacks) did "worse" (+14 percent).

With the exception of the measure of alienation, advantaged boys seem to do better than boys who are disadvantaged. Perhaps it would be more appropriate to say that advantaged boys are not affected as negatively as disadvantaged boys. As we go down the column of percentages showing differential change, and look only at those boys who are black, who were referred to the counselor, etc., we see a consistent differential which suggests more police contact for those in the work groups as compared to the controls. Items 6 and 7 are quite striking. Those boys who believed that their teachers would evaluate them positively showed little change if they were involved in the work group, as compared with the controls. However, those who felt that their teacher's evaluation was negative seemed to become more delinquency prone if they were involved in the work group, as compared with those who were not. A similar pattern seems to exist if one uses perceived evaluation of friends in determining self-concept.

The implications of these findings could be shattering. Obviously the boys we are most concerned about in any delinquency prevention program are those who are most inclined to be in trouble, those who have negative self-concepts, and those who are members of minority groups. Although the indicator of alienation runs contrary to the other ten items listed, the general pattern suggests that our work program did more damage than good, and that it had a particularly negative impact on those who were already at a disadvantage. However, let us examine Table 3.5. Using the same specific characteristics that were included in Table 3.4, we looked for differential change between those who participated in the teaching machine program and those who did not. Looking down the column of percentages, we are relieved to find a consistent column of minus signs. This indicates that those who were involved in the teaching machine testing program seemed to do better than those who were not involved. In eight out of the eleven indicators we also note that the disadvantaged boys showed a larger decrease than those who were advantaged. In a sense, the impact is just the opposite of that on those who were involved in the work groups. The differences between the advantaged and the disadvantaged boys are not very pronounced, but the general pattern suggests that the teaching machine testing program had a positive impact and was particularly positive for those who were disadvantaged.

Table 3.5
Impact of Teaching-Machine Program as Compared with Those Not Involved for Boys Having Specific Characteristics. Police Contact After Four Years.

Specific Characteristic of Boy		*Differential Change—TM Program Compared With No TM Program*
1. Race	White (74)	− 8%
	Black (115)	−11%
2. Referred to Counselor	Not Referred (102)	− 6%
	Referred (92)	−20%
3. Intelligence Quotient	High (44)	− 8%
	Low (131)	−10%
4. Teacher Rating of Boy	Good (96)	− 6%
	Bad (90)	−19%
5. Perception of Mother's Evaluation	Good (102)	−17%
	Bad (58)	− 0%
6. Perception of Teacher's Evaluation	Good (91)	−11%
	Bad (66)	− 2%
7. Perception of Friend's Evaluation	Good (100)	− 8%
	Bad (57)	−11%
8. Self Evaluation	Good (112)	− 8%
	Bad (47)	−13%
9. Perception of Teacher Assessment	Positive (127)	−10%
	Negative (32)	− 8%
10. Alienation	Not Alienated (54)	− 1%
	Alienated (106)	−15%
11. Attitude Toward Opportunities for Youth	Positive (132)	−11%
	Negative (24)	−17%

There are several plausible interpretations of these data. Actually, we would like to claim that our attempts to change "a boy's perceptions of how others expect him to behave" were successful in the teaching machine phase of the project, and that these data provide evidence in support of the theoretical scheme originally proposed. Unfortunately, we cannot ignore the unsuccessful results the work group experiences seem to have had, especially for the disadvantaged boys in the project. We have discussed the theoretical implications of this project in detail elsewhere (Hackler and Hagan, 1975), but the experience of others should lead one to be skeptical about the whole operation. If this study were replicated, the odds favour completely different results. Larger programs with more intensive treatment do not show consistency of results. There is little reason to expect Seattle Opportunities for Youth to be different. Even the negative impact of the employment program should be viewed with caution. The findings in regard to the work program could be influenced by factors quite unrelated to the work experience itself.

On the other hand, employment and vocational training programs, though worthwhile in themselves, have been disappointments in terms of modifying delinquent behaviour. One project working with girls at a vocational school in New York provides another illustration of a sophisticated project and results which suggest minimal impact (Meyer, Borgatta and Jones, 1965).

Another disappointing illustration comes from an ambitious vocational training program in New York dealing with delinquent boys. They were provided with vocational guidance, occupational orientation, placement in a work program; and, finally, after release from the institution, the boys received supportive aftercare and job placement aid (Zivan, 1966). None of this made any difference in recidivism rates. It should be noted that there were several elements in the New York community which were hostile to the program.

Our Opportunities for Youth Project did not deal with boys sentenced to a program even though there was a high delinquency rate in the neighbourhoods. In many respects Opportunities for Youth received extensive support from adults and other elements in the community. Of course one could argue that when the jobs ended the boys were frustrated because no other opportunities materialized. Furthermore, groups had been created which might have developed into delinquent gangs. But this is all speculation. To date, no one has provided clear evidence that work programs have been successful in decreasing delinquency.

Implications for Canada

The Opportunities for Youth Project has several characteristics which are worth noting for policy makers in Canada. Could we use the Opportunities for Youth Project as an argument for not conducting such experimental programs in Canada if we could get similar information in a much less painful manner? First, let us look at some of the fortuitous circumstances surrounding Opportunities for Youth which might not exist in another situation.

The community setting was particularly ripe for a delinquency prevention program. The only "competing" agency in the community was particularly cooperative and supportive. Other agencies and community organizations were enthusiastic and optimistic. In fact, their optimism may have made the negative findings particularly hard to take.

The project was especially fortunate in its relations with target communities. At a crucial stage, the project was able to obtain the services of a particularly capable black social worker who provided leadership for the project in many sensitive areas. We were viewed as an ally of the central community rather than as an enemy.

In addition, the project was fortunate to have the services of Herbert Costner, one of the most competent methodologists in North America, as a consultant. At that time, Professor Costner was new at the practical application of research programs in the community, but this blissful ignorance probably encouraged us to attempt a more ambitious experimental design. The warning by Hans Mattick, an experienced program director in Chicago, that the overly elaborate design could cause problems, was considered but set aside. Fortunately, as each of Professor Mattick's predictions turned out to be correct, and as experimental variables proved to be unrealistic, retrenchment was possible and the basic design remained intact. Other projects have not been so lucky.

Furthermore, the social worker directly in charge of the experimental program was alert to violations of the integrity of the experimental design and brought these to the attention of the research director. It is much more common to find those involved in the treatment eagerly sabotaging the whole design in order to "help" boys who are in the control group as well.

The seemingly inevitable clash between the researchers and the practitioners did occur, but in retrospect, this conflict was probably much less than that which has occurred in other projects. It is probably correct to say that it is one of the few projects which was able to complete its original plan. The chances of being so lucky again are not very good. Are the results worth such a gamble? Negative results are the most likely outcome of a sophisticated evaluation. How many agencies and communities are going to benefit from this painful experience? How about the impact on the working relationships between researchers and practitioners? Collaboration between researchers and practitioners on a project that is fraught with so many pitfalls probably leads to a decreasing willingness to work together in the future. In general, then, carefully designed experimental programs and rigorous evaluations can have negative implications for a community. Are there better ways to assess ongoing activities and glean the necessary knowledge which will provide guidelines for more effective policy decisions? Let me repeat the point made in the last chapter and argue that clear knowledge which is relevant to social policy will probably not be acted on unless political factors and other community pressures make such action acceptable. It is even more questionable whether one should spend scarce resources conducting careful evaluations which may have more negative than positive consequences.

Summary

The goal of this chapter has been to point out the dangers of believing that one can apply the rigorous scientific model for evaluating experiments to delinquency prevention programs without incurring some risks. Usually there will be difficulties in attempting to establish comparable experimental and control groups. Unlike white mice who stay in their cages in the laboratory, human subjects behave in ways that are outside the control of the experimenter. But even when things are going well, and it is fair to say that things actually went exceptionally well in the Opportunities for Youth Project, the attempt to be scientifically sophisticated can create problems.

The major point hinges on the fact that everyone concentrates on the *effectiveness* of most delinquency programs. In later chapters I will make the argument that very few programs seem to be successful. Hence, rigorous evaluation usually provides evidence of failure. Under such circumstances does it seem reasonable to make extensive sacrifices in order to learn that the experiment failed? My basic argument is that such rigorous evaluations are premature in Canada. It is possible that in some situations enough rapport has developed between researchers and program directors that the strains created by the experimental design could be tolerated. For those programs inside correctional settings focusing on relatively modest experimental changes, the traditional experimental design may be appropriate; but those programs that hope to have a wider impact and which attempt to modify characteristics of the community and the situations surrounding the juveniles concerned may simply pose too many barriers for such a rigorous design.

Before making recommendations for an alternative strategy, it will be appropriate to examine a few other projects that have been particularly careful and imaginative in their attempts to prevent delinquency.

Chapter 4

Programs Which Illustrate Inherent Difficulties

Men occasionally stumble onto knowledge; but most of them pick themselves up and hurry off as if nothing had happened.

—WINSTON CHURCHILL

Where Do We Stand?

It should be clear that conducting careful evaluations which meet rigorous requirements can be a difficult and at times an impossible task. The likelihood of success in maintaining the integrity of the experimental design is small and the necessary sacrifices may not be worth it. In Canada, as well as in most areas of the world where resources are somewhat limited, rigorous experimental designs are a poor investment. However, a careful theoretical rationale and the systematic search for interaction effects among several variables can be used in non-experimental designs. These are less costly and less threatening but they do require some thought and planning. The search for interaction effects can be done by computer at different stages of an evaluation without interfering with an ongoing program. The question is: can we gain the knowledge in a less painful manner without becoming enmeshed in political and public pressures? It is worthwhile to look at several experimental programs which stand out because of their contribution. These studies also provide a means of judging activities of a related nature in Canada.

The Provo Experiment

In this study (Empey and Erickson, 1972), delinquency was viewed as a group phenomenon and rehabilitation involved changing the shared delinquent characteristics. The treatment attempted to provide a social structure which would encourage delinquents to examine their behaviour and the ultimate utility of conventional rather than delinquent alternatives. Peer group interaction was the principle rehabilitative tool, because it permitted peer group decision making and granted status along with recognition for participation in treatment. The treatment program differed from group therapy programs in that the focus was not on analyzing individual personalities. Instead, the group leader played a less dominant role while the boys talked about their current situation and the possibilities for change. The project is one of the more interesting ones conducted, but I will focus only on certain aspects of the evaluation.

At an early stage in the evaluation, it seems that boys who were assigned to the treatment group did better than those who received institutional treatment. As one might imagine, it was not easy to develop adequate experimental and control groups, but, in general, the project directors were successful in having comparable groups in institutional care, in the community-based program and on probation.

It is interesting to note that the success rate of the boys on probation went up considerably during the project and was comparable to that of the experimental group. There is the distinct possibility that a certain amount of competition developed between those supervising probation and those in the treatment program. This is a fairly common phenomenon. An attempt to use a control group turns out to be unrealistic when the comparison group has been modified by the dynamics of the situation.

The complex analysis of the Provo experiment is difficult to summarize briefly. One could argue that the long-term impact of the experimental program was not demonstrably different from probation. It does seem clear, however, that the experimental program was significantly superior to incarceration. Although an occasional study has demonstrated better results with a more restrictive regime of physical custody as compared with a less restrictive regime (McClintock, 1961), the Provo experiment is consistent with a number of other studies which suggest that incarceration is both more expensive and has a negative impact on delinquency compared with most other alternatives.

Of course, you can always find someone who will argue that while a boy is in an institution he cannot commit any crimes. This assumption, though seemingly logical, turns out not to be true. In the Provo study the mean number of arrests per boy was calculated during the intervention period. One might assume that there should be no arrests for the boys assigned to the institutions, but it turns out that they had an arrest rate of .54 per boy held in custody! It seems that despite institutional restrictions, some of these boys committed new offences either when they were on furlough in the community or when they escaped from confinement (Empey and Erickson, 1972: 79). It is also possible that when a juvenile runs away from an institution, he is likely to steal a car or commit some other type of criminal act. Unless one is willing to adopt the philosophy of locking delinquents up and throwing away the key, training schools and other types of incarceration do not necessarily protect the public from criminal acts.

Using data from a Provo study, Fisher and Erickson (1973) have developed a time series experiment to examine the possible intervention effects of the project in more detail. They conclude that various types of social control intervention programs, not necessarily incarceration, can be utilized to reduce delinquency rates. Quite likely, this perspective is a minority viewpoint at the present time among researchers in this area, but it is clear that those who have been connected with the Provo project have made one of the major contributions to delinquency prevention literature.

The Silverlake Experiment

In Los Angeles, several years after the Provo experiment, Empey and Lubeck (1971) conducted an experimental program which utilized a residential community setting involving group meetings, school attendance, and weekends at home. Boys were randomly assigned to this experimental program and to the Boys' Republic, a private training institution, which was one of the more progressive training schools in the area. A systematic theoretical rationale was proposed and systematic attempts were made to test those ideas while testing the adequacy of the program. In a critical review of the book, *The Silverlake Experiment,* Travis Hirschi argues that the methodology was somewhat ritualistically applied and that it distracted attention from more basic questions (1972). Although it is always possible to argue that someone could have accomplished more by doing things differently, this systematic approach yields one of the clearest guides for evaluation research. The very fact that the theory was laboriously translated into hypotheses makes it possible to test both the theory and the program. Such an approach may not lead to great break-throughs, but it does lead to a careful assessment of the ideas that have been tested.

When this community-based residential program was compared with the more traditional training school, there seemed to be no evidence that the program was better than its control. A major contribution of this study, however, is the detailed way in which the program was described, complete with problems and crises. Anyone who has the audacity to attempt to construct a treatment program would be well advised to study the Silverlake experiment. Daniel Koenig, of the University of Victoria, in another review of the book (1972), points out that there was a staff of only two full time and two part time persons working with only twenty boys. In such a small program, there are a number of unique factors that can influence the outcome. For example, the influence of the personalities of the staff members could be very great. If this happened to be the case, and if the experiment turned out to be "successful," would these findings not lead future policy makers astray? The careful evaluation might credit the "success" to guided group interaction when in fact the changes were due to the accidental and unique characteristics of a staff member. Of course, the personalities of individuals can be an important influence on larger projects as well, but one can see how they can be a more serious factor in a small project. In other words, a careful evaluation of a small project could lead to interpreting unique findings as general principles and to future programs based on misplaced faith.

The reader should not interpret these comments as arguments against small projects. Rather, it is the combination of uniqueness and rigorous assessment of impact that creates the problem. A small project might be particularly well suited for studying various dynamic processes even though it would be unwise to emphasize the significance of the outcome of such a project.

The Silverlake experiment is not held up as a model of a program to follow but rather as a meticulous documentation of the dynamics and difficulties of a community-based program.

The findings of the Provo and Silverlake experiments do not provide us with any panacea to cure delinquency, but they do provide us with illustrations of carefully planned community-based programs. Their insights should help those in the future to avoid a few of the pitfalls. Since the *Report of the Task Force on Community-Based Residential Centres* (Canada, 1973) recommends the use of community-based residential centres, it would be worthwhile to pay attention to evaluations such as these. While they may not offer a cure, it seems that community-based centres are no worse than traditional training schools for juvenile delinquents.

The Atlantic Street Center

This program in Seattle, Washington, provided intensive social work services lasting from one to two years to "acting-out hostile boys" and their families in a central urban area. It is one of the few studies which utilized carefully matched experimental and control groups and gathered an extensive amount of information on the boys through the schools, the police, and the boys themselves. In a sense, it might be seen as a test of traditional social work practices when conducted with great care by a skilled staff. Rather than discuss the program in any detail, time can be saved by going directly to the outcome—the evaluation of the program showed that the untreated control group performed as well or better than the experimental group (Berleman, Seaberg and Steinburn, 1972).

But the reason for discussing the Atlantic Street Center is to note some of the informal characteristics. Since the Opportunities for Youth Project was launched in Seattle shortly after the inception of the Atlantic Street Center, and since the Research Director of the Atlantic Street Center and the Research Director of Opportunities for Youth were friends, it is understandable that there was some sharing of ideas. As we gained more experience in the field and noted the experiences of other cities, it became clear that such amicable relationships are the exception rather than the rule. Community agencies with a vested interest in certain activities often compete with other agencies for a variety of scarce resources, including funds, and the pressures to demonstrate success become very strong.

Unlike Opportunities for Youth, the Seattle Atlantic Street Center was an ongoing agency. The research component was an established part of the project and the staff was actively involved in its own evaluation. For a program to conduct such a thorough analysis and come up with such convincing evidence of their ineffectiveness is a rare display of integrity. Usually "in-house" research manages to find a certain degree of success. On the other hand "in-house" research may be better able to provide insights into the internal dynamics of a project. The emphasis on having independent, outside evaluations may be misplaced.

Other Inherent Difficulties in Evaluation Research

So far I have alluded to external difficulties that plague evaluation research. Other difficulties seem to be inherent in the process of evaluation itself, and despite extensive efforts to overcome them, they persist.

Biases which favour success

Even when attempts have been made to avoid biasing the results of an experiment in favour of a program, these biases can still creep in. In Table 4.1 Paul Lerman (1968) has utilized data from one of the California programs designed to prevent delinquency. There were 241 boys in the experimental group and 221 in the control group. The offences they committed were classified into low, medium and high seriousness. If one looks at those offences which are considered low in seriousness, it appears that the 241 experimental boys committed 376 offences, compared with the 114 offences committed by the boys in the control group. Note that the rate of parole violation was .02 per boy for the ex-

Table 4.1
Rates of Parole Violation per Offence Category for Experimentals and Controls— Community Treatment Project

	Experimentals 241 *boys*		*Controls* 221 *boys*	
Seriousness of Offence	Number of Offences	Rate of Parole Violation per Boy	Number of Offences	Rate of Parole Violation per Boy
Low	376	.02	114	.17
Medium	146	.10	100	.40
High	156	.37	140	.44

perimental boys but .17 for the controls. Although the experimental boys committed more offences, the boys in the control group had their paroles violated eight times as frequently! If we examine the offences in the medium seriousness category, we can see a similar phenomenon. The parole violation rate for the control group is about four times that of the experimental group (.10 vs. .40). When it comes to serious offences, the numbers and the parole violation rates are more comparable but they still favour the experimental group.

It is possible that the parole agents working with the experimental group were more aware of delinquent behaviour and, hence, gave the impression that the experimental boys were more delinquent. But even if we assume that the behaviour of the experimentals attracted more attention and should be viewed as similar to that of the control group, the response to that behaviour is remarkably different. Perhaps the boys were not behaving differently, but certainly the parole officers were. At least the system was responding differently, making it impossible to test the effectiveness of the experimental program.

While it may not have been possible to ignore some of the serious offences, it may have been easier for the less serious ones. Since most delinquent acts tend to be of low seriousness, one can see how workers with a desire to see clients succeed could ignore minor violations.

Such a bias is probably commonplace. In the Spring Street Project in Vancouver, a policeman was asked to evaluate the delinquent behaviour of the boys after their involvement in the project (Ratner, 1974). Certainly, it is possible for this to be an objective evaluation, but such objectivity is difficult. It would not have been surprising if this single policeman was familiar with the project and on reasonably good terms with project workers. It is interesting to note that while the policeman saw a decrease in delinquent behaviour, school teachers saw little change. Is it possible that the school teachers were more removed from the project and hence in a position to be more objective? This should not be viewed as a condemnation of the Spring Street Project. Given limited funds, this type of "soft" evaluation is both reasonable and meaningful. The likelihood of bias is a risk which is taken openly.

Obviously, biases could operate in the opposite direction. When the relations between the police and certain delinquency programs are strained, it seems that police have harassed and arrested youths who were involved in programs more frequently than those who were not.

Another illustration of bias which favours an experimental group is noted in an unpublished paper by Bottoms and McClintock (Hood and Sparks, 1970: 207). It seems that subjects in the experimental group of one phase of a community treatment project in California were more likely to receive parole suspension rather than parole revocation. Parole revocation (termination) was defined as "failure" in a project but parole suspension was a temporary situation which did not count as a "failure." When the experimental group committed minor offences, 44 had their parole revoked while 596 had parole suspended. For the control group, of those committing minor offences 87 had parole revoked as compared with 277 suspensions. It seems that the experimental group was treated more permissively than the controls. Hood and Sparks (1970: 209) also note that probation officers supervising the control subjects for the Provo experiment, mentioned earlier, may have been motivated to work harder to keep boys on probation.

Related to the problem of bias is the difficult problem of creating control groups and keeping them from being contaminated. I have provided some illustrations of how control groups are influenced simply by being involved in an evaluation. In addition, it is easy to see how judges and administrators would question the "justice" of randomly assigning a subject to an experimental group and another to a control group. In the Provo experiment, judges completed the process by which boys were sentenced to institutions. Then, by opening an envelope, certain boys were randomly assigned to the community treatment program in the community. Not surprisingly, this procedure drew some criticism. As long as everything we are doing is ineffective, one might argue that it doesn't matter whether a juvenile is in a treatment or a control group. However, this argument is not very palatable to most people, and perhaps it is not wise.

Obviously, I have only mentioned a few sources of bias. Although efforts must be made to control such biases, it is reasonable to assume that they will usually be present. In programs placing great emphasis on evaluation by means of the experimental design, such biases are very serious. In "softer" evaluations, which are not so intensely concerned with the specific impact of various experimental variables, these biases can be viewed as part of the dynamics of such programs. Could these biases be used as agents of change? For example, what is the eventual outcome of having social workers take unusual steps to keep those under their supervision from becoming official failures? This would bias the results of a rigorous evaluation, of course, but aside from making it difficult to assess the impact of the experimental variable, would it help the client?

The politicization of evaluation research

Carol Weiss (1970; 1973) points out that researchers who attempt to evaluate social action programs are beset by a number of problems arising out of pressures in the community. In addition to the problems mentioned above, there are problems related to careers of individuals, rewards for accomplishment, and political factors. In Canada, government agencies have probably been lenient with researchers in terms of standards of relevance and research quality. It is possible that political pressures from agencies funding the research are not as great in Canada as they are in the United States. On the other hand, very few members of a program staff are fond of having evaluators poking their noses into the operation of their programs. Despite noises about "accountability to the taxpayer" the evaluator is regarded as a snoop. Those in charge of programs feel they know that the program is doing well and believe that evaluation is of little use. Evaluation is frequently viewed as a threat and a barrier to helping clients.

But a major danger from the Canadian perspective is that evaluation may in fact serve the purpose of damaging innovative and venturesome programs while supporting traditional ones. The problem is that rigorous evaluation tends to reveal that programs have had a minimum of impact. When the evaluators are able to operate independently, utilizing rigorous techniques, and when the program is innovative and possibly struggling with other agencies, it is easy to show that the program has had little impact. On the other hand, well-established agencies have the means to resist the impact of negative evaluation. It is easy to argue that programs should not be abandoned simply because the results are disappointing at the initial stages, but there are few situations in Canada where long-term support for innovative programs will be encouraged if, in fact, the evidence suggests no impact.

In fairness, these pressures should not be viewed as detrimental. They must be recognized as meaningful factors in evaluation research. This phenomenon is not new. Donald Cressy noted some years ago that an agency organized around the administration of a particular program fills the needs of many employees and in one sense it has its *own* needs for survival (1958). As a result, any evaluative research which shows that a program is ineffective, and therefore threatens the agency itself, should be considered with considerable caution. The simplest method is to insure that evaluative research is not initiated, but that is an unpopular stand at the present time when everyone demands evaluation. Another strategy is to insure that the results will be "inconclusive."

It is not surprising, then, to find that sabotage of evaluations occurs. For example, the vocational training program at Children's Village in Dobb's Ferry, New York, met hostility from the education department of the institution, which believed instead in academic education. Staff hostility exerted subtle pressures of disapproval (Zivan, 1966). In addition, boys who went back to school before getting a job often received advice that conflicted with counseling from the vocational program.

Staff hostility to an innovative phase of any program and hostility toward an evaluator should be taken as a given in any evaluation. It is unreasonable to hope that it will not occur and then be shocked and dismayed when it does. To say that the status of the evaluator is "ambiguous" is to put it nicely.

Perhaps the political aspects of evaluation research are less clear in

Canada, but the large $21 million Mobilization for Youth Project in New York certainly provides an ample illustration of this problem. With approximately four hundred people on staff, it was not surprising that some opponents of the project were able to find staff members with "communist leanings." The size of the project alone guaranteed attention from the media and conflict with traditional institutions.

The battles between MFY and powerful groups in New York are not unique among action programs. Simply conducting such programs is hazardous. Evaluating them may be explosive. Since such political factors make objective evaluation close to impossible, we should heed the opinions of Robert Weiss and Martin Rein, who argue for a qualitative or process-oriented evaluation which attempts to learn what happened without attempting to make decisions concerning success (1969).

Research design and problems of interpretation

The reader may begin to believe that the major problem lies in the fact that self-interest among those working in and administering a program make worthwhile evaluation impossible. Let us be extremely naive and optimistic and assume that we have resolved all of these problems and see whether simply looking at data itself will provide clear directions for policy decisions. I have simplified the data gathered by Evelyn Guttman with the California Youth Authority (1963), but it serves to illustrate a very interesting point. In Figure 4.1 I have attempted to present the research design which was launched in two institutions in the California Youth Authority. I have simplified the experimental variables considerably. There were two types of institutions, one which I will call "pessimistic" and the other which I will call "optimistic." Let us simply assume that the staff in the "pessimistic" institution feel that there is little hope for clients who come into their program.

Let us further assume that an experimental program utilizing psychiatric treatment is going to be launched in each of the two institutions. Again, let us ignore the specific nature of the experimental program but simply assume that it is a meaningful, well thought out attempt to improve the performance of people who enter these institutions. As one can see from Figure 4.1 there are four different groups of subjects to be compared.

Figure 4.1
Psychiatric Treatment in Two Institutions

	Type of Institution "Optimistic"	"Pessimistic"
Experimental	1	3
Control	2	4

On the basis of information just provided, which group should perform best on some indicator of success such as recidivism rates? Most would be inclined to choose group number 1 as most likely to perform well. Furthermore, most persons would choose group number 4 as the group least likely to succeed. The ranking of groups 2 and 3 would depend on whether one feels the experimental program or the institutional milieu is more important. Many sociology students select the milieu over the experimental program and rank 2 over 3, but those with a counseling orientation might rank 3 over 2. But what actually happened? It turned out that the most successful group was group 4, the control group in the pessimistic institution. The group which did worst was number 2, the control group in the optimistic institution. The experimental groups fell somewhere in between with a roughly equal level of success.

Perhaps these findings are somewhat confusing. Let us change the conditions somewhat and assume that similar types of studies were made in Canada with slightly fewer resources and fewer choices in terms of 1) types of institutions or 2) the use of control groups. First, let us assume that we have only one institution to study, and it happens to be "optimistic." Further, let us assume that we have solved the problems facing experimental and control groups and can successfully compare groups number 1 and number 2. The finding is very clear, the experimental program did better than the control group. This is pleasing to the staff, and the recommendations made to policy makers are clear and unequivocal.

Let us now assume that the same study was done in a different locale, where the only insitution available turned out to be "pessimistic." This time we are comparing group number 3 with group number 4. The experimental group did worse than the control group. Again the policy recommendation is very clear. Don't establish this type of program permanently; it seems to do more damage than good.

Let us put ourselves in a third situation which does not use a control group. We want to attempt a different experimental type of program in the two institutions we have in our province, one which happens to be "optimistic" and the other which happens to be "pessimistic." Is it possible that our program will have a different impact in the two institutions? (Being sophisticated researchers, we are alert to the possibility of interaction effects.) We compare group 1 and 3 and find there is no difference. Our recommendation to the director of institutions is again very clear. The type of staff simply doesn't matter; the experiment is just as effective (or ineffective) in either type of institution. There is no need to hire optimistic staff members; pessimistic ones work just as well.

There is still a fourth possibility. We don't have the money, the imagination or the talent to launch an experimental program in our two institutions, one of which is "optimistic" and the other "pessimistic." However, we would like to see what sort of success rate the clients have who pass through these two institutions. Therefore, we compare group 2 with group 4. This time our evidence is even stronger and the inferences much clearer. The difference between group 2 and group 4 is large and those passing through the optimistic institution did considerably worse than those who passed through the pessimistic institution. Clearly, we must insist that the director of the institutions get rid of those optimistic people in the first institution and replace them with the most pessimistic staff members he can find!

Now the reader might be inclined to see this as a ludicrously unlikely situation, but it is sobering to consider what type of study might be launched in Canada or in any other area where the level of sophistication in correctional research is lower than that of the California system. There could easily be difficulties either in comparing two types of institutions or in comparing a program with a control group. In other words, the situations I have described above are much more likely to be conducted in reality in Canada or most parts of the world than the more complex plan which was launched in California. If we were to rely on the findings of any of these four types of studies, we would have come up with four distinct conclusions and four different policy recommendations.

This illustration further reinforces my argument that the evaluation of programs does not necessarily illuminate the problem. While the findings may be clear, they may still be incorrect. Is it possible that it is premature for us to use evaluation procedures for determining policy? Perhaps rigorous evaluation, at least in terms of assessing outcomes, is premature for most delinquency prevention programs in Canada. However, a more flexible approach might be worthwhile. Let us examine the difficulties of one recent Canadian evaluation of a delinquency prevention program and see if it illustrates some of the points mentioned above. Furthermore, we might ask how some of these difficulties could be avoided in the future.

The Vancouver Spring Street Project

The Spring Street Project in Vancouver was influenced by the detached worker programs which originated in the eastern United States and were later introduced into Canada. The most extensive application of this approach seems to be in Ottawa (Keech, 1962). The history and effectiveness of these detached street worker programs will be discussed in more detail in Chapter 9 but for the time being let us focus only on the evaluation of the program rather than on the program itself.

Following the guidelines of an ideal evaluation, the Spring Street Project tried to use an experimental design (Ratner, 1974). An attempt was made to create a control group. Unfortunately, the types of pressures which were apparent in the Provo Project, and which face almost all experimental programs, were also present in Vancouver. It became obvious that a true control group was not possible. An attempt to form a comparison group (incorrectly referred to as a control group in the report) uncovered the fact that 23 percent of the parents of boys involved in the experimental program were high school graduates whereas 57 percent of the parents of the boys in the comparison group were high school graduates.

Despite these differences Robert Ratner and his colleagues were able to make good use of this comparison group. They noted that there were other differences: 70 percent of the experimentals had positive self-images versus 80 percent of the comparison group. Similarly, 83 percent of the experimentals felt that delinquent behaviour didn't get you anywhere versus 93 percent for the comparison group (Ratner, 1974: 84). These, of course, are not impressive differences. Although the comparison group was different from the experimental group, it was possible to estimate the nature and size of those differences. Hence, a comparison group can still be useful as an approximate gauge when attempting to determine the impact of a program. By focusing instead on a fairly large comparison group, one might be able to select out portions of that comparison group which would resemble the experimental group. In other words, compromising with the ideal design at the beginning might save stress.

The Spring Street Project also illustrated other typical problems. The researchers were in an ambiguous status in the eyes of the social workers who were running the project. It is rare to find a major project where there has been an absence of strain between the researchers evaluating effectiveness and the staff of the program being evaluated. This project in Vancouver, like others, faced the problem of pressure to show success. Like any other normal human beings, those connected with the project wanted to view their efforts as effective.

Ratner asked the social workers to assess the effectiveness of the program as well. Interestingly enough, the workers were more conservative in their assessment than the supervisor. Again, if we are primarily concerned with an objective assessment of the outcome one could question the validity of such a measure; however, the social workers could have been much more alert than an outsider when it comes to distinguishing between weak and strong components operating within the program.

Note that utilizing these internal assessors effectively may require different strategies. For example, some of the social workers who were considered particularly effective rated the effectiveness of their own efforts somewhat lower than the self ratings of other workers. If one were to use these opinions as measures of outcome, it could be misleading. However, these ideas might lead to valuable internal modifications within a project.

Unlike the methodologically rigid research director of the Seattle Opportunities for Youth Project described in the previous chapter, Ratner also utilized "softer" indicators of success. He found that most of the boys and their parents approved of the project. Approximately half reported improvement in their family relations. Delinquent behaviour seemed to have decreased. True, these assessments may not convince those demanding a purer experimental design, but given the inconsistency from one project to the next, this type of information could be useful.

Summary

In this chapter we have examined several sophisticated delinquency prevention programs and their evaluations. In each situation the efforts to meet the standards of true evaluation added stresses to the program itself. Secondly, even sophisticated projects have trouble controlling for biases. Thirdly, political factors and the normal needs of agencies to demonstrate that they are doing their job competently frequently play a role. As a result, innovative programs are often more susceptible to evaluations than entrenched programs.

Incidentally, this does not mean that entrenched programs are automatically less effective than innovative ones. I simply argue that innovative programs might require the sort of evaluation that would nurture their strengths rather than expose their weaknesses. However, such programs are the ones most likely to face a rigorous evaluation emphasizing the outcome.

In Canada there are some promising indications that certain agencies are more protected from political pressures demanding evidence of success. For example, the Federal Penitentiary Service has encouraged careful evaluation of programs even though the findings have not been flattering to the programs involved. These programs are primarily concerned with correctional centres, however, and deal with only a few juveniles. Most juvenile programs are under provincial jurisdiction and are much more exposed to the pressures mentioned above. Some of the provinces, such as Quebec, Ontario, Manitoba, and British Columbia, have developed traditions for ongoing research. The larger provinces can also support full-time research units within their child welfare and criminal justice systems and may be able to develop the sophistication necessary to deal with these problems. If ongoing research were an established part of a criminal justice system, the continual examination of data and activities would appear less threatening.

However, sophistication is not the primary concern. Commitment to research as an ongoing process is needed.

Illustrations of this cooperative role of research can be found in Ontario. Lambert and Madden (1974, 1976) collaborated extensively with the staff of the Vanier Institute in their attempts to understand the dynamics of that ongoing program. Although interested in outcome, both staff and researchers were probing for insights within the institution and in the aftercare program. Another Canadian illustration of collaboration among researchers, staff members, and subjects is provided by Richard Walsh in Manitoba (1976). Perhaps such studies will provide guidance if we hope to avoid the politicization of evaluation research.

Even when many problems have been resolved, the interpretation of findings is still very difficult. The studies in the "optimistic" and "pessimistic" institutions mentioned above illustrate that clear policy recommendations rarely come out of a single evaluation. Even as evaluations grow in complexity and sophistication, they generate as many questions as answers.

Is not the message fairly clear? Even when systematic attempts are made, a multitude of problems manages to compromise the most carefully made plans. Is it realistic to pursue a direction where the likelihood of success is so minimal and the possibility of stress is so great?

Chapter 5

Alternatives to the Experimental Design

Parpalaid: *You may think me too much of a stickler for ethical standards, but doesn't your method subordinate the interest of the patient just a bit to that of the doctor?*
Knock: *Dr. Parpalaid, you're forgetting that there is an interest which is greater than either . . . the interest of medicine. I serve that interest and that alone. . . . You've given me a township inhabited by . . . individuals without direction. My function is to direct them, to lead them into a life of medicine. I put them to bed and see what can be made of them: tuberculosis, neurasthenia, arteriosclerosis, whatever you like, but* something, *for God's sake. Nothing gets on my nerves like that indeterminate nonentity called a healthy man.*

—JULES ROMAINS

Possible Strategies of Evaluation Research for Canada

The evidence cited in the previous chapters suggests that we should cut down on the number of delinqency prevention programs and avoid systematic evaluations, especially of innovative projects. Nevertheless, the desire to "do good" overwhelms logical arguments. A compulsion drives most of us to overlook, despite the overwhelming evidence, the fact that our attempts to improve things have little impact on delinquency. F. H. McClintock is an experienced criminologist who has been involved in an action research program at the Dover Borstal in England for a number of years. The final report for that project shows that the attempts to bring about significant changes in a group of youthful offenders came to the same end as do most programs—nothing much happened (Bottoms and McClintock, 1973). But in Appendix A of his book, McClintock, who has been involved in extensive action research in England for a number of years, shows that hope springs eternal from the human breast.

> It is hoped, however, that the report on this project fully justifies the confidence that was eventually accorded to those engaged in these joint activities, and that the results of this kind of evaluation are of

> sufficient penological significance to warrant the extension of this type of action-research design to other penological problems (415).

Similarly, the research workers in this project felt they had introduced some new approaches and techniques. Of course, they would be the first to admit that this work is still in its infancy, but they argue that "more resources will have to be invested in such work if refined and precise tools of evaluation are to be evolved (398)." The book ends noting the disappointing results but with the plea that any new proposals continue to be accompanied by proper research evaluation. The governor of the Dover Borstal, where the study was done, writes "with a little more help and a little more time we might very well have begun a breakthrough."

Is there any reason to think that Canada will learn from the experience of others? The reader will surely agree that our desire to "do good," while not rational, is at least understandable. Therefore, let us see what strategies would be most useful for a society that maintains unjustified optimism in the face of facts that indicate the futility of our actions.

The Merits of Careful Record Keeping

Very few people are opposed to careful record keeping. The point I wish to make is that careful record keeping may provide basic data for understanding, if not evaluating, some of the activities connected with the prevention of or supposed correction of delinquency. Unfortunately, the records on juveniles in Canada are not always kept in a manner which promotes the most effective usage. Assuming that there is data on every case which passes through our system, we might use them in the manner suggested in Table 5.1. This table contains information on four different types of programs for juvenile offenders being conducted in a hypothetical province. There are no control groups and the focus is on scrupulously collecting information as people pass through the system. The intention is to compare the effectiveness of three different institutional programs with each other and with probation. There is one maximum security institution, an "intermediate house" which is less restrictive, and a forest camp which is less restrictive again. As the years go by, it is noted that the recidivism rate for those who were in the maximum security institution was 56 percent, while for those who were put on probation it was only 30 percent. Naturally, these figures are not comparable because those placed on probation are usually a better risk than those who are sent to maximum security institutions. How can we make comparisons between the two types of situations?

Is there some way we can look at similar boys in the different types of institutional or probation settings? Let us assume that we feel that "family background" is an important variable. In Table 5.1 the cases are divided into those who have a "poor" family background and a "good"

Table 5.1
Evaluation Without Control Groups (Hypothetical)

		Family Background				
		Poor		*Good*		*Number of Boys in Each Program*
	Seriousness of Offence	*Serious*	*Not Serious*	*Serious*	*Not Serious*	
	Recidivism Rate	*Number of boys in each category in each of the treatment programs*				
Lakeview Forest Camp	32%	15	25	25	35	100
"Intermediate" House	45%	30	25	25	20	100
Maximum Security	56%	40	20	30	10	100
Probation	30%	5	40	10	45	100

family background. Similarly, it has been decided that the "seriousness" of the offence should be taken into account; therefore, the subjects are divided into those who have committed "serious" offences and those who have committed "less serious" offences. For simplicity, let us assume there are one hundred subjects who have been through each of the four programs. Note that the distribution of boys with different types of family background and seriousness of offence differs for each of the four programs. For example, in this hypothetical study, it seems that in the maximum security program forty of the one hundred boys came from a poor family background and committed serious offences. Only five of the one hundred boys in the probation program had a poor family background and committed serious offences. Is it reasonable to compare the forty boys in the maximum security program with the five boys in the probation program? If, in fact, family background and the type of offence committed are the most crucial variables in terms of determining success, then this is a reasonable comparison. If it turns out that other factors are more important (age, IQ, schooling, etc.), then perhaps they should replace or be added to the two variables chosen.

Table 5.1 contains a number of interesting comparisons. In the last column, are boys who came from a good family background and committed crimes that were not very serious. In reality, the number of boys in this category might be small; in fact, the ten cases which are hypothesized as being in the maximum security institution might be an overprediction. The important thing is to try to understand not just the results of each program, but the results for various categories of clients who are involved in each program. The simple design in Table 5.1 permits comparison of boys who had similar characteristics in each of the four programs. It is quite possible that the programs could have a different impact on different groups of boys, and not always in the predicted pattern.

One can use recidivism rates as a criterion of success; however, there may be better indicators of "success," such as success in school or finding a job. Perhaps it would be better not to talk about success at all, but simply to try to understand what seems to be happening in each program. Obviously, many other questions could be investigated. What percentage of the boys in each category are Indians? Is there a different pattern for boys with higher IQs? Lower IQs?

Table 5.1 uses two variables, family background and seriousness of offence. Theoretically, one could use more "control variables" in order to make more meaningful comparisons among clients of this system who are similar in other respects. Obviously, this is severely limited by the number of cases involved in each program. Various statistical techniques can be used to cope with modest numbers of cases and more variables. Such procedures approximate in a more sophisticated manner the logic suggested here.

The experienced researcher might react to these suggestions with the comment, "There is nothing new here. We have been using such techniques for a long time." Right! One advantage of using such simple procedures is that they are familiar to people with even elementary research skills. Furthermore, people in the community can understand what is being done. Sophisticated data analysis can be a barrier to communication between researchers and policy makers. My plea is for the systematic gathering of basic data which can be analyzed from a variety of perspectives. Unfortunately this suggestion is rarely heeded in Canada. Rather than criticizing our present procedures, I will focus on potential ways of utilizing this strategy.

Several things should be obvious. First of all, large numbers of cases would make it easier to make certain comparisons. If we dealt with *all* of the cases being processed through our systems, instead of selecting out certain portions for careful study, we would have large numbers to use in our analyses. Specific research projects take samples. These are appropriate at times, but if we use data generated by a good record keeping system, the large numbers permit simpler and clearer analyses. At the present time, much information about juveniles is collected unsystematically. If forms were devised so that the same information could be gathered more rapidly, no expense would be added to the present record keeping process. In fact, administrative procedures might be improved and eventually additional or more useful data would be collected.

Instead of using experimental groups to make evaluations, it might be better to create statistically comparable groups of subjects within each institutional program and compare them. These comparisons may not always be appropriate, but if we are using computer techniques, we may go back to the data several times and try to make them more appropriate. Agreement on a single measure of success is not really necessary. We are free to try a number of different indicators, either traditional ones or new ones. Instead of attempting to decide whether a program is "successful" or not, it might be much more worthwhile simply to try to understand what is happening. This activity should not threaten those launching programs. The steady accumulation of information may have little impact in the short run, but such information may later be useful in policy development.

The advantage of relying heavily on a large data base is that it provides great flexibility in analysis. In addition to offering a more economical way of generating routine reports, different investigators can ask different questions using the same data. It is true that using statistical controls to compare various groups of individuals is not as adequate as the ideal experimental program in which one has carefully matched experimental and control groups. On the other hand, it is much more economical to make comparisons by computer than by designing and implementing an experimental program.

Records linking vs. central registers

With good record keeping, other exciting possibilities are available. For example, the technique of "records linking" offers intriguing opportunities. Let us illustrate this point with a study which utilized seven thousand cases from a juvenile court in the United States (Simpson and Van Arsdol, 1967). An extensive amount of information is gathered on each individual when a national census is taken. Naturally, this is confidential information. Although many people see the computer as a threat to privacy, and indeed this may be true, it also offers the possibility of much greater protection than conventional techniques. If bureaucrats are continually pawing through folders to retrieve information, privacy can be lost. Computer techniques enable us to deal with thousands of cases without identifying the individuals concerned. Let us use the seven thousand cases in the study mentioned above to illustrate some of these points. Assume that we have information on Johnny Jones from juvenile court. We would like to know more about Johnny's parents and the conditions in which they live. Rather than trying to gather this information as a separate task, could we somehow match Johnny with the information gathered on his parents in the last census? Naturally, if Johnny has a social insurance number and we have a listing of the social insurance numbers of all the children whose parents were surveyed in the last census, the process would be much easier. Since this is not the case, the computer must try to match names (which are sometimes misspelled), addresses (which change), and ages (which are sometimes incorrect). It is a complicated task, but modern computers can do it and Canada has expertise in this area within Statistics Canada. In the study mentioned above, the delinquent juvenile and the adult in the juvenile's household were matched in 78 percent of the cases. There is good indication that accuracy can be increased considerably with experience and newer techniques.

The advantage of having such a body of information is to permit us to ask the same sorts of questions we asked before but with additional information about a child's family, housing, etc. Do boys who have taken part in certain types of programs across the country, who come from certain backgrounds, who live in certain types of dwellings, whose parents have varying levels of education, etc., have the same success rate on a variety of indices as boys with different characteristics? The questions which can be asked and the potential for interaction among variables are extensive. Note also that the logic of this procedure should permit us to follow these cases ten years later with the next census. It would also be possible, technically, to link information from our criminal justice system with welfare, manpower, and a variety of other data gathering agencies.

Naturally, it is necessary to guard against being able to identify a unique case. For example, there are very few Hungarian-born statisticians, earning high salaries, living in Ottawa, with two daughters aged such and such. Under certain conditions, unique individuals could be identified even from large numbers of cases. One way to combat this possibility is to change the exact number of cases which appear in any category. An article by Magundkar and Saveland (1973), entitled "Random Rounding to Prevent Statistical Disclosures," is an illustration of efforts by Statistics Canada to deal with this problem. In other words, it is possible to utilize such information successfully without revealing information on individuals. Our present sloppy systems of record keeping are a more serious threat to privacy.

The Province of Quebec has developed a system for providing centralized information. A multiple-copy form follows an individual through the legal-judicial system. Copies of the form are sent to Statistics Canada for reporting purposes, and also to the Central Registrar in Quebec City. This system should not be confused with records linking. A central registry refers to a common form which has been developed as part of mutual cooperation among several agencies. The records linking procedure has an advantage in that it does not require that agencies agree on the information to be gathered. Agencies gather any information they feel is pertinent. The advantage of records linking over a central registry is that it enables the collection of a much wider range of data, and agencies do not have to agree on the type of data which should be gathered. Note that records linking is not concerned about the loss of a few cases or even some incorrect matching. It is attempting to find *general* answers to broad questions.

A central registry may be the more effective way to deal with certain administrative requirements where complete knowledge of individual cases is needed for administrative decisions. However, certain agencies may have access to information about individuals which they do not need and perhaps should not have. Victor Matthews (1972) has discussed several precedents for central registry systems in his discussion of socio-legal statistics in Alberta.

Utilizing general records for evaluation has another advantage over other types of evaluation. It would be possible to look back at a number of projects over the years from a less pressured or biased standpoint. A boy involved in a particular type of action program may not develop a police record until much later. True, the information may be late in coming, but this may avoid some of the political problems, mentioned in Chapter 4, when programs are evaluated with the intention of making immediate changes. Hindsight may be less painful and permit more judicious policy making than attempts to assess programs immediately after their completion.

Another exciting possibility is to utilize computer simulation of judicial decisions. Alex MacEachern, a Canadian at the University of Southern California, has developed a number of techniques by which a judge can weigh his decision on a particular case against the effectiveness of alternate programs which have been utilized in the past. It is possible for a judge to maintain his own "box score" against past and future evidence. In the juvenile area, such decisions are moving more into the hands of directors of child welfare and similar persons, but the technique would be just as useful for anyone who must make decisions about the future of juveniles. Note, I am not suggesting that the computer makes the decision; it simply provides the decision maker with information about what has happened in the past when similar decisions were made.

Other research based upon careful recording keeping

With careful record keeping, studies of cohorts are possible, that is, a group of individuals who passed through a system at any one time can be compared with those who went through at a different time. Notice that a "system" could be many things—a school, an institution, or simply being born in a certain period. For example, Wilkins (1960) studied delinquency by year of birth in England. Looking at a period when the country was experiencing the pressures of war, he attempted to see whether or not young children were more inclined to become delinquent later in life as a result of this disruption. Jasinski (1966) used the same approach for Polish youth. These two studies contained a number of shortcomings. For example, grouping large numbers of cases into crude categories using official indicators does obscure important differences. Nonetheless, if detailed information were available on each case and records linking procedures provided us with more adequate information, the types of studies pioneered by Wilkins and Jasinski would probably yield more valuable information.

Another useful guide would be the study by Wolfgang, Figlio and Sellin, *Delinquency in a Birth Cohort* (1972). They followed all the boys born in Philadelphia in 1945 from their tenth to their eighteenth birthdays. Of the ten thousand boys in the cohort, 35 percent incurred one or more police contacts during their juvenile careers. Although some studies of this nature require extensive planning and sophisticated follow-up procedures, records linking would permit similar questions to be asked in the future with greater ease. These directions are particularly promising for Canada, as the technical expertise needed is currently available. It makes sense to build on our strengths instead of on our weaknesses.

Canadian studies utilizing promising techniques

Irving Waller's study, *Men Released from Prison* (1974), is an illustration of the type of study that was built on good records. Waller compared men who were released directly from prison with those who were released on parole. The groups differed in a number of respects, but Waller was able to get answers to his questions by using statistical techniques which approximated the logic suggested earlier in Table 5.1. Parole seemed to make very little difference in the ultimate recidivism rate. True, those paroled did have a better record than those released directly from prison, but the parolees were more inclined to be married. In this study, as in previous studies, married men were less inclined to return to crime than single men. When Waller controlled for marriage, being paroled or released directly from prison did not seem to make much difference.

Waller gathered information by interviews directly with the men themselves, and it is easy to see that this information could then be effectively linked with systematic records. If another researcher were to decide that he would like to compare Waller's subjects with a group of unemployed men with age, marital, and other characteristics similar to those of the ex-inmates, his task would be easier if Manpower had this information in a systematic form and if a records linking procedure permitted arrest rates to be added to the group with a history of unemployment. Note that these steps could be taken without identifying individuals if proper precautions were taken.

Similarly, Hogarth's study of Ontario judges (1971) could have been accomplished more easily if characteristics of agents of social control were systematically included in our record keeping. At present, suggestions to gather such information seem far-fetched. Compared with evaluating an action program though, this would be much less difficult.

Another type of research in this area being conducted in Canada is the work being done by R. Gordon Cassidy and his colleagues in the statistical division of the Ministry of the Solicitor General (Cassidy *et al.*, 1974). They are trying to develop computer simulation models of the Canadian criminal justice system. Eventually, they hope to be able to predict changes in one part of the system if changes are made somewhere else. Their work points up the need for resolving certain problems within our data gathering system. For example, the police may arrest a man for burglary. He may be released on bail and commit another burglary. The police lay two charges, but in court it is recorded as a single case. Police and court statistics, then, have different meanings. The resolution of such problems is necessary before data collected by the various agencies can be utilized effectively to describe the flow of cases from one agency to another. In addition, the process of resolving these issues helps to develop a clearer understanding of the operations of the criminal justice system.

A study by Brian Grosman (1973) provides another illustration of the types of questions which could be asked if we utilized data already systematically gathered. The police must make decisions as to which calls represent needs for police involvement. Every time someone calls to report an emergency, the communication officer must assess the other demands being placed upon available police resources and decide whether or not the call should be answered. His decision could be extremely significant. Clifford Shearing and others at the Centre of Criminology in Toronto have also been working on such problems. This data is being systematically recorded and the police in Canada are sophisticated users of the computer. Several studies being supported by the Law Reform Commission of Canada suggest that we have just begun to exploit the possibility of these data.

It is interesting to note that while the police are sophisticated handlers of data, the courts are not. In the studies done by Hogarth (1971) and Hagan (1974), extensive efforts were made to gather information, because the courts in Ontario and Alberta did not have the necessary data to deal with the questions they were studying. If our routine data gathering procedures included information on the people who operate these systems, such as judges, probation officers, etc., we might be able to deal better with some of the questions raised in regard to the operation of agencies of social control. Certainly, the characteristics of the people who run the systems are important to the outcomes. This is not to say that delinquency is simply the product of the response of the system.

Rather, gathering information on the various actors in the system would help us to answer some rather basic questions; for example, do different structural arrangements in certain types of juvenile courts lead to different results?

The main thrust of this argument is that separating out a significant portion of our resources for evaluating "action" programs is a poor strategy in a society which has limited resources for such activities. By devoting resources to tasks already being done, such as record keeping, we might in fact learn the answers to questions posed in such evaluation programs, for example, what sorts of strategies tend to have positive results? True, such information might come as a result of observing activities over a fairly long period of time, but experience should tell us that efforts to bring about rapid changes have not been particularly profitable.

An additional advantage of an efficient record keeping system is that agencies themselves could examine their activities more easily. They would also be more able to communicate with researchers who wish to perform complex analyses. In addition, administrative costs might be reduced. It is more expensive to prepare reports by fumbling through files and tallying items with a paper and pencil than it is to use a computer. If we were to use modern procedures for doing the routine administrative tasks, we might create the means for using that same data more effectively for a variety of research purposes. It seems unlikely that conditions will exist in Canada which would enable a delinquency prevention program to be adequately evaluated. On the other hand, even partial successes in improving our record keeping procedures would be beneficial.

When an Evaluation Is Necessary

Despite everything that has been said so far, evaluations of a specific program will continue to be demanded. Let us note some of the necessary conditions for a successful evaluation: (1) the maintenance of an experimental population and a comparable control group; (2) one or more theories which make specific claims about what should happen; (3) program personnel who are aware that most objectively evaluated programs in the past have failed but are willing to proceed anyway; (4) mechanisms which prevent people with vested interests from sabotaging the project; and (5) techniques for insulating the evaluators from a variety of pressures.

These conditions are hard to find, but some of them could be approximated if Canada were to use strategies similar to those employed by the California correctional system where a certain percentage of the correctional budget was dedicated to research. If Canada were to follow this method, instead of justifying specific projects which are poorly understood, it might permit concentration on ongoing research itself rather than public relations. Another feature of the California system was that program personnel were committed to conducting programs over a long period of time. In other words, personnel do not have to be dependent on the success or failure of a specific program for their future well-being or job security. The ongoing systematic commitment of funds to research had several obvious benefits over time. Aside from a steady stream of information that was available to policy makers, including studies on cost analysis (Adams, 1967; Robison, 1969), the availability of the data permitted secondary analyses that have provided new insights. For example, the well-known work on group homes and community treatment (Palmer, 1972, 1973a, 1973b) has been reanalyzed by Lerman (1975), who came to different conclusions.

In Canada, our research endeavours in delinquency prevention are usually done in fits and starts. We create commissions, launch new programs for evaluation and assessment but, until recently, we rarely developed agencies dedicated to the long-term process of understanding our criminal justice system. Occasionally, conditions may be ripe for a genuine evaluation and an experienced agency operating from a secure base might attempt it. For example, here in Canada, there are many advocates of William Glasser's "reality therapy" (1965). The strategy is widespread and it is reasonable to ask if it is really effective, instead of relying on the testimonials of those involved. While the technique certainly has its appeal, the argument could be made that a scientific evaluation is appropriate rather than the sort of subjective evaluations which are presently available. But one should weigh the consequences of such an evaluation. It is quite probable that this technique, like those in the past, will show no impact on delinquency. Such findings would not be well received and could lead to a number of stresses.

Are there alternative strategies which might permit a systematic evaluation to be less painful? Instead of proceeding in the conventional way and establishing experimental and control groups over a period of approximately one year, it might be better to go through several different stages. For example, in the first stage, a program might go through a shakedown in which the staff employs a critical attitude in assessing themselves and various aspects of their program. If there is some argreement that procedures are standardized enough, the staff may consider a second stage. It is not necessary to be convinced that the treatment is "good" but agreement is needed that there are one or more strategies which could be conducted with some consistency and that it would be worthwhile to investigate the impact of these alternative strategies. Many programs in Canada come to this point where staff members see weaknesses or questionable aspects in a project but would still like to see more systematic evidence before making changes.

In the second stage a traditional experimental design might be used with a relatively small number of cases. Expectations for this stage would be modest. Rather than attempting to answer the crucial question of whether or not a strategy is worthwhile, the emphasis may be on exploration of different strategies. Which strategies should be refined, which ones dropped, which ones modified? Should combinations be attempted? Should certain strategies be attempted under different conditions?

A third stage might return to refinement and standardization of those strategies selected as profitable. Data should be gathered at this stage as well as during the first and second stages, but the focus would be on defining the direction of the next stage and on developing data gathering procedures which would be appropriate to the larger questions.

Finally, a fourth stage might attempt a full-blown experimental design using past experience to avoid some of the problems which will certainly arise in the first three stages. In other words, it would be advisable to anticipate problems at stage 1, to expect minimal or no impact at stage 2, and to entertain the possibility that at the end of stage 3 it would be ill advised to proceed with stage 4. A long-term perspective may lessen the emotional commitment which usually creates tensions for any evaluation. If evaluations can be seen as long-term projects which help us to understand rather than as short-term attempts to provide information for policy decisions concerning a specific program, they may be more rewarding. Closer collaboration between researchers and treatment personnel over a longer period of time would also result.

Evaluation research as a long-term commitment

The reader might argue that such an evaluation plan would take five years or longer. A cabinet minister may complain that he might be out of office by the time anyone could answer his simple question. True. Quick answers to questions regarding delinquency prevention are not forthcoming. Instead of short-term, *ad hoc* attempts at evaluation, we should focus on ongoing evaluations which are not burdened with the responsibility of providing an answer to a policy question. This implies establishing research programs as part of an ongoing service agency for a ten- or fifteen-year period with the guarantee that there will be continuity of efforts even though findings are not particularly promising.

There are a number of separate functions which could be served by the same project (Hackler, 1967). In addition to testing the effectiveness of a specific technique, a project could permit the testing of related theoretical ideas. As far as the action workers in the program are concerned, it should be clear that their role should be evaluated in terms of the integrity which they have shown in carrying out the original plan. Unfortunately, action workers are sometimes considered to be responsible for the results of an experiment. If the procedure being used is in fact incapable of bringing about the desired changes, a worker who utilizes the procedure correctly will have no impact.

Another way of modifying the conventional experimental design would be to look carefully at those individuals who show considerable success or considerable failure in a given program. Those boys or girls who respond extremely well or poorly to various programs may have a variety of individual characteristics and unique life experiences. It would be worthwhile to search for patterns among such children and also ask whether these children had unique experiences as part of the program. Which social workers did they come in contact with? Were the dynamics created by their particular living group somewhat different from the others? It may not be possible to apply a procedure with any degree of uniformity, but an emphasis on examining more intensely what we are presently doing, either unwittingly or deliberately, might yield greater returns than spending so much effort thinking up new ways to "treat" kids.

But even if we were able to be much more sophisticated and much more flexible in conducting evaluation research in cooperation with administrators who are extremely secure and do not flinch at failure, is the procedure worth it? My basic argument is that it is a poor investment compared to careful record keeping. Although the careful analysis of data gathered as part of the systematic recording keeping procedure certainly has its limitations, these limitations come to light without being as disruptive as the discoveries which surface in an experimental design. The knowledge which would grow out of continued careful data analysis would probably come gradually. New questions would evolve and old questions would be viewed as inappropriate. Dramatic breakthroughs probably would not occur, but as information was steadily fed back into the system, this very lack of drama might lead to the more effective utilization of knowledge.

Here in Canada, we would probably learn as much by watching the experiments being conducted in the United States and Great Britain rather than launching such experiments ourselves. At present, we do not pay much attention to the work which has been done elsewhere. Canada seems to persist in launching programs that have been shown to be inadequate elsewhere. (See the "talk therapies" discussed in Chapter 9.) While a truly wise strategy may not be available to us, repeating the errors of others does not seem like the best use of our resources. Therefore, we should consider a strategy which focuses primarily on understanding our present system before we begin tinkering with it. Modest changes might be more effective in the long run than dramatic ones.

We should also question the basic assumption which underlies so many of our programs, such as those which attempt to reduce juvenile delinquency. We assume that if we can simply do something to these trouble makers, *they* will stop being delinquent, that delinquency is something nasty *they* do. Obviously the rest of the society and the agencies we have established to deal with various problems are basically sound. The problem lies within the delinquent. One does not need to be a Marxist radical to recognize the possibility that the basic question we are asking is irrelevant. If so, it is quite understandable that our attempts in the past to "cure" delinquency and "rehabilitate" offenders have naturally led to failure.

Chapter 6

Who Shall Lead Us?

What such enterprises do demonstrate . . . is that when social scientists enter the political lists, they are open to attack just like anyone else who plays the power game. Their anguished shrieks of "foul" and "unfair" when this happens are reminiscent of the cries of the Plains Indians who discovered that their magic vests, inspired by the Sun Dance, did not turn the bullets of the U.S. Cavalry. Politicians, like boxers, must learn to protect themselves at all times, but in modern society this requires full time specialization, and it is doubtful that we can be politicians and sociologists at the same time.

—EDWIN LEMERT

The Role of the Experts in Delinquency Prevention

In many areas of life we turn to experts for guidance. Perhaps our confidence in such persons is not completely warranted, but it is clear that most auto mechanics repair automobiles more effectively than most medical doctors, and most physicians are better at doing surgery than most mechanics. Similarly, the experts in delinquency prevention probably give better advice than the man in the street, but unlike the auto mechanic, it is more difficult to prove competence or incompetence in areas like delinquency.

There are several aspects to being an expert. One is searching for knowledge, doing research. Another is predicting what will happen if certain changes are made or are not made. Let us treat these two tasks separately. Most sociologists, psychologists and others who study delinquency are trained to do research. Eventually, one assumes that research will lead to useful knowledge. There is some debate, however, about the utility of much of the knowledge that has been gained in the study of delinquency prevention programs. Some would argue that in correctional research, attempts to assess the impact of various programs may in fact serve the interests of the criminal justice system rather than the interests of those being processed by that system (Robison, 1973).

But aside from this bias, there is also the question of whether or not research in delinquency prevention has come to the correct conclusions. Contradictory findings from project to project are common. Paul Lerman has reviewed the data gathered by some of the most carefully documented programs from California and argues that the original researchers came to incorrect conclusions (1975). Of course, most delinquency research findings will not be reviewed; therefore, the claims made after presenting findings will frequently be accepted. Since the experts do not agree on the facts, how much confidence can the public place in expert opinion?

In other words, what evidence do we have that "experts" are in a position to say whether or not a particular program is "good"? Since it is difficult to rate experts on this type of wisdom, let us turn to another aspect of being an expert in deviance, an area where there is more evidence: the prediction of dangerous behaviour. Perhaps it is unfair to use the ability to predict behaviour as an indicator of judgement in other matters; but if the claims of experts are invalid in one area, we have reason to question their wisdom in others.

The discussion that follows is primarily concerned with adult rather than juvenile behaviour, but the ability to predict dangerous behaviour should be seen as an illustration of a broader range of skills. I use psychiatrists as my main example, but the principle applies to social scientists, lawyers and other experts as well.

The Prediction of Dangerous Behaviour

In 1974 two policemen were killed in Calgary by a man who had been diagnosed as unbalanced. The public responded predictably and asked the age-old question: "Since the man was unbalanced, why wasn't he treated before someone was killed?" There are several problems. First, can we predict who is dangerous? And second, can we effectively treat individuals who are so diagnosed? The second question will be left to Chapters 8-11, where I discuss the efficacy of various treatment strategies. The question of predictability is related to the claims of experts and their capacity to make suggestions concerning delinquency prevention policy. John Klein, of the University of Calgary, responded to the Calgary killings and public outcry with a very lucid brief arguing that in order to protect society from the few truly dangerous individuals, the present state of psychiatric diagnosis would require that a very large number of "suspects" be locked up (1975). Almost all of the discussion in this section was taken from Dr. Klein's brief and recent article (Klein, 1976).

Klein notes that there is little agreement among psychiatrists when it comes to gross diagnostic categories (Ziskin, 1969) and even less as the categories become more specific (Danet, 1964; Stoller and Geertsma, 1965). Laymen seem to be as accurate as experienced clinicians in evaluating subjects (Taft, 1955). Certain situations seem to influence the psychiatrist to overpredict insanity. When a group of psychiatrists was presented with a case which had been characterized as "insane" by a "renowned authority," they too diagnosed the case as insane, even though the subject was, in fact, a stooge (Temerlin, 1970). Therefore, the confidence of the clinician in the accuracy of his judgement does not mean that his inferences are valid (Oskamp, 1965). Even when there is agreement among clinicians about the diagnosis, this does not insure that the evaluation is accurate.

> Psychiatrists seem to find sufficient strength and self-confidence in the consensual validation deriving from what they assume to be and view as shared expert opinion. . . . The findings reported here categorically contradict such a belief (Stoller and Geertsma, 1965: 65).

The evidence leads many social scientists to believe that accurate diagnosis in this area does not exist (Steadman and Cocozza, 1975). In addition, the tendency of psychiatrists to overpredict mental illness and dangerous behaviour is well documented (Scheff, 1964). As a result even with "the most careful, painstaking, laborious and lengthy clinical approach to the prediction of dangerousness, false positives may be at a minimum of 60 to 70 percent" (Rubin, 1972: 397). In other words, two non-dangerous persons may be incarcerated for every one who is dangerous. Frequently, psychiatrists and others in the social control system disregard the consequences of false positive decisions. This is illustrated by a study of 592 male offenders, most of whom had committed sex crimes and more than half of whom had a history of violence:

> The staff's initial diagnosis indicated that 304 of these persons were not dangerous, and they were released into the community after completing their sentences. Twenty-six (8.6 percent) subsequently committed serious assaultive (dangerous) crimes.
>
> The courts concurred in our diagnosis of dangerous in 226 cases and committed these offenders to our special "treatment" facility for an indeterminate period of one day to life. Following treatment for an average period of 43 months, 82 patients were discharged on recommendation of the clinical staff. Of these, five (6.1 percent) subsequently committed serious assaultive crimes, including one murder.
>
> Forty-nine of the originally committed patients were released by court order against the advice of the clinical staff. Of these, seventeen (34.7 percent) subsequently committed serious assaultive crimes, including two murders. (Kozol, Boucher and Garofalo, 1972: 371).

Kozol and his colleagues give these findings as if they support the accuracy of psychiatric diagnosis, and some readers will come to similar conclusions. But we should note that laymen, lawyers and judges do have some insights into dangerous behaviour. In the case of the 304 diagnosed as non-dangerous, the court agreed. In the case of the 49 released against the advice of the clinicians, the court was right in 65.3 percent of the cases and the clinicians were right in 34.7 percent of the cases. No one is arguing that the 49 cases did not involve a higher risk than the 304. The primary question is "How much should one weigh the risk of future offences against unnecessary incarceration?" The clinicians lean in one direction, the courts in the other; but the clinicians make more "errors" than the courts. Of course some would argue that it is better to keep two people in jail for life rather than have one person commit another violent crime, but this is a moral, not a scientific decision.

If we look at the 226 cases which were committed to "treatment," we note that 100 were released, 82 on recommendation of the clinicians and 18 against their advice. Of the 82 released, 6.1 percent committed violent crimes including one murder. Is this evidence of accurate psychiatric diagnosis? Definitely not. There is no reason for assuming that the courts believed the 18 were similar in risk to the 82, but the courts were "right" in 72.2 percent of the cases while the clinicians were wrong.

It should be noted that 126 remaining cases are still receiving "treatment" or are at least incarcerated, possibly for life. They are considered dangerous by the clinicians, but is it possible that approximately 70 percent of those who are treated for life would have avoided violence on the outside?

Let us return to the 82 who were released after almost four years of treatment. Does their failure rate of 6.1 percent, as compared with 8.6 percent for the original 304 diagnosed as non-dangerous, suggest that the treatment was effective? Or is it possible that they were similar to the original 304 but were not at risk for four years and were four years older? Violence tends to decrease with age.

Obviously, violent offenders are a problem. Many persons, in addition to psychiatrists, are able to distinguish between high risk and low risk cases. The pseudo-methodology used by Kozol, Boucher and Garofalo and their interpretation simply obscure the facts. These data do not show that clinicians predict accurately, but rather that they overpredict. Judges also distinguish between those who are more dangerous from those who are less dangerous. Like the psychiatrists and the rest of us, they make mistakes, but they are less inclined to overpredict dangerousness. Let us now turn to a study that deals with this question using more adequate methodology.

In February 1966 the United States Supreme Court ruled that Johnnie Baxstrom had been detained illegally because his sentence had expired and he had not received proper review for continued detainment as a civil patient. As a result, a number of patients in two of New York's correctional hospitals became known as Baxstrom patients. They had been passed over for many years (a mean of fifteen years) by psychiatrists as inappropriate for civil mental hospitalization. These patients were viewed as dangerous. Prior to the Baxstrom case, the same two correctional hospitals transferred 312 patients out of these hospitals. These patients were viewed as suitable for a civil mental hospital. By comparing the 312 patients that were considered "suitable" for release with the 967 who were diagnosed as dangerous but released against clinical advice, we can assess the accuracy of psychiatric prediction.

Steadman and his colleagues (Steadman, 1972; Steadman and Keveles, 1972) selected a sample of the Baxstrom males (199) and all of the females (47). This Baxstrom group was compared with the control group (those considered suitable for release). The control group was older (males, average 57 years vs. 47 for Baxstrom group; females, average 62 vs. 50 for Baxstrom group); had spent more years in the correctional hospital (male 22 years vs. 15 for Baxstrom group; females, 27 vs. 17 for Baxstrom group); were more inclined to be white (males, 70 percent vs. 50 percent for Baxstrom group; females, 64 percent vs. 45 percent for the Baxstrom group); and fewer had a history of violent crime convictions (males, 22 percent vs. 51 percent for the Baxstrom group; females, 6 percent vs. 30 percent for the Baxstrom group) (Steadman, 1972: Table 1). Even a person without psychiatric training would be able to predict that the older group, with fewer violent crime convictions would be less dangerous. In fact, 24 percent of the control group had died after four and a half years.

One might argue that if the clinical diagnosis of "dangerous" was reasonably accurate, the majority of such cases would commit assaults. After four and one-half years, 21 percent of the Baxstrom patients had been arrested for an assault. For the control group, 6 percent had been arrested for an assault. Again, we have evidence of overprediction on the part of clinicians.

Once transferred from the two correctional hospitals to the civil hospitals, how did the two groups perform in terms of patient release rates? It seems that the group of "dangerous" patients (the Baxstrom group) was more successful in obtaining releases from the civil hospitals than the control group and, in fact, more successful than usual civil (voluntary and involuntary) patients of similar ages and length of hospitalization. How did the 121 Baxstrom patients who were finally released into the community (from the civil hospital) compare with the 128 controls who were released into the community? The Baxstrom group had a 17 percent arrest rate, while the controls had a 12 percent arrest rate. Only two of the Baxstrom convictions and one of the control group convictions were for felonies.

It is important to keep in mind that we are discussing that small percentage of the population with serious behaviour problems. Was it right to have these people committed to special hospitals for the criminally insane for long periods, instead of civil hospitals? (The average commitments were over twenty years for the controls and over fifteen for the Baxstrom group.) Steadman concludes that the "low arrest and conviction rates of both groups after community release demonstrate the conservative estimates of psychiatrists employed both in hospitals for the criminally insane and in civil hospitals" (1972: 268-279). "The level of success of both patient groups highlights the psychiatrists' ascendance into an expert role for which they have unproven skills" (263).

It is no great achievement to categorize people into groups that are related to future behaviour. For example, Canadian Indians have a poor record of scholarship in college. One could argue that by not permitting them to go to universities we would save the taxpayers' dollars and maximize the success of those who are admitted. Our number of "false positive" predictions would be fewer than when psychiatrists predict dangerous behaviour. Obviously, society will not permit this type of "overprediction" as a means of screening unsuitable people from attending college. Yet we tolerate far greater overprediction when it comes to keeping certain people behind bars. While it is difficult to say what level of accurate prediction is required before we grant competence to experts, clearly we should demand better odds than the flip of a coin.

How does this discussion fit into our general theme of asking who is capable of guiding us in developing delinquency prevention programs? First of all, the psychiatrist should be seen as a single illustration of a general phenomenon: experts in the people changing business overrate their capabilities. Social workers tend to believe they are capable of being gang workers and changing gang behaviour, counselors are convinced their activities modify behaviour, sociologists are convinced they can achieve improvements by changing social structure, and lawyers are sure that good laws and properly functioning courts will cure most everything.

Specialists could make an important contribution to the delinquency problem if they were to develop a bit more flexibility and humility. This would be particularly true if they could view their own opinions as being formed by factors that influence any groups which interact, share ideas, and strive for status and recognition. Just as the ideas of others are subject to various influences, so are the ideas expressed by Ph.D.s and by those who have established careers in certain fields. As long as the experts are committed to ideologies or to particular technologies for dealing with individuals, we cannot expect them to be the wisest leaders in our search for effective delinquency prevention programs.

In other words, experts are *one* source of input into the delinquency prevention scheme. Most of us are willing to reject other simpleminded solutions to delinquency such as: knock more sense into them, punish the parents, etc. We should also reject the notion that the delinquency "problem" can be solved by turning it over to the experts.

Actually, policy makers have displayed a great deal of skepticism about experts. Instead of calling upon specialists, the government has frequently created commissions to look into a particular problem. While experts are sometimes involved, the favourite choice to head a commission is a judge, or at least a prestigious lawyer. Frequently, the mandate of a commission is to "find a solution to the problem." If the experts cannot lead us, perhaps the commissions can.

Government Commissions: Knowledge Producers or Vehicles for Political Discussion?

Usually the stated goals of commissions are the generation of knowledge and the application of that knowledge to achieve a solution to a specific problem. Such goals are probably unrealistic. However, commissions may accomplish other goals that were not stated publicly. If public sentiment and scientific knowledge seem to be coming together, a governmental commission may help certain forces to move in concert. It is not that the commission necessarily generates new knowledge, but frequently a commission can publicize and add public credibility to information that has been taken for granted among specialists.

But probably the most important aspect of the government commission is that it provides a marketplace for political ideas. Ideas should not be confused with scientific facts. A democratic society needs mechanisms for focusing interest on a given topic and the commission fulfils this function. These stated goals and actual accomplishments will be discussed in more detail utilizing some Canadian commissions as examples.

Knowledge

Let us first deal with the question of accumulating knowledge. In this area, commissions may be fairly effective. It should be noted that commissions in the area of crime and delinquency are usually headed by judges and lawyers, and sometimes have no representation from the behavioural sciences. One U.S. commission on crime had thirty members, but not a single criminologist. After a complaint from the criminology section of the American Sociological Association, one criminologist was invited to take part. In Canada, there is a similar problem, but perhaps it is more understandable. The legal profession has been one of the major contributors to criminology in Canada and social scientists in Canada have not made the contributions in this area that their colleagues have made in the United States. It is understandable that such commissions are made up largely of lawyers, since a large law firm can respond quickly and release one of its members. A social scientist at a university is usually unable to free himself for other activities until the end of the school year. Some Canadian commissions have dealt with this problem by utilizing people who live near Ottawa on a part-time basis so that they were able to contribute without giving up their normal positions.

The problem of gathering knowledge can bog down in several ways related to the composition of the commission: (1) a heavily legally oriented commission can persist with a rational model of man and fail to come to grips with the realities of individual and group behaviour which seem to defy rationality, or (2) a commission can become a debating session where people cling to strongly held opinions. Neither of these situations is likely to generate new knowledge.

Commissions are subject to and create political pressures. This was particularly apparent in the Board of Psychiatric Consultants which recommended to the Solicitor General that regional psychiatric centres be constructed for the treatment of inmates. In pushing for this general program for the development of psychiatric services in federal correctional institutions in Canada, this Board or Commission represented only one perspective—a psychiatric one. The suggestions of this Board reflected the biases of one profession and neglected knowledge which has been accumulated in the field by the social sciences arguing the inappropriateness of these psychiatric treatment centres for bringing about beneficial changes in an inmate population.

Even when commissions are selected so as to represent a diversity of viewpoints, it is difficult to discover new truths. It is possible, on the other hand, to collect available knowledge and make it accessible to the public in a readable form. For example, the Commission of Inquiry into the Non-Medical Use of Drugs (the LeDain Commission) was able to document carefully fairly well-known facts in its interim report (LeDain *et al.*, 1972). That interim report achieved a great deal of publicity and probably had an informal impact on Canadian society. It is fair to say, however, this information was already readily available to the government without creating a commission. In other words, we would be wiser to view such commissions as performing political functions rather than as fact finding bodies. If we see such commissions as creators of knowledge, we come to naive conclusions.

It should be noted that all government commissions do not have the same mandates nor do they respond to their mandates in the same way. In the middle 1960's the Ouimet Commission (Canadian Committee on Corrections, 1969) came up both with factual information regarding crime in Canada, a philosophy, and some recommendations. By contrast, the Law Reform Commission, about a decade later, has focused on specific issues within the legal system and tried to generate debate. Not surprisingly, the social sciences were hardly represented, but the one sociologist, Hans Mohr, does seem to have had some impact. Probably Mohr's impact was less the result of his specialized knowledge and more of his encouragement of a strategy that generated discussion as opposed to attempting to make specific policy recommendations.

In the United States, government commissions can play a somewhat different role. Their extensive resources permit the commissioning of quality research that could generate new facts. Or, one might argue that if you have the resources to commission many studies, the likelihood that some of them will be particularly useful is much greater. This, however, is not the case in Canada. Commissions can and do support original research which do add to our body of knowledge, but it is unlikely that these projects will be able to generate specific answers to the specific policy questions political leaders would like to have answered. Except for some of the commissions funded by the U.S. government, most commissions are launched with modest resources. They will help bring issues to public notice. They may also draw attention to certain facts, but it is unrealistic to expect them to produce many new facts.

For example, the LeDain Commission made certain facts widely known to scientists more acceptable to the public and to officials. Hence, the Commission may have influenced policy indirectly. Similar findings by government commissions in the United States at an earlier period were rejected by President Nixon and other government agencies. Also, the U.S. commission on pornography provided fairly convincing evidence that pornography seems to have few long-range negative effects on society (Commission on Obscenity and Pornography, 1970), but this finding had little impact on legislation.

In other words, finding facts may be a very secondary role for commissions. Even when their recommendations are based on hard evidence, other factors are often much more important in terms of influencing actual changes in policy. In delinquency prevention, or crime in general, the facts are even less clear. My complaint is not about commissions on delinquency or crime per se. They are sometimes useful semi-political bodies. They can also assemble facts and frequently bring issues to public notice. My concern is that they are viewed as bodies which come up with answers. Evaluations of specific delinquency prevention programs are viewed the same way. Both views are misleading.

The recommendations of commissions and their timing

The second stated goal of most commissions is to come up with recommendations. In this respect they are very similar to most evaluations. If a commission does come up with recommendations, should they be followed? The report of the Department of Justice Committee on Juvenile Delinquency (1965) contained over one hundred recommendations. That report evidently had little impact, but the report of the Department of the Solicitor General's Task Force on Community-Based Residential Treatment Centres (Canada, 1973) seemed to have had a fairly immediate impact on the British Columbia correctional system. Community-based residential centres were projected for the Vancouver area within two years of the report. Perhaps it is wisest to say that commissions are most likely to be effective when the time is ripe for their suggestions.

Sometimes there are complaints when the recommendations of a commission are not followed, but there is no reason to feel that these suggestions are particularly special. We have noted that the knowledge accumulated by commissions is probably a synthesis of what is available, but in the criminal justice area that knowledge is limited. Translating that limited knowledge into specific recommendations or into legislation does not automatically result in meaningful improvements, as the Poverty Program in the United States has demonstrated (Moynihan, 1969). Of course, there are times when society is ready for change, and when accumulated knowledge, specific recommendations and public sentiment come together. Under such conditions "knowledge is applied." The outcome may or may not prove to be wise, but we should be aware that policy making is a political, not a scientific, process.

The commission as political marketplace

It is important to distinguish between research activities and social policy formation. The first do not logically lead to the second. It is a mistake to believe that science can decide the many moral and ethical issues involved in plotting an appropriate societal response to crime and delinquency. Research is certainly not irrelevant. It can provide some useful building blocks, but policy decisions are political and the government commission provides a forum for the exercise of political muscle.

Those from the more influential professions serve most frequently on commissions. Lawyers and psychiatrists are influential in the correctional system. Social scientists play a less important role. When children are concerned, social workers seem to be influential. Sometimes this power is related to vested interests. One reason that social scientists may be less influential is that policy decisions do not have a great impact on their lives. Most of them will continue with their teaching and research activities regardless of most policy decisions related to criminal or juvenile justice programs.

Some social scientists are unhappy with their lack of influence, but it could be that the lawyers, psychiatrists and social workers provide an appropriate balance. Besides, the question should not be one of which professional group is represented, but whether there is an adequate diversity of views to make the political process work. Clearly lawyers, psychiatrists and social workers have widely divergent views within their professions, but possibly the social scientist could have something useful to add. However, there is no reason to believe that those who specialize in research on human behaviour can make more than a modest contribution to this essentially political process.

It is unreasonable to think that any government commission or any sophisticated evaluation program is going to eliminate delinquency. No one has convincingly shown that they can generate the "correct" knowledge, and there is considerable doubt today that science alone can save us. The experts and the commissioners do make their contributions and occasionally something positive comes out of the process. A problem may not be solved, but a clearer picture of what is happening is likely to result. In a society where knowledge and public policy interact, mechanisms for publicizing ideas, such as government commissions, are crucial.

Strategies for Those Who Are Suspicious of Experts

Although I claim that there is no clear direction to go in the delinquency prevention area and that many of the well-intentioned policies espoused by professionals and politicians have proven to be useless if not actually harmful in the past, some strategies do look promising. One of these is to encourage a great deal more humble research projects that ask modest questions about our criminal justice system. An M.A. thesis by Doug Heckbert at the University of Alberta provides an excellent illustration (1976).

Heckbert was interested in the impact of day parole on the inmate and on the correctional system. With the extensive cooperation of the Solicitor General's Department in Alberta, he tried to learn if the program in fact helped men support their families, decreased the costs to the correctional system, provided men with a nest egg after release, and perhaps taught good work habits. The results suggested that the men did not in fact earn much money and, when they did, it rarely went to support their families. The jobs they held were generally unskilled and did not provide much training for future advancement. One positive result was that the inmates experienced acceptance by employers and co-workers. One surprising finding was that the program seemed to work better for those under 25 than for those over 25. Work release has not been thought of as a program primarily designed for young offenders, but perhaps it should be considered more seriously.

Heckbert's study was primarily descriptive and suggested that the program only partially reached any of its stated goals. Why have I chosen this relatively insignificant project as an illustration of recommended procedures? Why do I not instead recommend massive research programs, directed by commissions made up of prestigious citizens who will conduct a "war against crime and delinquency?" When goals are clear and the problem is well understood, perhaps it is appropriate to rally the public in a unified effort. In the case of delinquency, the definitions are less clear, the questions that have been asked may be inappropriate, and the traditional evaluation techniques have not provided clear answers. Therefore, I favour the small inquiry that is accessible to program staff members and could lead to minor modifications. Heckbert's modest study could be a mechanism to improve the day parole program in Alberta. Of course, the unsophisticated findings of this study may be incorrect or misleading, but a number of staff members have given some thought to an innovative change and it is difficult to see how this could lead to more negative than positive consequences.

In addition to the simple research project that involves program staff, as suggested above, more sophisticated strategies might be applied to the juvenile justice system as a totality. We are interested in the "effectiveness" of our juvenile justice system, but the data presently being generated provide few insights into what is being accomplished or what type of specific changes would lead to full-scale changes in the system. Therefore, I favour research strategies and organizational changes that would permit the analysis of different aspects of the juvenile justice system.

Juvenile Justice as a System and Indicators of Change

Before describing juvenile justice as a system, let us look at some typical illustrations of complaints that arise among those who work with juveniles. In a detention centre for juveniles, for example, the average length of detention may have been increasing steadily in spite of efforts to reduce it. Some staff members could interpret this as failure to rehabilitate delinquent youngsters. However, this type of change could have been brought about by a number of factors. For example, if the police followed a diversion program which resulted in a higher release rate for minor offenders, the result could be a proportionate increase in detention of juveniles for more serious offenses (Klein *et al.*, 1971). In other words, the meaning of the length of detention at a centre for juveniles can vary. Such a change might be the result of an effective program somewhere else. Similarly, monitoring system rates for various units within the juvenile justice system does not automatically tell us if that particular unit is "effective" or not, but such monitoring increases the likelihood of assessing various changes.

Systems techniques have been applied to a number of large industries and other bureaucracies characterized by monolithic administrative structures. Juvenile justice, however, is administered by many autonomous and diverse administrative units whose ultimate goals are related but whose responsibilities under the law make them more or less independent. If effective delinquency prevention programs are to be developed, it is important to keep the different parts of the system from cancelling each other out. On the other hand, it is possible that harmful practices by one part would be recognized more readily if there were a way of assessing the various components.

A criminologist from the University of Southern California, working with three others on this issue, was explaining systems analysis to a group of practitioners. He likened the criminal justice system to a driver and his automobile stuck in a snow bank.

> The driver-auto "system" was working perfectly, yet each action of that system merely spun the wheels of the auto, thereby sinking it further into the snow. The analogy, while useful, was criticized by an experienced systems analyst who said, "No, no—the real system here includes the driver, the auto, *and* the snow bank. All of them must function together to produce the desired movement". (Klein *et al.*, 1971:359).

In other words, in considering the juvenile justice system, we must include not only the agencies, but also aspects of the community. Klein and his colleagues list six system rates or indicators that help us to understand the total system. One of these is the "community absorption rate."

> It is a highly significant and consistent characteristic of criminal justice systems everywhere that the majority of criminal acts do not lead to the apprehension of an offender (to say nothing of convictions). There are a number of reasons for this. Some criminal acts are never detected. Some are detected but not "solved." Some are detected but the offender is handled informally by citizens and not reported to officials of the criminal justice system. Finally, some are detected but the offender is handled by various community agencies in lieu of being introduced into the system.

> It is these last two "absorption" procedures—detection without introduction into the formal system of criminal justice—which represent processes most open to change by the system. A community absorption rate requires procedures to estimate the number of processable criminal acts that actually take place and accurate data on the proportion of such acts "handled" by unofficial agencies and other informal mechanisms (363).

Another indicator is the "processing rate." Although the community absorbs many criminal acts, some criminals are apprehended, leading to an apprehension rate. Once apprehended, processing in the system could take a number of different forms.

> At probation intake, juveniles may be released or may be formally placed back in their homes, in foster homes, in institutions, etc. Courts may dismiss cases, hold them over, reduce charges, etc. Each of these decision points will yield a processing rate that expresses the proportion of persons handled in a particular fashion by the system. Some of the rates are important expressions of the criminal justice system's philosophy of the administration of justice (363).

Without going into detail about the other four system rates suggested, the reader can see that there are various indices that can be used to illustrate what is happening in the system. When developed, system rates of this nature could provide some very important functions for the juvenile justice system.

1. They will permit a comprehensive assessment of the current efficiency and effectiveness of various system components or combinations thereof.
2. They will permit assessment of efficiency and effectiveness over time, showing trends which might otherwise go undetected and therefore uncontrolled.
3. They will suggest areas for investigation and/or action.
4. They will provide ready-made measures of the impact on the system of changes introduced anywhere within it.
5. They will, in the very process of being developed, encourage interagency procedures to be planned and carried out with their systematic impact carefully considered (361).

This fifth point may be the most important for the Canadian scene today. It may not be possible, or even desirable, to have a truly integrated juvenile justice system. However, it would be a worthwhile goal to be able to examine more objectively the various changes that are taking place in different parts of the complex semi-integrated structure that currently exists.

Some people could argue that this approach is inherently conservative, that it would simply lead to the perpetuation of the evils of the system. There is no reason to believe that understanding how a system works will automatically lead to one type of political action or another, and I have argued earlier that policy decisions in the criminal justice area will be heavily influenced by political considerations. Findings using a systems approach might provide the basis for dramatic and revolutionary changes, but the reader should not assume that scientific research on the topic of delinquency leads to the same conclusions as the political interest inherent in all social policy.

Conclusions

Selecting ideas from the cafeteria of knowledge dealing with juvenile delinquency is not a scientific process but rather a political one. The connoisseur who advises us on the choice of dishes will reflect the tastes of "important" people in society, but the meals actually chosen by the public may not be the most nutritious. It is not enough to pay attention to which choice is made. We need to know how choices are made.

Delinquency prevention programs are not the only illustrations of how scientific knowledge fails to influence policy. The problems are just as serious elsewhere. We know the natural gas in Alberta will soon be gone, but we still use it to generate electricity and use it in questionable ways. We know that the private automobile compounds transportation problems in large cities, but few governments are willing or able to struggle against certain popular practices.

Knowledge-seeking, then, should take into account the manner in which knowledge is applied. Therefore, I advocate two types of knowledge-seeking strategies. One would emphasize extensive collaboration with program staff members who help to define the questions. Such research would be largely descriptive, but should improve communication between research and action workers. A second strategy would attempt to establish indicators that would measure the activity of various components in the juvenile justice system. Other strategies may also be profitable, but approaches that emphasize "cures" for delinquency and evaluations which rate "success" in specific terms should be approached with caution.

Many will not be content with humble, gradual approaches. While delinquency itself may not be dealt with effectively by vigorous action, the needs of leaders in society frequently require active responses. Hence, advocates of popular causes will arise in response to these needs. Recently diversion has been a popular course of action tried on delinquents. Earlier, it was reality therapy. The debate between the rehabilitation advocates and those who favour "due process" has taken on renewed vigour. But the loudness of the voices is a poor indicator of wisdom.

Recommendations relating to delinquency prevention do not spring directly from scientific knowledge. They reflect the needs of those playing different roles in society. In addition, the knowledge itself is far from reliable.

Chapter 7

Preparing for the Great Stumble Forward

The welfare of the people in particular has always been the alibi of tyrants, and it provides the further advantage of giving the servants of tyranny a good conscience.

—ALBERT CAMUS

Choosing Among Cynical, Optimistic and Gradualistic Perspectives

Our current perspective on delinquency is similar to that of a drunk who wakes up to find himself lying in the gutter. Placing one hand on the sidewalk, he mutters to himself, "By golly, I'm going to climb over this wall if it takes me all night." We are simply not in a position to make significant advances overnight. Our problem is to determine which way to stumble. Many contradictory voices beckon. These can be divided into the cynics, the optimists and the gradualists.

Those with a cynical perspective argue that our attempts to rehabilitate deviants have been completely unsuccessful. The attitude of Robert Martinson (Lipton, Martinson and Wilks, 1975), expressed here in a personal letter, is typical of this viewpoint.

> Must Canada recapitulate the history of the United States in these matters? I certainly hope not. There are surely alternatives to enriching the prisons with expensive "treatment" personnel. Buy them some barbells, a chess set, and some dirty movies. Give them access to a law library. None of this does any good either, but it also doesn't do any harm—and costs quite a bit less (1974).

The cynics do not, however, downgrade the work of those treatment advocates who have fought against overwhelming odds to humanize the handling of criminal offenders (Wilks and Martinson, 1976). Basically, they argue that it is unrealistic to expect the criminal justice system to be parent, teacher, disciplinarian, reformer, and also protector of criminal offenders, while at the same time reducing the crime rate. Nor would they deny that positive changes have been made in the correctional systems of North America, but they would argue that we have reached a point of diminishing returns in regard to treatment. At a meeting in Calgary in 1975, Martinson stated that even though he felt that reform programs do not work, there was no reason to believe that punishment does. In other words, the cynics should not be confused with those who favour harsh punishment. Most of those who feel that the rehabilitation movement has been a failure would probably favour David Fogel's justice model for corrections (1975). He advocates flat-time sentencing, with no opportunity for parole or early release. Most advocates of the justice model do not discard rehabilitation programs but argue that they should be voluntary.

The optimist is well aware of the problems involved in launching delinquency prevention programs, yet nevertheless feels that slight gains have been made as the result of systematic and meticulously monitored research programs. Optimists emphasize the low productivity of research in any field. Stuart Adams's work on the PICO project, mentioned earlier, is an illustration of sophisticated evaluation research. He disagrees with the claim that nothing has been accomplished because little or no evidence of efficacy can be found in recent evaluations. In a personal letter he writes:

> This, of course is the history of science. Progress is snail-like, and those who do not like the pace can be merciless to those who are doing the crawling. Fortunately, not all interested onlookers insist on "immediate and full gratification" through research. Du Pont's stock holders have not insisted on firing all Du Pont's presidents because only 5 percent of Du Pont's research ultimately pays off (1974).

In other words, the optimist believes that modest gains have been made and does not allow his hopes for a dramatic breakthrough to obscure the value of less significant advances.

The cynical and optimistic perspectives are neatly contrasted below.

> With few and isolated exceptions, the rehabilitation efforts that have been reported so far have had no appreciable effect on recidivism. . . . The history of corrections is a graveyard of abandoned fads. (Martinson, in Martinson, Palmer and Adams, 1976).

> . . . a number of promising leads do indeed exist within the field of correctional intervention. (Palmer, *ibid.*)

> The Nothing Works doctrine is a meaningless, unanchored, indeterminate piece of correctional "wisdom." It offers no credible basis for planning, decision making, or research in correction. (Adams, *ibid.*)

A third perspective on delinquency prevention argues that despite the lack of evidence of effective rehabilitation resulting from past and present programs, the criminal justice system has been made more humane in the last quarter of a century. Hans Mohr of the Canadian Law Reform Commission has argued that this in itself should be viewed as a major accomplishment and a trend which should continue in the future. The fact that "nothing works" does not negate the value of necessary changes on the criminal justice system itself. For example, at the present time there is preferential treatment of people of high status who break the law over lower status offenders. When lower class thieves go to jail to be "corrected" and high class embezzlers are put on probation, one wonders whether society has lost sight of the concept of justice. If middle class members of society were more inclined to be clients of correctional treatment programs, the system would likely come under much closer scrutiny. It is possible that sentences given to youthful middle class marijuana offenders have had some impact in this direction.

Despite many disappointing findings that programs have not had the impact that practitioners anticipated, the gradualists favour retaining a rehabilitation orientation even when success is not demonstrated. Without this orientation an unhealthy environment would surely result. At the 1975 Calgary conference, Seymour Halleck, a psychiatrist, pointed out that drug therapy, electronics and biological controls will be increasingly used as modes of treatment. Without a commitment to the rehabilitation model, Halleck warned, these potentially powerful techniques could be applied for control purposes alone. The offender would be regarded as merely a body to be warehoused for a certain period of time, and morale among staff and inmates in correctional institutions would dangerously deteriorate. Halleck also emphasized that many programs have indications of some minor improvements even though the formal criteria do not show positive changes. For example, in one North Carolina study, Halleck noted that although recidivism rates were not reduced by the rehabilitation program, the subsequent offences were less serious.

The debate over treatment is slightly different for juveniles and young offenders in contrast to older criminals and the mentally ill. Few people advocate jail sentences for juveniles except in unusual circumstances. In addition, some sort of treatment is more or less assumed. While aware of the limitations of their efforts, gradualists would argue that sympathetic teachers, staff members who attempt to relate to juveniles, courses on auto mechanics, etc. may have merits in their own right. Failure to reduce recidivism rates does not call for automatic abandonment of a program.

Many gradualists would be somewhat sympathetic toward "radical non-intervention" (Schur, 1973), but they recognize that the juvenile justice system is under constant pressure to take some form of action. Although many agree with the criticism that the juvenile court is poorly equipped to act like a parent, and hence favour more formal proceedings in the courtroom, there is less agreement on what should be done after the courtroom experience. The gradualists are less convinced than the optimists that something constructive can be done, but they assume that society will demand that something be done.

There is merit in each of these three orientations, and it is probably unprofitable to line up behind one perspective or another. However we should remain aware that the perspectives held by researchers, policy makers and the general public tend to become factors in policy development.

The problem of setting a policy on delinquency prevention is further complicated by different authorities viewing the same data in different ways. For example, LaMar Empey, whose work with the Provo and Silverlake experiments has been discussed earlier, reviewed what is considered to be the "bible" of the cynics, *The Effectiveness of Correctional Treatment: A Survey of Treatment Evaluation Studies,* by Douglas Lipton, Robert Martinson and Judith Wilks (1975). In his book review Empey (1976) notes that "treatment" is usually not compared with "no treatment" but with other types of treatment.

> A finding of no difference in outcome between two or more correctional alternatives does *not* demonstrate that correctional programs have no effect. The only way that can be determined is if an experimental design is set up in which one of the controls involves *no intervention whatsoever,* no action by officials on convicted offenders. Yet, there are precious few, if any, instances in which this has been done. Instead, findings of no difference between two or more correctional alternatives are often incorrectly interpreted to mean that correctional programs have no effect, or that the effect is deleterious (583).

In addition, Empey does not feel that this review of 231 studies of correctional effectiveness demonstrates the total bankruptcy of all approaches to rehabilitation. Rather, "It is laced with suggestions that under some circumstances, and for certain types of offenders, some correctional techniques have made a difference" (582).

The Institutional Alternative: A Stumble Backwards

Prisons have done little to reform individuals. Even when they are called reformatories, training schools or correctional centres, the evidence is overwhelming that children and young adults are not reformed as the result of their experiences in these institutions. Since this evidence has been carefully documented elsewhere (Street, Vintner and Perrow, 1966), I will focus primarily on the specific debates in Canada and secondarily on empirical data.

The claim that institutions do not reform does not mean there are no delinquents who are dangerous or that we should do away with all of our prisons. However, we would be more honest if we saw prisons as institutions for punishment and control and did not engage in the self-deception that such places are primarily for the purpose of reforming offenders. Of course prisons or training schools should be humane and various educational and other programs should be available on a voluntary basis. Attempts to mitigate the negative impact of prisons are worthwhile, but they should not be confused with the belief that a benevolent prison system can somehow "treat" individuals so that they will be "safe" when they are returned to society.

Richard Ericson (1973), of the University of Toronto, argues further that incarceration cannot be viewed as a more effective individual deterrent than sentences which allow the offender to remain in the community. He agrees with Leslie Wilkins (1969), who argues that in terms of the welfare of the offender, "by doing as little as possible we may be doing as little harm as possible" (1973:76).

One reason for emphasizing this point is that many judges who could be classified as enlightened tend to use incarceration in the belief that such treatment actually will improve the individual. In his study of magistrates in Ontario, John Hogarth (1971) found that the institutional alternative was selected for both punitive and treatment reasons. The judges tended to believe that they were able to punish and treat offenders at the same time. Similarly an earlier study of juvenile court judges suggested the possibility that better read, better educated, and less punitive judges believed training school helped to rehabilitate (Wheeler *et al*, 1966). William Outerbridge made the inconsistency of this stand very clear in his address before the Canadian Congress of Criminology and Corrections in 1973 by selecting a particularly eloquent quotation from George Bernard Shaw.

> Now, if you are to punish a man retributively, you must injure him. If you are to reform him you must improve him. And men are not improved by injuries. To propose to punish and reform by the same operation is exactly as if you were to take a man suffering from pneumonia and attempt to combine punitive and curative treatment. Arguing that a man with pneumonia is a danger to the community and that he needs not to catch it if he takes proper care of his health, you resolve that he shall have a severe lesson, both to punish him for his negligence and his pulmonary weakness, and to deter others from following his example. You therefore strip him naked and in that condition stand him all night in the snow. But as you admit the duty of restoring him to health if possible and discharging him with sound lungs, you engage a doctor to superintend the punishment and administer cough lozenges made as unpleasant to the taste as possible so as not to pamper the culprit. A board of commissioners ordering such treatment would prove thereby either that they were imbeciles *or else that they were hotly in earnest about punishing the patient and not in the least in earnest about curing him* (Outerbridge's italics).

Therefore, when we learn from Hogarth that Ontario magistrates who give maximum weight to the reformation of offenders pass the same type of lengthy prison sentences as magistrates who sentence on the basis of punishment or deterrence, we have to take Shaw's comments seriously.

It is also difficult to hide behind the argument that somehow Canadian institutions are different from those in the United States. Carlson

(1973) in his study of the Ontario reformatory system presents data which support the findings of U.S. studies. Among the "first incarcerates" to an adult institution, those with institutional experience as juveniles have the greatest chance of being caught for further crime. Naturally, we must be careful about the interpretation of these data, since those who were the most serious offenders were possibly those who had institutional experience as juveniles. This study also argues that long periods of imprisonment are just as ineffective as short periods in terms of preventing recidivism. Carlson concludes his article with the comment, "The current emphasis on educational and vocational training within a disciplined setting does not seem to have proved remarkably successful" (1973:408).

Frequently it has been argued that different training programs within training schools would lead to different outcomes. Unfortunately, the type of "treatment" tends not to make much difference. It is possible that the changes which are imposed on these institutions have meaning in the eyes of the staff, but they do not reflect meaningful differences in the eyes of the clients—those who are being treated. In England, the Whitegate School shifted to a new "treatment" approach which was to view the boys as having individual problems influenced to a large degree by their family backgrounds. The hope was that the staff would help the boys work out individual solutions to their problems. However, when the boys in the training institution were studied and their views solicited, they had very different opinions from those of the staff concerning the role the institution should play in changing their lives (Gill, 1974). They still saw the training school as an attempt to condition them, to develop socially acceptable behaviour patterns. This study of the Whitegate School in England indicates that changes in policy and genuine attempts on the part of the staff to act differently may not in fact result in actual change in terms of those being processed by the system.

Canada would be wise to look at the varieties of regimes which have been tried within the various Borstal schools in England. Different types of programs have been attempted, but there is little indication that any of these institutions for young people have been particularly effective. After World War II, British Columbia decided to import the "Borstal system." Staff members were recruited and S. Rocksborough Smith was brought to Canada to lead this activity. The history of the New Haven experiment in British Columbia should naturally be examined, but it is probably unrealistic to think of this experiment as being much different from those that have been attempted in England. There was a period, however, when the staff at New Haven was particularly optimistic and this climate may have had an impact on the clients. Systematic attempts were made to bridge the gap between the institution and the outside world. For example, a New Haven Alumni Association was formed, and this might be seen as an illustration of an unique response to problems faced by institutions of this sort. As larger numbers of clients passed through the court system, New Haven became inadequate and the Haney Correctional Institution was developed. Perhaps the smaller, more intimate setting of New Haven was not particularly effective, but it is even clearer that the large, modern and efficient institution at Haney should not be viewed as a superior device for reforming offenders.

In general, there has been a growing awareness that institutional settings are unlikely places for rehabilitation. Whether this is because an inmate subculture tends to develop in such institutions, such as the one described by W. E. Mann (1967) in the Guelph Reformatory, or whether it is simply because programs do not have meaningful links to conventional roles on the outside, is not clear.

A promising counter-trend is illustrated by the interim program outlined in 1973 for the Manitoba Youth Centre. Many juvenile treatment programs are beginning to develop community treatment centres to permit removing more young people from the institutional setting. However, the reader should also be aware that individuals sharing a certain personality profile (a minority of juveniles), as classified by a California system, have responded *better* to the more restrained institutional setting than they have to community treatment programs, as we will point out later in Chapters 8 and 10 (Warren, 1974).

The Boscoville Experiment.

Despite the unimpressive record of institutional treatment, there is good reason to believe that many training schools will still be maintained in Canada. Frequently, other alternatives seem to be lacking. Therefore, a policy that would favour the minimum use of institutions for juveniles does not mean that we ignore programs that take place in institutional settings.

At present a study at the Boscoville School in Quebec is being conducted by Marc LeBlanc and his colleagues from the University of Montreal. It will probably be the most thorough evaluation of an institutional program for juveniles in Canada (LeBlanc *et al.*, 1973; LeBlanc, 1977). The program has a well-educated staff and utilizes some features of a therapeutic community. (See the section on Group Therapy in Chapter 8.) The program of activities was developed following the ideas of Piaget and Erikson leading to a four-stage developmental process of reeducation.

It is too early to speak of the effectiveness of this program because the results are not yet available, but we would have the reader keep in mind several points regarding an evaluation of this type.

1. Because of the poor record of institutions in modifying recidivism rates, etc., we should not anticipate dramatic results from Boscoville. It would be unfair to both Boscoville and the researchers if findings of no impact were to lead to stress. The public and the government should not

place unrealistic expectations on either the institution or the research team.

2. Aside from evaluations of effectiveness, research from this project could provide useful information for other programs. How does one avoid the damaging effects of a prison subculture? To what extent do serious delinquents gain status by spending time in an institution? Even findings that a particular program is effective may be of limited value because other institutions may not be able to create the same environment. Several experts in this field have expressed their feelings at various conferences that it is very difficult to duplicate a given delinquency prevention program. On the other hand, there are certain common features in most institutional settings that plague program staff, such as the development of subcultures that thwart organizational goals. Insights into these features may be an important byproduct of such a study.

3. Because of the wealth of data being gathered by the Boscoville study perhaps it will provide a better understanding of some of the processes involved in the juvenile justice system. For example, a study of those cases that do well after their institutional experience may provide some clues to those variables that play a meaningful role in turning the frequently negative experience of a training school into something positive.

Boscoville will be worth watching; but if too much emphasis is placed on proving that an institution can "rehabilitate" delinquents, disappointment could be severe and many of the potential benefits of this extensive research project could be lost.

Our concern in Canada at this time is not with those institutions which are attempting to decrease the numbers in residence and which are working on a variety of strategies to keep these young people in the community. Rather, our concern is with those who accept the school of thought which argues that in the face of failure, we must redouble our efforts at treatment. In an appropriately entitled article, "The Tyranny of Treatment," William Outerbridge warns us of this particular perspective.

> Well aware that behavioural scientists now possess the ability to change people's minds by the use of coercive psychological techniques, supporters advocate not only a more aggressive employment of efforts to change behaviour by "treaters," but a concomitant increase in their authority as decision makers over the destiny of those they treat (1968:384).

It is hazardous to generalize about trends involving incarceration in Canada; therefore the reader is asked to consider this discussion primarily as speculation. There currently exists in Canada pressures toward an increase in the use of prison facilities plus involuntary treatment for young adults and at the same time a reverse trend for juveniles.

Since the government agencies responsible for adults and juveniles are frequently separate, this is possible. This could mean that in Ontario, where the age limit for juveniles is 16, 17-year-olds would be handled by agencies for adults. In Quebec and Manitoba, where the age limit is 18, 17-year-olds would be handled by juvenile agencies.

The evidence for these two opposing trends is by no means conclusive. The psychiatric centres program in the federal penitentiary system could easily increase the institutionalization of young adults. This can be construed as evidence for the existence of a trend to imprison and/or treat young adults involuntarily. An examination of the number of juveniles placed in training schools in the past few years suggests that the current trend is not to institutionalize them.

Several years after Outerbridge expressed concern about the tyranny of treatment, *The General Program for the Development of Psychiatric Services in Federal Correctional Services in Canada* was issued by the Solicitor General of Canada (1973). The expansion of psychiatric facilities in the federal penitentiary system is viewed with alarm by many. Richard Ericson, of the University of Toronto, has been a severe critic of this proposal (1973, 1974). The involuntary application of psychiatric techniques, many of questionable value, in an institutional setting, could lead to abuses under the guise of treatment. When a client moves from the "offender" category to the "sick" category, he could end up being treated more harshly, for a longer period of time and without the safeguards that exist in traditional penal institutions. In addition to being a possible backward step in the correctional system, the expansion of these facilities may be part of a general Canadian tendency to use prisons to a greater extent than other countries.

The Use and Abuse of Institutions in Canada

It is commonly believed by those working in criminology and corrections that Canada utilizes prisons more than the United States and more than most countries in Western Europe. An opposite position, reflecting the views of a small minority, will be presented first. Waller and Chan (1974) state that the way in which prison rates are measured vary tremendously and make international comparisons unreliable. For example, in 1971, 36,271 persons were sentenced to prison in adult courts in Canada. However, on any one day there were approximately 20,127 in prison. Waller and Chan used data gathered as part of a United Nations study that sent a questionnaire to national correspondents to establish the number of persons in prisons on an average day. They note that disparities are large in various provinces across Canada with higher rates tending to prevail in the west. Disparities are also great in the United States with the west and the south keeping a higher than average portion of their population behind bars. Table 7.1, reproduced from the article, is of particular interest. It does not rank Canada higher than the

Table 7.1
Selected Countries Ranked in Order of the Number of Persons in Prison Per 100,000 Persons in the Population for the Most Recent Year Information Was Available

Rank	*Country*	*Year*	*Imprisonment Rate Per 100 000 Population*	*(Remand Rate Per 100 000 Pop.)*[6]
1	U.S.A.[3]	1970	406 531/203 200 000 = 200.0	
2	Poland[1]	1972	62 748/ 33 070 000 = 189.7	(88.8)
3	Australia[1]	1972	16 615/ 12 960 000 = 128.2	(9.2)
4	Finland[1]	1972	4 947/ 4 630 000 = 106.8	(11.0)
5	New Zealand[4]	1972	2 643/ 2 850 000 = 92.7	—
6	Canada[1]	1972	19 668/ 21 850 000 = 90.0	(11.0)
7	England and Wales[5]	1971	39 708/ 48 900 000 = 81.3	(6.1)
8	Denmark[2]	1971	3 350/ 4 800 000 = 69.8	(22.0)
9	Sweden[2]	1971	4 977/ 8 090 000 = 61.4	(6.9)
10	France[1]	1972	31 573/ 51 700 000 = 61.1	(21.8)
11	Italy[1]	1972	27 812/ 54 350 000 = 51.2	(27.8)
12	Japan[1]	1972	49 241/105 990 000 = 46.5	(7.9)
13	Spain[1]	1972	13 826/ 34 680 000 = 39.9	(16.6)
14	Norway[2]	1971	1 432/ 3 870 000 = 37.1	(13.7)
15	Netherlands[2]	1971	2 919/ 13 120 000 = 22.4	(10.4)

Sources:
[1] UN Census of Prison Population (1972). Population as of December 1, 1972.
[2] Great Britain Expenditure Committee Report (1971). Population as of January 1, 1971.
[3] Estimated from total of State and Federal Institutions, local jails, and juvenile institutions. Sources: *National Prisons Statistics Bulletin,* US Bureau of Prison No. 47 (1972); *National Jail Census* (1970) US Department of Justice; *Children in Custody* (1971) US Department of Justice. In 1965, the equivalent statistics were 404 049/194 240 000 = 208.0 (US Task Force Report 1967).
[4] Report of the Department of Justice, New Zealand (1973). Average daily population.
[5] Home Office. Report on the work of the Prison Department (1971). Average daily population.
[6] Remand rate is not restricted to those awaiting arraignment or their first trial. In some European jurisdictions such as Italy, this includes those awaiting a hearing in a court of second instance.

Chart from Irvin Waller and Janet Chan, "Prison Use; a Canadian and International Comparison." *Criminal Law Quarterly* 17: 47-71 (1974).

United States in terms of proportion of population in prison, but rather as sixth, with the United States being at the top of the list.

In effect, Waller and Chan claim that the common wisdom among professionals is wrong and that in 1972 Canada had about half as many people in prison as did the United States, and only 25 to 30 percent more than Denmark and Sweden.

The reader should be aware that the majority of professionals in the correctional field would be more inclined to agree with the following quotation which reflects quite a different perspective.

> The Canadian judicial system is more likely than other judicial system(s) in the Western world to consider incarceration as an appropriate response to problems of crime and delinquency. In Canada during 1960, the rate of incarceration of adults over the age of 16 was 240 per 100,000. This was higher than the rate of 200 per 100,000 in the United States, and markedly higher than the rates for other countries, such as the United Kingdom where the rate was 59 per 100,000, or Norway, where the rate was only 44 per 100,000 (Cousineau and Veevers, 1972: 10).

We should be careful about using our adult institutional statistics as an indication of societal reactions to delinquency. These official statistics can be particularly misleading when we deal with data pertaining to juveniles. To illustrate this point, let us examine statistics dealing with both juvenile and adult institutions in Canada. If we look at the rate of incarceration across Canada, we see a pattern which is fairly traditional (Evans, 1973: 85). British Columbia has the highest percentage of people behind bars with Alberta close behind. One might assume that a similar pattern should exist for juveniles. Because British Columbia has not been reporting the number of juveniles in training schools since 1969, it is impossible to make any calculation for that province. But in 1969 Alberta seemed to have only one juvenile in training school for every sixteen thousand people in the province, making it one of the lowest rates in Canada (Statistics Canada, 85-208, 1970). Quebec typically shows a low rate for adult institutions but a high rate for juveniles—about one juvenile in training school per five thousand. Ontario, with an intermediate standing in terms of overall incarceration rates, has about one juvenile in a training school per six thousand. We should note, of course, that the age for juveniles in Quebec is eighteen, for Ontario it is sixteen, and in Alberta it is eighteen for girls but sixteen for boys. We note also that Quebec admitted one-third of its cases as "children in need of protection."

Interpreting this data is difficult for a variety of reasons. Probably the category of "child protection" in Quebec is applied to children who would be classified as delinquent elsewhere. The fact that Quebec deals with sixteen and seventeen year olds probably inflates its delinquency rate. In Alberta, placing juvenile corrections under the Director of Child Welfare may have led to a different philosophy from that which was previously applied when the jurisdiction was part of adult corrections.

Nova Scotia and New Brunswick also display confusing patterns. In general, the Maritimes tend to have lower crime rates than the rest of Canada. In terms of the percentage of adults in jail, Newfoundland and Prince Edward Island are predictably low, whereas Nova Scotia and New Brunswick in 1970 ranked rather high. However, the percentage of juveniles in training schools in Nova Scotia was almost twice as high as that in New Brunswick, with Nova Scotia's rate being the highest in the nation. Again, we should be cautious about interpretation. Inmates and juveniles involved in a community-based activity, work camp, or some other type of program might be classified as being in a "training school." The point of this exercise is not to point out that one province is "better" than another. We should be aware that programs for juveniles and programs for adults could vary tremendously within the same province as well as from province to province. Classifying these persons for statistical comparisons can thus be misleading.

Although I ask the reader not to use these statistics to make comparisons among provinces, I will speculate about general changes in Canada in recent years. Of course, future analyses could easily prove me wrong, but the juvenile courts may in fact be sending fewer juveniles to training schools than they were in the past. In 1949 14.4 percent of the delinquents who came before the juvenile court were sent to training schools. By 1968 that number had dropped to 8 percent. In the province of Alberta, the use of institutional care has dropped considerably in the past few years, even though a commissioned report in the late 1960's recommended the building of new facilities. It is quite likely that the shift of juvenile corrections in Alberta from the Department of the Attorney General to the Department of Health and Social Development in the early 1970's was accompanied by a major shift in correctional thinking for juveniles. Similar trends seem to be influencing Canada as a whole.

Trends are difficult to study from official statistics, however. If more juveniles are being picked up by police and processed by the courts, we should anticipate that even though more children are placed in training schools, the percentage of those appearing in court who end up in training schools would decrease. By looking at some recent data we may be able to show whether the use of training schools in Canada has been changing.

Trends in institutional usage for juveniles

Although it is even more difficult to make sense out of juvenile delinquency statistics than those for adult crime, a few tables may offer some insights. (Note: It sometimes takes several years before such statistics are available for public use. Hence, 1973 statistics are the latest ones available at the time of writing.)

In Table 7.2 the actual capacity of training schools in each province is shown for 1969 and 1973. By actual capacity we mean the number of juveniles in the training schools at the end of the month. It would be useful to have a longer time period, but as the reader will see, these statistics are still evolving in Canada, and as a result, meaningful long-term trends are difficult to establish.

In the third column of Table 7.2 I have calculated a rate showing the number of juveniles in training schools per 100,000 population. According to this column, Quebec appears to have a high percentage of juve-

Table 7.2
Actual Capacity in Training Schools in Canada, 1969 and 1973; by Province

	December 1969	*December 1973*	*Per 100,000 Population 1973*
Newfoundland	80	78	14.4
Nova Scotia	193	134	16.6
New Brunswick	66	36	5.5
Quebec	1152	1108	18.2
Ontario	1066	633	7.9
Manitoba	159	64	6.4
Saskatchewan	28	35	3.8
Alberta	89	—[1]	5.2[2]
British Columbia	—[1]	—[1]	—

[1] No report
[2] 1969 rate
Source: Statistics Canada, Catalogue 85-208, 1970, Appendix I and 1973, Appendix I.
N.B. Prince Edward Island did not report.

niles in such institutions while New Brunswick, Saskatchewan, and Alberta have relatively few. Of course, it would be more meaningful to calculate these rates on the population aged ten to nineteen, but that would only make slight changes. Other factors play a larger role. For example, the age limit for juveniles in Quebec is eighteen, for Ontario it is sixteen. In addition are group homes classified as training schools? Did Alberta include juveniles who were placed in privately operated "schools"? In detention centres? Does Quebec have a wide range of activities which come under the heading of "training schools"?

Without utilizing other information, we do not know if few juveniles are spending long periods in these institutions or if many juveniles are spending short periods. Nor can we assess whether there are meaningful seasonal variations. For example, in Ontario in December 1969, the absolute capacity was 1066 (Statistics Canada, Catalogue 85-208, 1970 and 1973). In May 1970 it was up to 1,468. By December 1970 it was down to 606. Why is December a low month for Ontario? Do children go home for Christmas? We notice the same pattern several years later. In December 1972, absolute capacity was 472. In May 1973 it was 1360. By December it was down to 633. This pattern does not seem to be apparent in the other provinces.

These data make more sense if we look for changes over time. In Table 7.2 we can compare the number of juveniles in training schools in 1969 and 1973. Almost all of the provinces show a decrease. Although there are probably many facilities housing juveniles which are not specifically designated as training schools, one fact seems to be clear: there has probably been no increase in the use of training schools in the last few years. If anything there has been a decline. Despite pressures to increase the capacity of institutional care, the Canadian juvenile justice system has resisted attempts to expand this portion of the system. Whether deliberate or not, the policy makes sense.

On the other hand, the adult correctional system in Canada seems to be adding more facilities. Some claim this will permit the closing of older facilities. Notice that changes taking place in the adult system have an impact on juveniles. Those who are seventeen in Ontario go to adult prisons, while seventeen-year-olds in Quebec go to juvenile institutions. Therefore, as far as seventeen-year-olds in Ontario are concerned, expansion of adult facilities counterbalances the more cautious use of institutional care in the juvenile system.

The policy decisions which lead to such changes are the product of a number of social concerns. These concerns are not necessarily based entirely on scientific knowledge. For example, group homes have been one method of reducing the population of training schools. Attempts to locate a halfway house or group home in a suburban area frequently provoke an outcry from the neighbourhood: "We're all for halfway houses, but *not* in *our* neighbourhood." Launching programs, then, is not simply a matter of making rational decisions based on what is best for juveniles.

Such attitudes influence the options open to the juvenile court. Table 7.3 shows that training schools are a relatively rare choice of final disposition (2.3 percent). However, it would be unwise to assume that the 2.3 percent of the cases sent from court to training schools in 1973 could be compared with the 14.4 percent reported in 1949.

Table 7.3
Disposition of 1973 Juvenile Cases Appearing in Court

Total Cases	16,599
Cases in Juvenile Court	15,948
	Percent
Dismissed	3.5
Adjourned	21.9
Probation, court	23.4
Probation, family	5.3
Fine or restitution	23.4
Training school	2.3
Suspended disposition	15.8

Source: Statistics Canada, Catalogue 85-202, 1973.

Table 7.4
Disposition of 1973 Cases Appearing in Juvenile Court—Percentage Sent to Training School by Province

	No. of Cases	*Sent to Training School*	*Percent Sent to Training School*
Newfoundland	388	25	6.4%
Nova Scotia	515	31	6.0
New Brunswick	609	44	7.2
Quebec	10,929	258	2.4
Saskatchewan	733	5	.7
British Columbia	3,320	9	.3
Alberta[1]	3,742	—	—
Manitoba[2]	8,961	40	.4
Ontario[2]	14,869	679	4.6

Source: Statistics Canada, Catalogue 85-202, 1973.

[1] All cases sent to Director of Child Welfare.
[2] Manitoba and Ontario have reporting systems that differ from those of other provinces.

N.B. Prince Edward Island did not report.

In Table 7.4 it appears that the Maritime provinces use training schools more frequently than Quebec, Ontario and British Columbia, but is it possible that the cases which finally get into court in the Maritimes are more serious than those that appear in court elsewhere? If we calculate the appearance rate in juvenile court per 100,000 persons for Newfoundland, it was 72 in 1973, while for Nova Scotia it was 64. In Quebec, Ontario, and British Columbia, the appearance rate was 180, 187, and 143. One could argue that there are more delinquents in Quebec, Ontario and British Columbia than in the Maritimes, but it is also possible that the juvenile justice system in the three more populous provinces draws a larger percentage of juveniles into its system at one end and utilizes a wider range of options at the other.

In addition, Table 7.4 must be viewed with a number of obvious reservations. The second column shows only nine cases in British Columbia going from the juvenile court to training school. Although British Columbia no longer has any official training schools, clearly many of the programs which house juveniles in British Columbia resemble training schools in the rest of Canada. These data show differences in the way data are handled more than differences in actual programs. In Alberta, for example, no training school population is indicated. In fact, all cases from the court which were formerly sent to training schools must now go to the Director of Child Welfare, who may or may not send juveniles on to the various training schools that exist, even though that is not the term currently in vogue.

The Manitoba statistics are also noteworthy. Like Alberta and Ontario, Manitoba has developed a reporting system somewhat different from that of the other provinces. The 8,961 cases in Manitoba give it a rate of 898 per 100,000, making it almost five times as delinquent as Ontario. More interesting is to compare Manitoba with its neighbouring province of Saskatchewan, which has a population of comparable size (just under a million) but with only 733 juvenile court appearances, about one-tenth of Manitoba's. True, the age limit for delinquents in Manitoba is eighteen while it is only sixteen in Saskatchewan, but instead of believing that juveniles are more delinquent in Manitoba, it is safer to assume that something is diverting cases before they get into the record keeping system in Saskatchewan. With the increasing use of diversion systems in Toronto, Kingston and elsewhere, it is quite likely that the high Ontario rates noted above will drop considerably. This probably will not mean a change in juvenile behaviour, but it will be interesting to see if someone tries to take credit for lowering the delinquency rate.

According to unofficial data from the Montreal police in 1973, there were 4245 juvenile court referrals in 1965 and 4782 in 1970. Of these 259 were institutionalized in 1965 but only 142 in 1970. Although interpretation is risky, the institutional alternative may have become less popular.

It is important to realize that these figures are quoted, usually inappropriately, as evidence that someone has been "doing a good job" (or doing a poor job, as the case by be). Furthermore, officials, the mass media and the public use these data, again inappropriately, as the basis for new action programs. And to compound horrors, many people persist in believing that the presentation of such data is in itself an "evaluation" of correctional and prevention programs.

Tables 7.2, 7.3, and 7.4 then, while providing possible insights into the different procedures used in the various provinces, do not permit comparisons in terms of either delinquency or delinquency prevention programs. Nor are they valid indicators of institutional patterns in various provinces. At present these data may be useful for making comparisons over time, assuming that other changes do not complicate the interpretation within each province. Basically, however, there is a general indication that the juvenile justice system in Canada has not been opting for an increased use of institutional care.

It is possible that I have been overly harsh on some institutional programs. Many institutions now offer a variety of settings. Some training schools attempt to house juveniles while they attend schools in the community. Although the Silverlake experiment and other such programs do not show striking success, they constitute an effort to keep juveniles in touch with the community where they must eventually live. In other words, as training schools modify their programs so that they attempt to keep a larger percentage of juveniles in contact with the community and thus counteract certain subcultural tendencies, many of the criticisms mentioned above lose their force.

Let us now turn to some of the cost factors connected with institutions, delinquency and crime in general. I shall try to tie together several related themes. One is the cost of the correctional apparatus itself. It seems that some of the most expensive features of this apparatus yield the lowest returns in terms of a decrease in crime and delinquency. The second theme is the cost of criminal behaviour. Since much delinquency is concerned with theft, and data on such costs are scarce for juveniles, I will utilize some figures on adult crime.

The Cost of Institutional Care and the Cost of Crime and Delinquency

Compared with other alternatives, institutional settings are expensive. The high cost of crime may in fact be due to the extensive use of incarceration (Robison, 1969). One must be careful how one calculates the cost of crime. Although many automobiles are stolen, 90 percent are recovered. Do our statistics on the cost of crime take this into account? We might also ask what the total cost is to society. When a $500 typewriter is stolen from an office, then resold to a fence for $100 and finally ends up in the hands of a college student, how much did society lose? An insurance company may reimburse the office for the cost of the typewriter, making other businesses more inclined to take out insurance and thereby helping to keep insurance agents employed. True, a crime has been committed, but how does one assess the economic consequences of this "transfer" of property compared with the behaviour of a salesman who manages to sell an overpriced refrigerator to a naive customer? Why is laying asphalt over agricultural land to build a highway recorded as a gain to our Gross National Product, while the replacement of a safe for one destroyed by a safecracker is seen as a loss to society?

One U.S. study points out that a major cost of crime is the justice system itself. James Robison argues that the cost of robbery to victims in the United States in 1965 was between $27 and $65 million while the cost of corrections for those involved in robbery was $59 million and the cost of the rest of the criminal justice system was $81 million (1969:pp.79-97). For burglary the loss to victims was $251-$500 million, while the cost of corrections and the criminal justice system for those involved totaled $820 million. We must consider the possibility that using incarceration to deal with certain crimes is the major factor in making these crimes expensive to society. Is crime any more expensive to society than say, for example, smoking? Canadians spent $1.45 billion on cigarettes in 1973. It is difficult to estimate the medical costs in terms of cancer and heart disease. Should the increased burden on hospitals, families, insurance systems be seen as a cost or should these increased fees, premiums, etc. be viewed, in economic terms, as a contribution to an increased Gross National Product?

Of this $1.45 billion spent on cigarettes, perhaps a third came back to the state in the form of taxes. About $50 million was profit. Approximately 120,000 acres of prime agricultural land were used to grow tobacco; 95 percent of this land is in southern Ontario near population centres where the cost of transporting food to the market would have been minimal. How does one assess the costs of the loss of this land? What penalties do we pay when we consume energy to bring food from California that might be grown near urban centres.?

When we read of juvenile vandalism in the newspapers, we are typically outraged by the senseless destruction. The same outrage doesn't seem to exist when we consider the behaviour of adults that leads to preventable heart attacts. At the 1976 Canadian Cardiovascular Society and Canadian Council of Cardiovascular Nurses joint meeting, Dr. E. S. O. Smith argued that heart disease in about 49 percent of males could be prevented. He calculated that preventable heart attacks cost the Canadian economy at least $630 million a year in medical bills and lost income.

The point should be clear—it is difficult to assess either the economic or social costs of much human behaviour. However, several conclusions are apparent: attempts to treat juveniles in institutional settings yield a very low return on the investment. In addition, the cost of juvenile crime is rather trivial compared with the financial costs involved in cigarette smoking, alcohol consumption, auto accidents, income tax evasion, and many other activities which are accepted, or at least tolerated by society. Even institutions for juveniles are not excessively expensive. They are simply similar to other wasteful aspects of our society. Our major concern with institutional treatment should be its *social* costs.

Marc LeBlanc, of the University of Montreal, notes other reasons for being wary of institutional treatment. He expresses the more general concern that applied criminology, of which correctional treatment is a major component, runs the risk of becoming an instrument of control to be used against certain populations (1973). If we look at proposed programs in criminology, we can see the possibility of serving present bureaucracies without asking basic questions. If departments of criminology and social work cooperate with government agencies to develop an orientation toward better institutional treatment it could lead us away from alternatives to incarceration.

Since information on the better known American studies is readily available to the reader (Lipton, Martinson and Wilks, 1975), I will close this section by referring to a recent study done in Vienna, Austria. A six year follow-up study compared boys who were sent to a training school for an indefinite period with boys on probation and those who received a suspended sentence. This Austrian study (Hinsch, Leirer and Steinert, 1972) came to conclusions very similar to those of parallel studies done in the United States. The three different groups of boys (training school, probation, and suspended sentence) were not directly comparable. The most serious cases were sent to the training school and the least serious cases were simply given a suspended sentence. Therefore, the researchers utilized a logic for analysis identical to the one suggested earlier in Chapter 5.

When one examines the recidivism rate for each of the three groups, those who received a suspended sentence did not recidivate in 57 percent of the cases. We might say they had a 57 percent "success' rate. The comparable figures for those with a probation officer were 43 percent, and for those in the training school 15 percent.

But these three groups were not comparable. In order to make more meaningful comparisons, three types of "handicaps" were devised. The first was based on previous crimes, the second on the quality of family life, and the third on educational and occupational training. Each of the three comparison groups was classified into low, medium and high "handicapped" boys. As expected, a rather high percentage of those in the training school were classified as having a "high handicap."

Interestingly enough, the controls for the type of handicaps did not alter the picture as much as one might have assumed. Recidivism rates were higher for those who were in the training school and lower for those who received a suspended sentence, even when comparisons were made within categories of the handicap. That is, controlling for background characteristics did not change the impact of institutional treatment. For example, those in the least handicapped group who were sent to the training school had a 74 percent recidivism rate in the first year. Surprisingly, this failure rate was even higher than the most handicapped group, which had a recidivism rate of 52 percent. One might argue that incarceration was harder on those inexperienced in crime, from better families, and with better education than on those less fortunate. It is also possible that those incarcerated from better families had very strong inclinations toward delinquency, and that the institutional experience may have reinforced these tendencies.

By simply looking at the first-year performance of those who were least handicapped and most handicapped, we discover the major theme of this Viennese study. (In Table 7.5 we have eliminated the column for the medium handicapped boys, to make the illustration clearer.) We can see that the recidivism rate for those who were sent to the training school during the first year is very high regardless of the type of handicap (74 percent and 52 percent). For those on probation, the recidivism

Table 7.5
Recidivism Rates in Three Alternate Delinquency Prevention Strategies in Vienna

	Degree to Which Delinquents Were Handicapped[1]	
	Least Handicapped	*Most Handicapped*
Training School	74% (30)	52% (82)
Probation	18% (40)	23% (48)
Suspended Sentence	10% (90)	15% (40)

[1] A combined variable taking into account: (1) previous crimes, (2) the quality of family life, and (3) educational and occupational training (Hinsch, Leirer and Steinert, 1972).

rate for the least handicapped group was 18 percent and the most handicapped was 23 percent. For those with a suspended sentence the rate was 10 percent for the least handicapped and 15 percent for the most handicapped. The suspended sentence seemed to work "best" regardless of the degree of handicap.

It is possible that the attempts to control for the type of "handicap" were inadequate, but obviously previous crimes, family life, and educational and occupational training are relevant to continuing delinquency. While the type of analysis presented here may not be as convincing as a controlled experiment, it offers a strong suggestion that the training school was a poor choice. When those who are "least handicapped" do so badly, even worse than those "most handicapped," there is reason to believe that the training school experience increases the likelihood of crime.

It is interesting to note that boys are no longer being sent to the training school in Vienna which was under study. Perhaps this is an illustration of how knowledge *did* influence policy. It is also interesting to note the compatibility of these particular findings with the general recommendation of critics of institutional programs: doing the least seemed to do the least harm.

When we take into account the fact that many juveniles who are not considered to be delinquents but only in "need of supervision" are placed in various institutions, we have reason to be concerned. One study in New York showed that the median institutional stay for delinquents was nine months. For those in need of supervision the length was thirteen months. One might argue that the median was influenced by many short sentences for delinquents; however, the average stay was 10.7 months for delinquents and 16.3 months for those in need of supervision. Regardless of the measurement, institutionalization was longer for boys sentenced for juvenile status offences (such as being in need of supervision) than for boys convicted of criminal-type offences (Lerman, 1971).

My preference for a conservative approach precludes my recommending that all juvenile institutions be closed, as they were in Massachusetts, but a systematic reduction in the number of juveniles sent to them seems to be a reasonable goal. It is possible that a hard core of problem children will still have to be placed in institutions, but we should not deceive ourselves that this is effective treatment. Justice may demand punishment in some cases. In other words, we may simply be desperate. Instead of insisting that child welfare or corrections departments work out "meaningful" programs for every lawbreaker, it might be healthier to admit that there are some cases that baffle us. Locking them up, in reasonably humane conditions, may be all we can do.

The Consequences of Doing Nothing

As one can see from the previous discussion, even institutions operated by humane staff members offer little hope of effective delinquency prevention. It is difficult to make wise suggestions in the face of this evidence. There is always a certain number of juveniles who end up in institutions because reasonable alternatives are lacking, but society should consider other possible approaches. First, we should view doing nothing as a reasonable choice. Even though the family situation seems to be poor and the environment conducive to delinquency, the milieu where these young people live may in the long run be more benevolent than an institutional setting. We should keep in mind the insights gained by John Mack in his studies of "rough" families in England and Scotland and the delinquent children who came from such families. True, theft and other delinquencies were more common than among the "respectable" families. The rough families may have been seen as more of a problem for society, but is it possible they were also capable of solving certain problems?

> The family structure of the rough family is on the one hand ill-adapted to swim in the mainstream of social progress, but it is not too badly adapted to some of the murky backwaters (Mack, 1956:12).

If modern society creates a number of murky backwaters, it is possible that the lower classes have developed ways of dealing with them more effectively than the artificial institutions created by government bureaucracies.

A second suggestion is that institutions need to make considerable effort to see that their clients stay with them only a short period of time and that they maintain as much contact as possible with the outside world. There is some indication that this is being done in Canada. The decreasing numbers of children in such institutions suggest that alternatives to incarceration are being used more frequently than they have been in the past. And finally, for those who must spend time in a training school, a variety of steps can be taken to minimize the negative impact. Although some of these procedures do little to rehabilitate juveniles, we should acknowledge the possibility that they keep these institutional situations from making things a great deal worse. Frequently, critics of the system are impatient and are unsympathetic to those institutions that are doing what they can to mitigate the damage being done to juveniles. When one is grasping for straws, preserving the humaneness of an institutional setting should be seen as an achievement.

Factors Which Make Meanings Obscure

Before we turn in the next chapter to a review of various delinquency prevention strategies, we need to be aware of some of the factors which make it difficult to interpret them. One problem is the inconsistency of findings. Usually, the expense of carefully evaluated prevention programs means that relatively small numbers of juveniles are involved. The combination of factors that influences one program may be slightly different from another combination influencing another program even though the same experimental variable is used. A few unique personalities among the staff may be the major factor in determining the outcome of a given program. To compound matters, increasing numbers of programs make it more likely that some studies will fall into the ".05 level of significance," that is, things can happen by chance. While the odds of five to one hundred may be good enough to accept the findings of a specific project, if one hundred programs are attempted, we would expect five of them to show success even if things happened randomly. Of course, we would also expect another five to show a significant failure rate compared with experimental groups. In other words, it is difficult to place credibility on a single study even though it suggests clear success or clear failure.

In an earlier chapter, we pointed out that four years after the completion of the Seattle Opportunities for Youth project there was some evidence that boys involved in the work program did worse than those in the comparable control groups. We also found that boys involved in the teaching machine testing program seemed to do better than those in comparable control groups. Naturally, we attempted to work out a rationale to explain these phenomena, but if these experimental variables were utilized again, what is the chance that they would yield the same results? When we note the inconsistency which results when studies have been replicated by sophisticated researchers, we would have to predict that results similar to those obtained in the Opportunities for

Youth project would be unlikely. Hence, social policy based on the results of those few studies which do have adequate evaluations and clear policy implications is hazardous.

Aside from the lack of comparability among delinquency prevention programs, the very fact that one attempts to do something seems to change the situation. In recent years this has frequently been referred to as the Hawthorn effect.

One of the classic studies in industrial sociology attempted to learn what sort of work conditions led to greater output in the factory (Roethlisberger and Dickson, 1937). Under carefully controlled conditions, the engineers and other researchers in the Hawthorn plant of Western Electric near Chicago varied the size of light bulbs, numbers of minutes worked and other variables. Each time working conditions were altered, even in such a manner as to make work more difficult, the output went up. It soon dawned on the researchers that the social environment which made these workers "special" was the most important variable. In other words, people usually respond favourably when someone pays attention to them.

Similarly, if young people think they are being treated in some special way, they are liable to respond favourably regardless of the nature of the experimental variable. As described in Chapter 2, the introduction of a gang worker into a street gang with a tough reputation may be enough to change the behaviour of that gang. Changes may take place even if the gang worker does nothing. Those who undergo counseling frequently have similar experiences. As long as someone is listening to their problems, they feel better. The ramifications of the principles illustrated by the Hawthorn experiment have led to insights in a number of related fields. Much has been written which relates these phenomena to the study of deviance. For our purpose it is simply important to note that introducing changes in human situations generates other changes which are not necessarily related to the nature of the initial stimulus. It is difficult to control this influence in a delinquency prevention program. Whereas the medical researcher can use a sugar-coated pill which looks like the real one, it is frequently difficult to give a placebo to a control group in a delinquency prevention program. For this reason, programs which seem successful at first sometimes lose their impact as time goes on. It may be wise to consider utilizing the Hawthorn effect as part of a treatment program. This possibility will be explored in more detail in a later section.

In Chapter 4, Table 4.1, we saw an illustration of bias in terms of parole violation for boys who were involved in an experimental group versus those who were in a control group. Although boys involved in the experimental program committed as many or more offences than boys in the control group, their parole was not violated as often. In this case, the responses of those in a position of authority probably had a direct impact on the criterion for success or failure. However, the responses of others can operate in even more subtle ways, which make it very difficult to detect their influence. The responses of social workers, teachers, counselors, police, etc. who are involved in an experimental program can change simply because of that involvement. Furthermore, as they talk with others as part of their normal interaction patterns in an experiment, they may have an impact on school principals, policemen, probation officers, etc. The dynamics of these activities will quite likely be reflected in the data gathered by researchers.

These factors influencing the findings coming from various delinquency prevention programs provide another argument for not investing scarce resources in sophisticated experimental programs and their evaluation. The alternative research strategies suggested in Chapter 5 are a cheaper way of dealing with the factors mentioned above which can lead us astray. True, careful record keeping and data analysis will not eliminate those factors that obscure the meaning of the data, but such confounding factors are more devastating to the carefully constructed experimental program than to research procedures not dependent upon assessing the effectiveness of a given experimental activity.

I began this chapter with a debate. Cynics argue that our attempts to rehabilitate offenders have been completely unsuccessful. Optimists feel there has been progress. At present there seems to be no clear answer, but there is some agreement on which strategies are ineffective. The traditional training school seems to offer little hope for meaningful change. Since North America, and possibly British Columbia and Alberta in particular, seem somewhat inclined to attack a number of social problems using concrete and steel, it is worthwhile emphasizing this point.

Although institution building seems to be a frequent societal response to adult crime in Canada, it has been a less frequent response to juvenile delinquency. And yet the distinction between juveniles and young adults is frequently an arbitrary one. A portion of this group may fall under the jurisdiction of one bureaucracy while the others will be dealt with by another system. Societal response will differ according to an arbitrary age line. Although young people are not transformed when they cross from seventeen to eighteen, bureaucratic response to their behaviour can differ markedly. Hence, it makes no sense to think of delinquency prevention or youthful crime prevention as a logical and rational response to a clearly defined problem. We must take into account many factors that are not directly related to delinquency if we are to develop an intelligent, if not completely rational, response.

Conclusion

Still focusing on institutionalization, this chapter went on to note that such programs were expensive and that, in general, our response to crime and delinquency may be more expensive than crime and delinquency itself. However, we felt that an economic argument was of secondary importance in this particular issue.

Next, evidence of the negative impact of a training school in Austria was offered to convince the reader that the points we were making are valid for Europe as well. Perhaps they are, but we acknowledge that one cannot rely on one small study.

Since the purpose of this chapter was to prepare us for stumbling ahead, it is important to emphasize the blind alleys. We will have enough trouble with the highways that appear to lead us into the distance. Some danger signs are clear, but others are difficult to read. Leaping forward can be dangerous. I also have an inclination to improve the world and help juveniles in particular, but I am aware that hasty and dramatic responses to what I perceive as an emergency can result in the creation of new problems. There is, however, a limit to restraint.

In the following chapters I will examine some specific programs, keeping in mind that despite the sophistication shown by the researchers who conducted these evaluations and assessed the outcomes, the hazards discussed in the past chapters were present. And finally, I cannot resist making recommendations. Our goal is not to give a false sense of security by making a clear case for a particular strategy. The best direction is not obvious. The road signs are confusing. I prefer to reflect that confusion and caution the reader that the largest and brightest coloured road sign could point in the wrong direction.

Chapter 8

A Focus on the Community and Group Dynamics

The facts are important, but they vary in their importance and they change. . . . A thoughtful style of analysis need not be revised every year, however. It need not endure forever either, but a way of thinking may represent a style where collections of facts about specific issues are, like fashions, fleeting.

—GWYNN NETTLER

Community Treatment and Residential Programs

The report of the Task Force on Community-Based Residential Centres (Canada) came out with a strong recommendation in favour of the use of community-based residential centres for a larger percentage of persons serving sentences (Canada, 1973). This report has encouraged a movement that is already underway in Canada. We should look carefully at such programs because they are compatible with a philosophy of attempting to maintain close contact between young offenders and the community.

The California Community Treatment Program

California has had experimental programs in community treatment since 1961. The careful assessment of the various phases of the Community Treatment Program (CTP) must definitely be taken into account if new programs in Canada are to take advantage of these experiences. Eight hundred and two boys and 212 girls participated in the California program to find out whether certain kinds of juvenile offenders could be allowed to remain in their home communities, if given intensive supervision and treatment within a small-sized parole case load (Palmer, 1973a). The program took place in Sacramento, Stockton, and San Francisco. Youths who had been sent to the California Youth Authority for offences such as armed robbery, assault with a deadly weapon, or forceable rape did not take part in the program; however, it was still possible to include 65 percent of all boys and 83 percent of all girls who were serious delinquents in these three cities. The presence of marked drug involvement, homosexuality, chronic or severe neurosis, occasional psychotic episodes, and suicidal tendencies did not, in themselves, mean exclusion from the experiment. In other words, this particular study was not based upon a selected group of youths who were different from traditional delinquents. The youths were randomly assigned to experimental and control groups, with the controls being sent to an institution for several months prior to being returned to their home communities, where they were given routine supervision in standard-sized parole case loads. In the experimental group the youths were assigned to parole officers who worked with no more than twelve youths.

For purposes of analysis, the youths were classified by their personality characteristics. Those in the first group were referred to as *passive conformists*.

> This type of youth usually fears, and responds with strong compliance to, peers and adults whom he thinks have the "upper hand" at the moment, or seem more adequate and assertive than himself. He considers himself to be lacking social "know how," and usually expects to be rejected by others in spite of his efforts to please them (Palmer, 1973a: 5).

This group accounted for 14 percent of the population in the study. The researchers note that this type is far more common at the city and county probation level than within the California Youth Authority itself. The passive conformists in this study would probably be seen as "immature conformists" according to a typology of personalities developed by Marguerite Q. Warren (1969) which I discuss later in Chapter 10.

The second category was referred to as *power oriented*.

> This group is actually made up of two somewhat different kinds of individuals, who, nevertheless, share several important features with one another. The first likes to think of himself as delinquent and tough. He is often more than willing to "go along" with others, or with a gang, in order to earn a certain degree of status and acceptance, and to later maintain his "reputation." The second type usually does not wish to conform to peers or adults. Not infrequently, he will attempt to assume a leading "power role" for himself (Palmer, 1973a: 5).

This power-oriented group accounted for 20 percent of the 1961-69 sample of boys and would resemble the "cultural conformist" and "manipulators" in the typology developed by Warren.

A third category of youths was labelled *neurotic*.

> Here again, we find two separate types of youth who share certain important characteristics with one another. The first type often attempts to deny to himself—and to others—his conscious feelings of inadequacy, rejection, or self-condemnation. Not infrequently, he does this by verbally attacking *others* and/or by the use of a variety of "games" and distractions. The second type often shows various symptoms of emotional disturbances—e.g., chronic or intense depression, or psychosomatic complaints produced by feelings of failure, inadequacy, or underlying guilt (Palmer, 1973a: 5).

This neurotic category would probably be classified as "neurotic acting-out" and "neurotic anxious" in the Warren system. This group made up 53 percent of the boys in this study.

Some researchers would criticize this classification scheme as leaving little room for a "normal" delinquent. Other scholars have indicated that they have found the majority of delinquents to be quite normal. Despite possible debates over this classification scheme, it should be noted that these three types accounted for 88 percent of the boys in the study and provided useful information related to the impact of the program.

For the group classified as neurotic, the CTP program seemed to be a better alternative than the traditional institutional treatment plus standard parole. The controls were arrested 2.7 times more often than the experimentals. On a 24-month parole follow-up the recidivism rate was 66 percent for controls and 45 percent for experimentals. Within 60 months of the time of their first release to the community, 40 percent of the controls versus 77 percent of the experimentals had been officially given a favourable discharge. Within the same period, 40 percent of the controls versus 17 percent of the experimentals received an unfavourable discharge. Within 48 months after having left the jurisdiction of the Youth Authority, controls recorded an average of 1.88 convictions versus 1.58 for the experimentals. Whether or not one quibbles with the label neurotic, it appears that some of the youth so categorized seemed to benefit from the community treatment program. Perhaps it would be better to say that it was worthwhile avoiding the institutional experience.

The power-oriented youths, however, did worse in the CTP program on three out of four indicators than those in the traditional program. On the 24-month parole follow-up, the recidivism rate was 66 percent for controls and 40 percent for the experimentals; however, despite the better showing by experimentals on the 24-month recidivism index, 53 percent of the controls versus 43 percent of the experimentals received a favourable discharge from the Youth Authority within 60 months of their first release on parole. In addition, 15 percent of the controls versus 23 percent of the experimentals received an unfavourable discharge. Within 48 months after having left the jurisdiction of the CYA, those who had been given a favourable discharge had an average of 1.47 convictions for the controls versus 2.55 for the experimentals.

The passive conformists provided a mixed picture. While under Youth Authority jurisdiction, they seemed to do better in the CTP program compared with the traditional program. However, those experimentals who received a favourable discharge from the CYA performed somewhat worse than their controls in terms of convictions (but somewhat better in terms of arrests).

Taken together, the boys who participated in the CTP program performed substantially better than those in the traditional program during the period they were under the jurisdiction of the Youth Authority. After leaving the Youth Authority, an examination of those who received a favourable discharge shows that those in the traditional program had 1.42 convictions within 48 months after they left the CYA compared with 1.67 for those in the CTP. In terms of arrests, those in the traditional program had 1.72 versus 1.94 for the CTP boys. This outcome seems to reflect the rather good performance of a large number of power oriented boys among the favourable dischargees.

Analyses for individuals who received an unfavourable discharge were not available, since approximately 50 percent of these cases were sent directly to prison upon discharge from the California Youth Authority.

Since there are few programs which provide such careful analyses, these findings should be weighed carefully. First of all, being able to categorize delinquents seems to be important. Secondly, the performance of boys *during* parole supervision is not necessarily a good indicator of performance *after* that period of supervision ends. One must also consider the possibility that a parole officer with only twelve cases to supervise may have been able to influence the criminal justice system more directly. Could he have kept a boy who committed a minor delinquency from returning to jail by intervening with the authorities? This might be desirable, but it is not the same thing as preventing delinquency (Table 4.1 in Chapter 4).

We must also ask whether the positive impact of the CTP program during the supervisory period is the result of the small parole case load or the *avoidance* of the influence of serving time in a traditional training school. In one study of gangs in Boston, it appeared that gang leaders who were recently released from jail tended to increase their criminal activity upon reassuming leadership positions in order to solidify their positions. Once they reestablished their status in the gang, their criminal activity decreased (Miller, 1969). In other words, under some circumstances, institutionalization could lead to an increase in crime because of the need for youths to reestablish social roles which were interrupted. Therefore, involvement in a community treatment program would not keep such youths from criminal activities, but it might avoid contributing to an increase. By contrast, Richard Ericson (1975) found that boys recently released from an English detention centre felt constrained by a fear of return to the centre. For several months they avoided delinquency producing situations. It is not clear whether these differences from Miller's findings in Boston reflect local or larger cultural factors.

Furthermore, as we learned from the Provo experiment, incarceration does not automatically lead to an absence of crime while the boys are serving time (Empey and Erickson, 1972). Escapes are common from juvenile institutions and during these escapes the likelihood of crime is quite high.

In the California Community Treatment Program, the findings for the sample of girls did not provide a clear picture. On some indicators those in the community treatment program appeared to do better, but on others, those in the traditional program came out ahead. The basic conclusion was that no substantial overall difference was observed.

Not surprisingly, the sophisticated 1961-1969 study in California provided an inconclusive picture. The more recent study, from 1969 to 1974, was built on this experience.

Community Treatment Plus a Special Residential Setting, 1969-74

Utilizing a sample of youths from the greater Sacramento area, the California Youth Authority established a special residential setting which was used prior to sending youths out into the community under its CTP program. The idea was that this special residence period might enhance the effectiveness of community treatment. The facility normally housed 23 to 25 youths, with minimum security, and was staffed by people in close contact with the CTP program. Some parole officers even had their offices in the facility. The question was: would an initial stay in this type of residence be better than releasing the individual directly into the intensive community treatment program as was done in the 1961-1969 experiment?

Subjects for this program had been diagnosed as either (1) troublesome and restive, and therefore needing this residential setting, or (2) as not needing such a residential setting. Once categorized the two subgroups were divided again. One portion of each subgroup was appropriately placed while the other portion was inappropriately placed. Figure 8.1 illustrates the four different experimental groups. In the RR cell we find appropriately placed boys who were diagnosed as needing the residence and were placed in the residence. In the RC cell boys were diagnosed as needing the residence but placed in the community. In the CR cell boys diagnosed as not needing the residential centre were placed in the residence. In the CC cell boys diagnosed as appropriate for the community were appropriately placed in the community treatment program. Within each of the four cells, the average monthly offence rate was noted for the eighteen months the boys were on parole in the community. The highest rate of .140 was in the RC cell, those boys diagnosed as in need of the residence but placed in the community. Ninety-four percent of this group chalked up one or more offences during their first eighteen months on parole. In contrast, the RR group, diagnosed as needing the residential setting, had a .066 monthly offence rate and 58 percent of them committed offences. In this situation, placement within the residence before beginning the CTP program seemed to result in a significant improvement.

How about those boys who were seen as less troublesome and restive

Figure 8.1
California Community Treatment Program
Residential Setting, 1969-1974

Diagnosed as Needing Residential Setting	Placement: In Residence	Placement: In Community
Yes (troublesome and restive)	Appropriately Placed .066 RR	Inappropriately Placed .140 RC
No	Inappropriately Placed .086 CR	Appropriately Placed .068 CC

Rates refer to monthly offence rate after 18 months on parole.

and who should have done all right in the community? Those who were appropriately placed, the CC group, had a monthly offence rate of .068, about the same as the group of restive delinquents in the RR group. Those inappropriately placed in the residence, the CR group, had a higher monthly offence rate of .086. Again, the combination of classification and program seems to improve success rates. Palmer and his colleagues point out, however, that the consequences of inappropriate placement in this particular study was much more damaging for those boys diagnosed as troublesome and restive. The difference between the less troubled boys who were appropriately or inappropriately placed was not statistically significant. The inappropriate placement of a better adjusted youth may not have been as much of a hardship as he was better equipped to cope with the residential environment.

At this stage I am obliged to mention an extensive critique of the Community Treatment Project and the California Probation Subsidy Program (Lerman, 1975). Using data generated by these projects, Lerman reanalyzes the material and concludes that they were more costly and no more effective than traditional programs. He claims that juveniles were detained more frequently than treated in spite of the official goals of the program. In addition, Lerman suggests that probation subsidies were frequently associated with greater institutionalization or some other form of detention.

To some this might come as a shock, but to readers who have been toughened by the experiences described in the earlier chapters of this book, such a critique seems reasonable. I feel the work done by Palmer and his colleagues still deserves detailed review, not because it is "right," but because it is some of the best research in the field. By now we are aware that there is no such thing as a sacred study which provides evidence that we can accept without reservation.

Occasionally, a reanalysis of data produces positive findings. Fisher and Erickson (1973) performed time-series analyses on data gathered in the Provo experiment (see Chapter 4). They argued that intervention, either in the form of detention or some other attempt at social control by the juvenile justice system, such as a community-based program, did have an impact on delinquency. Their findings provided little support for labeling theory. Hence, it does not seem reasonable at this particular time to believe that we can weigh the evidence and conclude that certain techniques are clearly effective or not. Aside from the formidable difficulties of interpreting data, the unique characteristics of each project make it virtually impossible to compare it with another.

These studies show that simplified answers or extreme claims are not helpful. The battle between the "lock all of them up" advocates versus "the keep everyone in the community" may be inappropriate. If either side wins, we may be worse off because of it. There seems to be a majority of youth who might benefit from community-based programs, at least as compared with institutionalization, but there seems also to be a few difficult-to-reach youth who adjust poorly if placed directly in a community-based program. Some sort of residential treatment may in fact help. In his summary of this twelve-year experiment to date, Palmer notes the very important point that what goes on *within* a given setting seems to be more important than just the setting itself (1973). This probably applies to community-based and residential settings alike.

Many advocates of community treatment programs argue that they are less expensive than traditional training schools. While this is probably true, it is clear that community treatment programs similar to those run in California are fairly expensive operations. I personally have misgivings about the application of cost accounting techniques to delinquency prevention programs, but it is understandable that governments wish to take such factors into consideration. Naturally, the cost of future incarceration as an adult should also be taken into account. Stuart Adams, while working with the Los Angeles County Probation Department, used cost accounting techniques to assess the financial impact of a gang worker program (1967). This topic will be treated separately in a later section utilizing Canadian data (Murphy 1975).

Community work by offenders, some English programs

Community work programs have been developed in England, Sweden, and other countries. The program I wish to mention briefly, which exists in London, England, is actually designed for adults rather than juveniles, but it illustrates a few principles not found in most community treatment programs for juveniles. The 1972 English Criminal Justice Bill made provisions for community work by offenders. The idea was to make it possible for certain persons who would normally be sentenced to prison to remain in their normal jobs and in addition work for up to eight hours on Saturdays and Sundays as part of a supervised work project. Some of these supervised settings would include providing recreational facilities for children, the handicapped and the elderly, as well as clearing derelict areas. There would also be opportunities for men to work in less structured settings. The present plan calls for having men work in small groups under the direction of a supervisor (Collie, 1972).

A Home Office report (Pease *et al.*, 1975) describes these "community service orders" in six jurisdictions. Although the effect on the offender is as yet unknown, and the penal theory underlying the scheme somewhat uncertain, the program seems to be viable. Like many other programs, it can be subverted. As yet there is no indication which type of work placement has what type of influence on different individuals.

Such a strategy may be meaningful for juveniles in Canada. Instead of continuing with a "treatment" model which may be of questionable validity, an expectation that one must "pay one's debt to society" may in fact be much more comprehensible to the delinquent and to law-abiding, tax-paying citizens. A sense of accomplishment and contribution to the community may also come out of this type of project. It will be interesting to observe the results of these experiments in England.*

Obviously, there are a number of variations on community-based programs. Some, like the Grierson Centre in Edmonton, Alberta, deal with inmates from the Federal Penitentiary Service who have received long sentences for serious crimes. The majority of these men are holding jobs in the community while living at the Centre. The Temporary Absence Pass has also allowed inmates to be gainfully employed, pay taxes and support their families. Although such programs sometimes face public resistance, the advantages seem to be worth the risk.

Juvenile institutions are finding that it is possible to send a portion of their wards into the community on a regular basis. Whenever an institution has a portion of its population going out into the community every day while another portion remains within the institution, problems will arise. Experience shows that youths from institutions who attend school or who work during the day sometimes bring contraband back into the institution. However, problems of this nature may not be very different from those which occur in institutions that attempt to maintain tighter security.

---

*Community service programs are being used in Montreal and elsewhere in Canada, but we do not know of any systematic research connected with them.

It is reasonable to assume that community correctional programs will be launched in most communities without rigorous attempts to evaluate them. As the reader knows from previous comments I feel this is a wise strategy even though the failure to evaluate is usually not a deliberate decision. On the other hand, a continuous critical look at such programs on the part of insightful staff is important. The tendency for some people to have unbounded faith in new programs leads to a lack of caution, which can have severe repercussions. There is also a tendency for new programs to select those clients who will increase the likelihood of success. In Canada, there is the distinct possibility that community-based programs will leave Indians behind in institutions. A well-meaning social worker might be hesitant to place a fourteen-year-old Indian girl, who had been engaged in prostitution, in a community-based program. If such programs are to be meaningful, we must examine our biases more carefully and openly. Community programs could be unjust. They may favour those who are already advantaged.

As I describe other types of programs, it should be clear to the reader that a number of combinations is possible. Most programs are mixtures. This is probably desirable, since it permits flexibility. As yet we do not know whether the interaction effects of different experimental variables are influential, but at the present time it would be inappropriate to say that one particular strategy is clearly superior to another. One strategy, in some situations, might be helpful for certain types of juveniles but might prove disastrous in other settings or with other types of individuals. For the majority of juvenile delinquents, keeping in touch with the community seems to have more advantages than disadvantages. It is worthwhile to seek alternatives to incarceration.*

Group Therapy

Despite the extensive overlap in strategies used in these various programs, it is useful to describe several studies which utilize the group itself as the basis for initiating changes in delinquent behaviour. Some strategies bring youths together in a residential setting. Others utilize some form of group counseling. Many specialists in this business have distinguished between guided group interaction and other forms of group counseling. It is possible that the variations which exist in actual practice are so wide that it is inappropriate to think of guided group interaction as a single strategy. However, there is usually agreement that this procedure involves the group members in a very active way.

The Vanier Centre

The Vanier Centre in Brampton, Ontario caters to women who have up to two years to serve in an Ontario provincial institution. It consists of several modern one-storey buildings and large grassy areas, enclosed by

*For a thoughtful discussion of such alternatives, see Empey, 1967.

a fence. Four resident cottages, each housing a maximum of 24 women, plus the administration and activities buildings, are located within the fence. One similar cottage is outside the fence. The institution is committed to the concept of "therapeutic community treatment" as advocated by Maxwell Jones (1953). It encourages open communication between staff and inmates and includes participation in program planning by inmates.

A study was undertaken to assess the social climate in the different cottages over time (Lambert and Madden, 1974; Lambert and Madden, 1976). As expected, staff tended to hold more positive attitudes toward the program than inmates, but generally the attitudes of the residents were positive. Comparisons among the cottages provided useful information and the cyclical patterns indicated that there was considerable agreement between staff and residents. They seemed to share periods of optimism and gloom. Some of the interesting findings included the fact that although two-thirds of the residents were under 25, those over 25 were more favourably inclined to the program. Women with special interests and those who were involved in group activities held more positive views of their environment.

While clear guidelines for other programs may not be forthcoming from this particular study, a healthy research environment was created that bodes well for the future. Some critics will claim that the research tells us little about the "effectiveness" of the program in preventing crime. True, but as the reader has seen from previous research, most studies do not answer that question, and when they do, the answer is not particularly helpful. As yet relationships between social climate scores and various indices of rehabilitation are not available, but the recidivism rate of a specific sample followed for one year was only 22 percent, which is fairly low.

The study of the social climate at the Vanier Centre further suggests that an "inmate code" was largely avoided. Communication between staff and residents seemed to be reasonably effective and may have helped to avoid the counter-productive tendencies generated when the inmate code is strong.

The most significant finding to come out of the Vanier Centre study relates back to the previous theme—ties with the community. Those who left the Centre and had stable employment records had significantly lower recidivism rates (Lambert and Madden, 1976). True, one could argue that those less criminally inclined were more likely to find stable work, but this is nevertheless a hopeful sign. Since teenagers and young males in general have high rates of unemployment, the lesson should be obvious.

Naturally, the Vanier Centre has its critics. Some female offenders, especially older ones, prefer to serve their sentences of less than two years in the decrepit Toronto Don Jail, the older portion of which, incidentally, is slated for demolition. Some women prefer the harsher setting to all the "head stuff" that goes on in the Vanier Centre. On the one hand, the opportunity to choose between the Vanier Centre and the local jail may screen out a portion of those female inmates who would not benefit from a guided group interaction program.

If the data from the individuals involved in the Vanier Centre can be linked with data from other sources, a longitudinal record might be created that would permit comparisons according to the strategy suggested earlier in Chapter 5. Although control groups are not available, one could compare the "success" of different types of women with comparable women who chose to serve their sentences in the Toronto Don Jail.

It should also be kept in mind that the Vanier Centre is not a "pure" treatment type. The therapeutic community, reality therapy, and a variety of other dimensions are involved. At this stage it would be difficult to assess the impact of the various dimensions. At least the recipients of the services are being asked what they think of the situation, a step researchers and policy makers usually ignore.

Evaluations of group programs in the U.S.

A look at some of the carefully researched projects in the United States provides some insights. One of the better known programs is the Highfields study, which compared boys in a group therapy program in a residential centre with sixteen- to eighteen-year-old male delinquents who were sentenced to the state reformatory at Annandale, New Jersey (McCorkle, Elias and Bixby, 1958; Weeks, 1958). The initial research findings from that project suggested that the boys at Highfields did better than comparable boys who were sent to the reformatory. Critics of this evaluation have pointed out that the meaningful differences between these two alternatives were largely due to the superior performance on the part of black youths in the Highfields project as compared with the reformatory setting. One could argue that the reformatory setting was punitive and had a high concentration of blacks. When the black youths were placed in a more congenial setting, it is not surprising that their level of delinquency decreased.

Several years after Highfields, the Essexfields Program was launched. It was a non-residential program. The boys were permitted to return to their home each night and remain at home during the weekend. Essexfields did screen out boys who were emotionally disturbed and those with previous institutional experience. Admission was limited to those boys who were known as "socialized" or "adaptive" delinquents. In other words, those who were seen as capable of responding to a subcultural way of life rather than those who were seen as "lone wolves" (Scarpitti and Stephenson, 1966). About twenty boys at one time were accommodated by the project, which consisted of a work program at a county mental hospital where the boys ate lunch and dinner. The work itself was seen as part of the total learning situation, as boys were encouraged to discuss their problems and activities with each other during the work period, while riding the bus, and at meals, as well as at the formal guided group interaction session which began at seven P.M. The results of this project suggest that it was somewhat superior to a residential program, but the boys who were simply placed on probation did even better.

One study of group therapy involved 70 institutionalized adolescent girls in Kentucky. Half were randomly assigned to mandatory group therapy with therapists chosen for their qualities of empathy and nonpossessive warmth while others were in an untreated control group. During the three years prior to therapy, the two groups had similar records in terms of time spent outside of institutions. During the year after release from the institution, the therapy group spent 54 percent of the time out of institutions while the control group was out only 40 percent of the time. Greenberg (1977) notes that the measure of success was an official reaction: neither offence rates nor measures of seriousness of offence leading to institutionalization were reported.

More systematic evaluations of a variety of group therapy programs have been completed in California over the years. While some moderate improvement does seem to exist for short periods after such programs, long-term effects seem to be negligible (Palmer, 1972). It is interesting that despite these findings, regular group counseling and small group counseling has, as a matter of policy, been made an integral part of the building unit programs at all California Youth Authority reception centres, institutions and camps (Seckel, 1974). Here we have an illustration of programs that might not do much good, but probably do little harm.

There have been a few studies which suggest some impact from group psychotherapy (Jew, Clanon and Mattocks, 1972; Persons, 1967; Truax, Wargo and Silver, 1966), but the pattern for these studies is similar to the evaluation of delinquency prevention programs in general. When the programs have a relatively small number of cases, when some compromises have been made from the truly rigorous experimental design, and when one looks at relatively short-term effects on indicators of crime, a positive impact is more likely. When large numbers are utilized to deal with the problem of statistical significance, when tests for interaction are sought, when stringent demands are made to preserve the experimental design, when longer-term impact is assessed, the evidence suggests that there has been a minimal effect (Kassebaum, Ward and Wilner, 1971; Robison and Bass, 1970; Seckel, 1965). In addition, one must be very cautious about any studies which claim success. Even when sophisticated researchers have made sincere attempts to avoid biases, it is not unusual for reevaluation to show that a number of factors can lead an initial evaluation astray (Robison, 1973; Lerman, 1975).

Resentment against group therapy

Since none of the studies of juvenile group therapy seem to offer the depth of detail that one finds in *Prison Treatment and Parole Survival* (Kassebaum, Ward and Wilner, 1971), it is worth noting some of their findings. In some cases group therapy actually seemed to generate hostility. A poem, discovered in a man's cell in a California prison, expresses a view of group counseling that is different from the image intended by the program initiators.

> The guard brought a duckett, on it it read—
> group councling tomorrow.
> Be their or you are dead.
> The object of this meeting is as far as I can see.
> Is to squeel on each other.
> The biggest fink goes free.
> . . . . .
> So lets knock off this shit of talking to the man,
> and let him figure
> It out for him self the best way he can.
> (Kassebaum, Ward, and Wilner, 1971: p.v).

In addition to resentment, the researchers found that they had difficulty observing the situation without altering the climate. Inmates frequently tried to solicit criticisms from the researchers that would discredit the program. However, it is possible that some of these negative aspects were heavily influenced by a strong inmate subculture. In juvenile institutions such resistance might be easier to overcome, but we should be sensitive to suspicion and resentment of all this "head stuff." When staff members talk to juveniles in these programs, they must be particularly careful to hear what they are saying about the program and not simply listen for their comments about their families and their personal problems.

Since most group therapy with juveniles is proposed as part of a community-based program, there may be other differences that decrease hostility, but perhaps we are being unrealistically optimistic. It is hoped that these group therapy programs, like the Provo experiment described in Chapter 4, do not do much damage. They seem to be less harmful than institutional programs, including group therapy in institutions, but they seem to have little advantage over traditional parole in terms of recidivism. If staff members gain greater insights into the nature of the individual, however, group therapy may make an indirect contribution to our understanding of deliquency.

Under these circumstances, what seems to be a reasonable policy? There are several factors which have to be taken into account. Bernard Murphy, a psychologist with the Canadian Penitentary Service in British Columbia, would argue that it is possible to utilize experimental designs in such a way as to give clearer assessments of treatment programs. Although the experience in California makes me somewhat pessimistic about the success of experimental designs, it is necessary to continue launching programs and examining them. (I prefer the word examine to evaluate or assess). Our attempts to measure success in terms of future recidivism rates provide an incomplete picture. Changes may be taking place in clients, staff and in institutions which are difficult to detect and understand. Therefore, disappointing research findings do not automatically mean that we should give up programs such as group therapy. It is possible that even positive changes in personalities, interpersonal relations, etc. will not be reflected in changes in arrest rates and similar variables. Perhaps the factors which influence future incarcerations are outside the reach of correctional programs.

The other extreme should also be avoided. Efforts to greatly expand and intensify group therapy, or other treatment programs, are not justified. Those who do launch such programs need humility. Admittedly, it is difficult to be enthusiastic while being aware of the limitations of such programs. Some clinicians are self-critical, humble, yet still eager to interact with clients. By paying close attention to the insights of these professionals and their clients, maintaining flexible programs, and avoiding intensive programs based on the latest fad, some modest gains may be made.

Group Homes

Group homes do not necessarily imply some form of group counseling. They do, however, offer another alternative to larger and more impersonal institutions. In Toronto a study was made of children who were placed in group homes for the period of July to December 1969 (Wilgosh, 1973). The study suggests that placements for longer than six months seem to be more beneficial than shorter placements. It should be noted that the criterion for a positive outcome relied heavily on the rating of the parents and perhaps it is not surprising to find that parents who had positive attitudes toward the child and toward the placement in the group home tended to rate the results as more effective. Unfortunately the Toronto study by Wilgosh does not permit us to compare the group homes with institutional treatment, parole, or simply being sent home. A more thorough record keeping procedure, which attempted to gather systematic data on every case passing through the court, might have permitted some meaningful comparisons.

The Silverlake experiment has already been noted in Chapter 4. This group home was compared with a more traditional residential school located farther away from the community (Empey and Lubeck, 1971). Even though the study reported no significant differences in outcome for the two programs, the meticulous documentation of this experiment makes it one of the most valuable sources of insights on group homes. To date, it is difficult to find clear evidence that favours group homes over other alternatives, but the increased use of group homes seems to make sense: when in doubt, take modest steps. The group home is a modest alternative to other more dramatic programs. Probably, the activities which go on within these various group homes are much more crucial than the concept of a group home itself.

In the last few years, the province of Alberta has adopted a deliberate policy of utilizing small group homes as alternatives to institutional care. There seems to be no predictable pattern for success. Some of the apparently successful house parents are quite young while others are elderly. Both the variety of settings and the different factors which influence these situations may make it almost impossible to conduct a systematic research project to determine the effectiveness of group homes. It may be unrealistic to think that such an assessment will be available in the near future.

Again we might draw on the California experience. Group homes were operated within the structure of the community treatment projects described above. Although overall evidence on group homes is somewhat confusing, a recent study of eight group homes in California suggested that boys who were placed in such homes did better than those who were not (Palmer, 1972). One interesting informal conclusion suggested by this study was that the optimal number of youths in these homes was three or four. (This excludes the home operator's own children). It is possible that group homes are a beneficial alternative to foster homes. The uncertainty of foster homes may be quite damaging for some children. While the group home is no substitute for a genuine family, the presence of other children in a similar situation, along with more opportunities to assess the future, may provide greater possibilities for adjusting to reality.

Community treatment, group therapy and group homes constitute sensible, though modest, attempts at delinquency prevention. Let us now turn to diversion programs, where attempts are made to stream juveniles away from the formal aspects of the juvenile justice system.

Diversion Programs

Clearly, the current fad is diversion. It has been the major program effort in the United States for several years, and instead of waiting the traditional decade before following the U.S. pattern, Canada is in hot pursuit. Fads are neither right nor wrong. It is just that when programs are being enthusiastically launched, many deficiencies will be obscured by the dust stirred up by traditionalist versus radical battles. My cautious tone should not be misunderstood. Diverting juveniles from being processed through the court system makes as much sense as any of our other programs. However, I feel that objective knowledge on diversion will not be carefully weighed and discussed until there has been a few more years' experience with such programs. And of course we must acknowledge that the police and others have been using unofficial diversion for years.

There is some hope that Canada will be able to profit from American experiences in this area more than it has in the past. Marie-Eve Hart, National Consultant on Diversion, comments in the November 1976 issue of *Liaison* that there is real concern in Canada to avoid the tyranny of treatment in the name of diversion. Rather, it should offer a logical response to the delinquency committed. For example, if a person steals, he should return the money.

Of course, diversion can take a variety of forms. In Halifax, Nova Scotia, one unique diversion program has involved about thirty youngsters in archaeological digs (*Liaison*, November, 1976). Their finds have led to a small museum where the kids tell the story of each piece to visitors. The artifacts belong to the youngsters who found them and can be removed from the museum at any time. As a result of this interest, the boys have been reading about Halifax history and talking with old-timers.

Kingston may have one of the more enlightened family courts in Canada, and the Frontenac Diversion Program represents an attempt to apply social science knowledge to the criminal justice system. The concepts of diversion, non-intervention and restitution provide the rationale behind the objectives of the program. Some of these goals are: (1) to prevent children from being referred unnecessarily to Juvenile Court; (2) to avoid the establishment of juvenile delinquency records; (3) to minimize the delay between the time of the offence and the time of the final resolution of the problem; (4) to allow the child to be actively involved in undoing his wrong; (5) to restrict the degree of unwanted intervention into the lives of the child and other family members; (6) to develop among members of the community an attitude which recognizes that delinquent acts are a community responsibility and wherever possible should be resolved informally in the community (Thomson, Barnhorst and Barnhorst, 1975).

These objectives typify the strategy of most diversion programs. They frequently include the notion of restitution. As these programs unfold, it will be important to consider the following points:

The impact of labelling

The philosophy of diversion has been influenced by the "labelling approach" to deviance. It assumes that the stigmatization arising out of the formal processing of a juvenile in the criminal justice system tends to reinforce or even create deviant behaviour. Diversion attempts to avoid that stigmatization.

Recently, however, more people have been questioning the validity of the labelling perspective (Gove, 1975; Fisher and Erickson, 1973). To what extent is the behaviour of the juvenile well established before the child appears in court? While labelling has had tremendous emotional appeal among students of deviance for the last decade, it is possible that its claims are overstated. If so, a major argument on behalf of diversion will be lacking.

The possible increase of injustice

Diversion could lead to even more injustice. Middle class children and those who have certain desirable characteristics may be favoured by this informal process. Indians, other minority groups, and those from "inadequate" families may not qualify. These "undesirable" cases may be left in the formal system, which may treat them even more harshly now that many of the "better" cases have been diverted.

Restitution compounds the problem. A middle class child may be better able to compensate the victim and to "be actively involved in undoing his wrong." The lower class, poorly socialized child might not view his behaviour as wrong. In other words, diversion contains the same seeds of potential bias that have always existed, and could lead to even greater stigmatization for those not diverted.

An expansion of juvenile supervision

Diversion is not new. The police, juvenile probation officers and others have traditionally diverted many juveniles from the criminal justice system. At times this has taken place without the approval of judges and others in the system. It is not clear what the implications are when more formal procedures are used to divert cases that were previously handled informally. It is also possible that diversion will keep children from being processed by one agency, the juvenile court, only to be processed instead by another agency. For example, in British Columbia some juveniles have been given the choice of "voluntarily" taking part in an outdoor program or being processed through the juvenile court. This could be viewed as diversion, but it should be noted that authority over the juvenile may simply end up in a different agency. Instead of being diverted from official agencies, the juvenile could find himself facing more treatment, supervision or other agency processing.

In Los Angeles County, diversion sometimes was viewed as an opportunity for the police to do something with the juvenile as opposed to letting him off scot-free. Juveniles who would normally get "counsel and release" were those most likely to be diverted. Instead of reducing the overload and scope of the justice system, diversion may extend it by involving other agencies. Rehabilitation, rather than being directed toward juvenile offenders, might now apply to those who had formerly been released outright (Teilman, Klein and Styles, 1975).

The informal role of police, clerks and others

The police and others may not be pleased with a system which gives them less control of the situation. Traditionally, the police argue that very little happens to a child when he is brought to juvenile court. While doing very little may be a reasonable response in terms of the future of the juvenile, the police can justifiably feel that their efforts to capture juvenile criminals are in vain. As yet we do not fully understand how much the morale of the police influences delinquency in the long run.

It should be noted that the police are specifically involved in certain aspects of the Frontenac Diversion Program. They may decide to refer a juvenile to the Restitution Project rather than lay a charge. If such a referral is seen as a new option for the police, they may be more supportive of such a program. In other words, police and others should be allowed to participate in diversion and restitution projects so as to avoid feeling their authority has been curtailed.

Studies of diversionary dispositions with juvenile offenders in Ontario and British Columbia are currently under way. These findings may permit other diversion projects to avoid certain pitfalls. However, it may be difficult to generalize from one situation to another. For example, John Klein, a sociologist at the University of Calgary, has launched a restitution project that will attempt to draw up contracts for offenders at various stages of the criminal justice process. Even at the initial stages of the project it became obvious that certain people in the system can make or break the program. To illustrate, the enthusiastic support of the court clerk in Calgary was clearly crucial. She had the power either to expedite or frustrate a contract.

One of the major contributions which can be made by the Ontario, British Columbia and Calgary projects is to identify those roles which are crucial to the smooth operation of diversion programs. It is possible that judges and others who sit on juvenile court committees are much less important than court clerks and others who handle the day-to-day operations. To date, Canadian studies are based primarily on the laws and formal rules that guide the criminal justice system. Researchers and evaluators often describe what *should* be happening. They rarely study the clerks and others who make seemingly routine decisions. While principles are important, we need to examine the day-by-day operations of these systems. This may be particularly true of diversion programs.

For example, in Vienna, Austria, a complex information network involving youth officials, police, and court social workers supplied fifteen judges with information so they could make decisions. A good portion of the critical information was funneled through a single liaison officer, who advised all of the judges (Hackler, 1975). This person may have been the most influential person in the entire system.

Diversion as a beachhead

The failure to examine some of these informal roles in juvenile justice systems makes it difficult to take advantage of diversion in a more meaningful way. For example, diversion programs are directed primarily at the juvenile court, but it might be wiser to use them as mechanisms that intervene in other institutional procedures. Let us illustrate this point by borrowing some ideas from a team working on different ways of implementing diversion (Galvin *et al*, 1977).

Instead of beginning with the court, let us go back to the school setting and note certain conditions that are conducive to delinquency. In most schools peer groups form that reflect the relative status of the individuals within the school system. This involves future status anticipated by the boys as well as their present status in the educational system. Youth who are doing well in school and who anticipate careers as lawyers, doctors, etc. tend to form peer groups. Similarly, youth who do poorly also tend to congregate together. Access to rewarding aspects of school social life can be reinforced by the formal demands of the system. For example, minimum grade standards may be required for participation in sports. While this requirement makes sense to educational administrators, it further excludes weak students from status-enhancing activities. The result is that higher status students can partake of the offerings of the school fully, but lower status students tend to operate outside the school among others who find school a drag. They search for other types of rewards. Such low status youth are likely candidates for delinquency.

Some diversion programs may recognize educational skills as being related to delinquency, but they may ignore the status problem and create conditions that lower status even more. For example, a diversion program concerned with education might provide extra classes at a different site for low status students without offering any credit courses that would enhance the student's school record. Although the diversion program means well, it could further contribute to the negative labelling of students involved. Their records would show that they were in a program for "problem boys" and hence would not be candidates for the more academic courses or some of the other enrichments that high school could offer.

It is not easy to deal with status problems, but some school programs provide job placement activities that combine genuine work experience with school. Some of these activities can be seen as rewarding and can gain status for those involved. The tendency of much secondary education is to segregate students into the "college-oriented" and the "vocational." The status distinctions are obvious. However, in some countries, such as Yugoslavia, vocational programs have better paid teachers, have lower teacher-student ratios, and are viewed with a respect that is hard to find in North America.

Diversion can be a beachhead for dealing with some of the institutional deficiencies that currently encourage delinquency. However, in the illustration provided above, one can see that diversion might simply reinforce present problems. There is also a tendency for diversion programs to become trapped by the treatment philosophy that focuses on "correcting" individuals. In other words, if diversion means that we now have another device for "doing something" it will simply provide employment for a few more social workers without making basic changes. On the other hand, if diversion programs can provide juveniles with improved status in the academic and occupational sphere, such programs may become more than the latest fad.

The lack of government support for appropriate research

In order to deal with the above issues constructively, we need to understand the processes operating in the juvenile justice system and its links with other societal institutions. Canada has been particularly negligent, compared with the Scandinavian countries and the United States, when it comes to studying its systems of social control, such as the juvenile justice system. We have done slightly better at the adult level, but most of the federally funded work has been highly legalistic. We are only vaguely aware of implications of the tremendous variety of ways in which juvenile justice is dispensed in Canada. The struggle to achieve agreement across Canada on the age of the juvenile delinquent shows how different factors make a uniform policy difficult. The response to these problems has been to propose new legislation dealing with "young offenders in conflict with the law." Unfortunately, these actions ignore the reality that the various ways in which juvenile justice will be delivered in different parts of Canada will persist regardless of legislation. Diversion programs are dependent on understanding the processes operating at the community level. A program that seems effective in one location could be completely impractical elsewhere.

The fact that the juvenile justice system provides its services in a variety of ways across Canada does not mean that there are no similarities. Although there is little enlightening Canadian research, superficial examination of juvenile courts in Austria, France and elsewhere suggests that similar patterns may exist across different cultures and under circumstances that appear to be different. The challenge is to understand what these patterns mean in terms of attempts to modify the system, such as the introduction of diversion programs. For example, in Kingston, one youthful judge may develop effective communication networks with a variety of others which would expedite a diversion program. However, in Edmonton, the five juvenile judges may have greater difficulty sharing information with city probation officers who work in different buildings and provincial social workers who work in another location. In a still larger city like Vancouver, juvenile justice services are decentralized and provided by courts serving areas of the city. The

Kingston experience may actually be applicable to a large city like Vancouver, because of decentralization. On the other hand, the Kingston experience may be completely inappropriate for medium-sized cities like Edmonton, which have developed citywide, medium-sized bureaucracies that have distinctive functions and less informal communication with other agencies in the juvenile justice system.

In other words, Canadian communities differ in their organization of juvenile justice, but the variety is not infinite. Discovering essential similarities as well as differences should be one goal of research on juvenile justice processes. Unfortunately, much money is being spent on the planning of diversion projects and even on the "evaluation" of such programs without parallel efforts to understand the informal procedures that are necessary to adjust legislation and broad social policy to local situations. While we should be alert to the American findings on diversion, and note the cautions raised in such publications as the October 1976 issue of *Crime and Delinquency*, we can still create many unnecessary headaches by attempting to launch diversion programs without making attempts to understand the dynamic elements operating in our juvenile justice systems.

There is an additional reason for decrying this deficiency in research programs supported both at federal and provincial levels. Instead of always being a borrower of ideas in this area, Canada could be a contributor. We could study juvenile justice systems in the sparsely populated north, in our highly concentrated ethnic communities, as well as in various urban centres to develop a cross-cultural perspective. This could contribute to the study of juvenile justice systems in other parts of the world. Compared with those in many other nations, workers in our juvenile justice system tend to be self-critical, open with researchers, and willing to experiment. This provides a promising forum for the exploration of the processes that lead to differences among court systems. Yet government-funded research is rarely sensitive to the subtle workings of the juvenile justice system.

Our tendency has been to form commissions on the naive assumption that they will devise intelligent social policy by sampling the opinions of the influential. True, commissions can sponsor sensitive research, but they often appear irrelevant to those working at the grassroots level in the juvenile justice system.

I do not wish to give the impression that research into the processes operating in our agencies will automatically provide the necessary facts for clear policy decisions, nor do I favour delaying innovation until "research gives us the answer." Policy making is still a political process and research in this area frequently generates more questions than answers, but certain types of research could provide a better basis for the discussion.

Like the seven blind men who attempted to describe an elephant, there are many people viewing the "delinquency problem" from different perspectives. But the important issue is not necessarily whose image of delinquency is correct, but what happens to the elephant. If the blind men are responsible for the care of the elephant, if they decide everthing by majority vote, and if four out of the seven blind men grasp the tail, the elephant could end up in a zoo for snakes. Our problem is to learn how the blind men communicate, how they resolve differences, and how they finally arrive at decisions. Do they speak the same language? One may speak socioıogese, another psychologese, still another legalese. Others may simply be chanting "diversion, diversion." Do some scream while others mumble? Nevertheless, they must reach a consensus regarding the treatment of the elephant.

Juvenile justice systems do come to decisions, but at present we are focusing on the decision itself. We are not sensitive to the way in which decisions are made. Even if we feel that one type of outcome is more desirable than another, change may not be possible if the components of the system are organized in certain ways. Diversion is one alternative which may not be feasible if many components of the system have reasons for rejecting it.

Conclusion

Let us conclude this section with a review of some of the questions which need to be asked. Could diversion lead to an increase in the treatment of juveniles? Do we understand the importance of the clerks and other less-studied roles within the juvenile justice system? They may be crucial to the success or diversion programs. Have the differing structural characteristics of communities or organizations that are active within these communities been taken into account? Will diversion screen out the advantaged and leave the disadvantaged behind in a juvenile justice system which has become less tolerant? And finally, will attempts at assessment create so much friction that potentially valuable projects will have to be abandoned?

In a few years we may be able to evaluate juvenile diversion and restitution programs more adequately. For the present, cautious support seems appropriate. The past suggests that unforseen negative consequences will arise and that positive gains will be modest, if any. This cautious approach may avoid major disappointments and, in the long run, incorporate positive features of diversion and restitution into the criminal justice system.

Let us now turn to individual psychological counseling and other approaches which focus on changing the individual delinquent.

Chapter 9

A Focus on the Individual and Changing Attitudes

When God threw me, a pebble, into this wondrous lake, I disturbed its surface with countless circles. But when I reached the depths I became very still.

—KAHLIL GIBRAN

The Talk Therapies: Individual Psychological Counseling

Probably the most common response to delinquency in the last fifty years has been to provide counseling. It is difficult to discuss this topic without noting that a large number of professionals have a vested interest in this form of treatment. The advocates of counseling naturally believe that it changes people. Admittedly, the subjective experience of individual counselors and of clients would lead one to believe that something positive does occur but the objective evidence supports neither the claim that counseling changes behaviour or that it has any impact on delinquent behaviour. Since this battle has been fought for many years with little impact on social policy or programs, it seems pointless to repeat the arguments or to launch an attack on the advocates of counseling. Instead, it would be more constructive to look at some of the underlying factors that contribute to the continuance of counseling as a popular form of treatment.

Three persistent assumptions support the counseling movement. The first assumption is that delinquents are "sick." This is not the place for an extended debate on the mental health of delinquents, but there is evidence that the vast majority of delinquents and criminals tend to be quite normal, in the psychological sense. The tendency to use delinquent behaviour as evidence of psychiatric abnormality is still common, but the inadequacy of this argument has been known for years. This argument does not deny that some delinquents have psychological problems; but even in such cases, evidence that counseling helps is lacking.

The second assumption is that the problem lies within the individual, and the rest of society is adequate. Admittedly, some sociologists err in the other direction by claiming that the entire problem lies with society. Along with an increasing awareness that there are societal conditions as well as situational factors which influence delinquency, most social scientists are willing to acknowledge that individual characteristics, possibly induced by environmental factors, do play a role. However, the traditional emphasis on the individual as the source of the problem has led to attempts to change individual behaviour through some form of "talk therapy." The lack of evidence that such practices bring about positive change has not lessened their popularity.

The third assumption is that psychiatric diagnosis is reliable and valid and that psychiatric techniques enable psychiatrists to predict and even change future behaviour. Unfortunately, this is an area where scientific knowledge and practices do not coincide. Paul Meehl has been quoted by Mishel as saying:

> Personally, I find the cultural lag between what the published research shows and what clinicians persist in claiming to do with their favourite devices even more disheartening than the adverse evidence itself (Mishel, 1968: 146).

It is important to note that the gap between knowledge and practice is chronic and long standing. Hans J. Eysenck in his chapter on psychotherapy in his *Handbook of Abnormal Psychology* (1961) criticized psychiatry for making unwarranted claims. During the 1950's and early 1960's other outstanding psychiatrists and psychologists were making similar criticisms within the profession. For example, Dr. Benjamin Pasamanick noted that unless more systematic procedures were used, psychiatry would remain an art rather than a science (Ubell, 1962). Jerome Frank of John Hopkins University, Henry K. Beecher of Harvard, and Lawrence S. Kubie expressed similar views (Ubell, 1962). Despite the lack of evidence of success, the popularity of the "talk therapies" continued to grow in the 1960's. Nettler voices the same concerns today.

> Since the principle instrument of this kind of effort [psychotherapy] is words, these attempted cures—and there are many types of them—are often called the talking therapies. Until recently they have constituted the most popular form of treatment for the mental disorders in Western countries. As with the magical remedies, the popularity of the psychotherapies is as much a manifestation of faith as it is a consequence of results (Nettler, 1976: 79).

While few of the attacks on the psychiatric approach to deviant behaviour have been as severe as those leveled by Michael Hakeem (1958), criticism continues to mount concerning the inability of psychiatrists to diagnose, predict and change behaviour utilizing the "talk therapies."

Counseling as an illustration of problems associated with changing behaviour

There are several points of similarity between the deficiencies of psychiatry and other scientific and pseudo-scientific activities. First, initial scientific insights usually lead to many ideas about application. The science of human behaviour is still in its infancy and naturally it spawns speculation. It is also normal that many of these speculations will turn out not to be well-founded. Secondly, the world is always looking for cure-alls. Psychiatry, like so many theories, has been expected to work miracles, just as religion was once supposed to do. Thirdly, not unlike religion, psychiatry has become institutionalized and resists criticism and change. It is normal for groups with power to pursue traditional patterns, believe in their own effectiveness, and resist change.

Returning to the link between new scientific insights and their application, it seems that in some areas, an apparent immediate gain is later revealed as a step backward. Insecticides provide an obvious illustration. In the area of counseling, we have definitely gained insights into human behaviour, but only recently has it become evident that these insights rarely transfer to other situations. True, behaviour can be modified when the counseling situation is under the control of the experimenter. For example, people obviously respond to the reward-punishment structure of behaviour modification therapies. In the next chapter, it will be seen whether this changed behaviour transfers to the larger social setting.

Counselors and psychiatrists are not alone in facing difficulties applying their insights. When sociologists were given a chance to deal with poverty in the United States, they did rather badly. Philosophers and political scientists occasionally are in positions to influence governments, but rarely are they effective. Economists have given advice on curing recessions and preventing inflation for years, but the wisdom of their advice has not been demonstrated.

But academics are not the only ones with a frustrated desire to share their wisdom. A group of Eskimos who visited a white settlement were dismayed at the white man's inability to live together in peace. Upon returning home they discussed sending missionaries to the white man to teach them cooperation. Although these ideas could have been very useful, it is likely that the Eskimos would have had trouble winning converts. This illustration should not be seen as frivolous. People with power are allowed to play the role of "advice givers" to those who do not have power. The reverse is rare, regardless of the quality of the advice.

The reader, then, should see counseling as an outgrowth of one of many persistent theories of human behaviour. It is not necessarily more harmful than other delinquency strategies, but it is highly institutionalized and hence harder to change. As such it becomes a barrier to more meaningful procedures.

Since individual counseling is such an excellent illustration of the points we have just made, we do not apologize for returning to our critique; but the reader should be aware that parallel criticisms would apply to many child-saving programs. It may take us a few more years to document the negative evidence to the same degree it has been documented for counseling. Notice also that we are not denying that something happens during counseling. People may feel better, etc. Nor are we differentiating among the various talk therapies, nor denying that outcomes are different. But the major point is that they do not seem to have much impact on that big outside world where delinquency takes place.

As noted in Chapter 6, clinicians have in the past been poor predictors of dangerous behaviour and display a tendency to overpredict. While populations diagnosed as dangerous *do* display higher rates of violence than those diagnosed as nonviolent, laymen are able to make such predictions just as well as professionals. Let us try to understand why this professional goal of diagnosis and prediction, and the ability to make changes, has been so hard to attain. Even when clinicians agree on diagnoses and predictions, the accuracy of their evaluations does not increase. John Klein, of the University of Calgary, argues that this phenomenon may be an outcome of the setting in which the patient is seen, the social class of the patient, and the biasing effects of fellow clinicians' reports.

> The effect of this last factor is vividly illustrated in Temerlin's (1970) research in which mental health professionals and non-professionals observed an interview with a healthy man after having a renowned mental health professional, acting as a confederate, characterize him as psychotic. Both professional and nonprofessional subjects then tended to diagnose the healthy man as mentally ill, even though his behaviour was healthy by multiple criteria. As well, Chapman and Chapman (1967) found that one does not even need the suggestion of a "renowned professional" to obtain similar results (Klein, 1975: 5).

The tendency of people to be influenced by "experts" is a well known characteristic. Clinicians are not unique—they are simply not immune to this type of influence. The following statement by Seymour Halleck, a psychiatrist specializing in deviance, seems appropriate:

> The psychiatrist has few more important functions in criminology than evaluating the probability that a given offender is likely to do violence to his fellow man. It must be reluctantly admitted that there is little science to be brought to this task . . . If the psychiatrist or any other behavioural scientist were asked to show proof of his predictive skills, objective data could not be offered (1967: 313-314).

Let us turn from the ability to predict to the ability to change behaviour. The Illinois Institute for Juvenile Research has pioneered studies in this area for many years. One study of a group of emotionally disturbed children, some of whom received psychotherapy while a control group received no treatment, was made by Dr. Eugene Levitt. After five years there was no difference between the treated and untreated children.

Later Dr. Levitt surveyed 37 investigations involving eight thousand patients given psychotherapy at different clinics. He found no differences between the treated and untreated groups. Even fifteen years ago there was an awareness that the comments of Hans Eysenck should be taken seriously; namely, that therapeutic procedures have not lived up to the hopes which greeted their emergence fifty years ago. He suggested it might even be advisable to discard the psychotherapeutic method.

In the last decade psychology and some branches of psychiatry have made a great deal of progress, but the debate continues within and outside these fields. Despite the popularity of the "talk therapies" the professional literature contains very few illustrations of carefully controlled scientific experiments to test the effectiveness of these techniques. The reader should be careful not to confuse the "talk therapies" with other therapies, such as behaviour modification, where there exists convincing evidence that behaviour can be changed. The fields of psychology and psychiatry provide an interesting illustration of rapid progress occurring in certain areas while vested interests and dogma restrict progress in others.

One could argue that long-term counseling might be more effective than specialized psychiatric care. The Cambridge-Somerville study is one of the few projects where intensive and long-term counseling was provided to potential delinquents under careful experimental conditions. The counseling lasted for approximately seven years (Powers and Witmer, 1951). The long-term impact on delinquency was disappointing. Of those boys who appeared in court, 96 had been in the treatment group and 92 had been in the control group. Among those convicted for offences, 264 were in the treatment group and 218 were in the control group. If the long-term counseling had any impact on the boys it did not manifest itself in lower rates of delinquency. These data have been reanalyzed and more data were gathered as the 650 boys involved in the study grew older (McCord and McCord, 1959). In 1977 a thirty year follow-up showed that those boys who had more frequent contacts with counselors were more likely to be failures (McCord, 1977). While this study has yielded some excellent insights, the evidence seems clear that counseling had no impact on delinquency.

Gwynn Nettler summarizes the case rather well:

> Attending to talk alone is not the best way of knowing the other person. It is not the best way of knowing his beliefs, or predicting his behaviour, or changing his conduct . . . Evidence for these allegations is to be found in studies of clinical prediction and in the weak (even negative) contribution made by the "talking therapies" in the cure of unwanted behaviours (1974: 198).

Let us turn now to other studies which pose different dilemmas. In California the Preston School of Industry utilized classical insight therapy while the Nelles School for Boys was more reality-oriented and included extensive informal contact between youths and therapists in recreational activity. The boys in the Nelles program were considered to be amenable (Guttman, 1963) while the Preston program included both amenable and nonamenable boys. Both studies utilized treatment and control groups. Success on parole was measured fifteen months after release. For the Preston group, 58.5 percent of the boys receiving classical insight therapy had failed while the control group had a failure rate of only 47.7 percent. The difference was statistically significant at the .05 level. One could argue that in this case classical insight therapy was damaging. At the Nelles School the failure rate for the treatment group was 59.7 percent and 73.8 percent for the controls. While this difference was not statistically significant at the .05 level, it was at the .10 level. Some would propose that this could be seen as evidence of success for reality therapy.

But if we were to compare the boys who received reality therapy with those who received classical insight therapy, we would not see any difference. True, the two groups are not comparable, but the boys in Preston included nonamenable boys whereas at Nelles there were only amenable boys. This should have increased the failure rate of the boys at the Preston School. The average age of the boys at Preston was 17.4 and at Nelles it was 14.8. It is possible that the older boys at Preston were beginning to leave the delinquent pattern or that they were more skilled at avoiding detection. As with so many good studies, there are more questions at the end than at the beginning. These two studies reaffirm the need for modesty among clinical psychologists.

Greenberg (1977) summarizes two other experimental studies of the effect of individual interview therapy on delinquent teenage girls in California institutions.

> One [study] found that neither individual nor group therapy, nor both taken together, led to recidivism lower than that of untreated girls; the other study found individual therapy slightly superior to the combination of individual and group therapy, much better than group therapy alone, and slightly better than doing nothing (unpublished manuscript).

Inconsistency, then, seems to be a normal product of most careful evaluations. This fits with the hypothesis that the changes taking place are random and have little to do with the theoretical variables being tested.

The above study summarized by Greenberg produced another finding: the girls in therapy with social workers had a revocation rate very much lower than that of girls whose therapists were psychologists or psychiatrists (Adams, 1961). The argument that highly trained personnel are needed to achieve successful results in counseling is certainly not supported by this study.

Obviously, counseling will continue to be used as a delinquency prevention strategy. Certainly, it is reasonable for someone to be available to listen to delinquents who wish to talk. In addition, counselors might gain insights and be able to make more positive suggestions for social change. For the delinquent, a counseling session may be a beginning step in a process which leads to a better job, knowledge about educational opportunities, etc. There is no evidence, however, that counseling itself leads to such steps. Unfortunately, a philosophy that focuses on the "needs" of disturbed youth prevails in Canada, and, if a recent article, reiterating the conventional methods of treating the "untreatable" adolescent, in *Canada's Mental Health* is an indication, it is not likely that evidence showing the ineffectiveness of this approach will change the pattern (Finlay and Randall, 1975).

The major problem seems to arise in the fact that many counselors feel that if they can work on a child long enough, they can "straighten the kid out." Such assumptions may simply make it more difficult for counselors to provide meaningful links with the larger world.

The Use of Volunteers and Victims

The Youth Centre in Winnipeg utilizes a number of strategies including an emphasis on volunteers (Manitoba, 1973). In Edmonton, city social services have maintained volunteer programs involving college students on a one-to-one basis with juveniles for a number of years. Informal assessments of the volunteer programs with juveniles tend to be positive.*

A particularly valuable document on volunteer programs has been prepared by S. Pirs for the Ontario Ministry of Correctional Services (1975). I shall draw heavily from it in describing a Toronto-based program and also for a summary of other studies.

Often professional probation officers have mixed feelings about volunteers. This was also the case in Toronto. Probation officers were not able to decide on the amount of responsibility or the types of cases volunteers should handle (Juozapavicius and Wegessy, 1974). Not surpris-

*It should be noted that volunteers working with adults may face different and more difficult problems; but since one of the most interesting Canadian studies of volunteers involved adults, I mention it here.

ingly, probation officers felt that personality variables were the most important consideration in the activities of volunteers.

Another Toronto study involved undergraduate community volunteers and young incarcerated offenders in short-term structured counseling (Andrews, Young, Wormith, Searle and Kouri, 1973). When compared with a control group of offenders, those in the discussion group decreased their identification with criminal others while tolerance for law violation remained the same. The control group showed increased identification with criminal others and increased tolerance for law violations.

An additional study utilized recreational activity with community volunteers, but this program failed to produce an increase in favourable attitudes toward the law (Andrews, Wormith, Kennedy and Daigle, 1973). On the other hand, a comparable group involved in structured discussion with community volunteers did show a positive attitude change. Naturally, it is difficult to assess the significance of "decreased identification with criminal others" and attitudinal changes as measured by various test instruments, but such findings encourage some guesses about the quality of interaction which takes place in recreation versus discussion groups.

The parents of juveniles on probation sometimes have a mixed response to volunteers, but another Toronto study showed that 70 percent of such parents perceived volunteers positively (Pitman, Strecker and Yip, 1973). These positive feelings were not related to "changing" the probationers, but rather to appreciation of the attention shown toward them.

There are, of course, many illustrations of volunteer programs in the United States. One of the better known programs was launched in Lincoln, Nebraska (1975). Volunteers and probationers were carefully matched and the evaluation showed dramatic reductions in delinquency in contrast to a control group. This program was designated as "exemplary" by the Law Enforcement Assistance Administration (LEAA). Since demonstrating success would be one of the characteristics of an exemplary project, could the LEAA be increasing the political pressures discussed earlier in Chapter 4? Certainly the Opportunities for Youth project, which demonstrated its lack of impact in great detail, would never be considered "exemplary." Is it possible that such a recognition by the LEAA will add to the difficulties of conducting honest evaluations?

Volunteer programs have increased rapidly in the past few years in various parts of North America, but it is possible that after a period of high initial enthusiasm, positive changes within programs will tend to taper off. Perhaps these periods of initial enthusiasm are when much is accomplished. A constant level of activity may, in the long run, not be as valuable as surges of enthusiasm.

Many volunteer programs are concerned with characteristics of probationers *and* volunteers with the hope that combinations will be discovered which are particularly effective. One exploratory study in Indiana indicated that differences in age as well as differences in marital status may have a significant effect on the amount of satisfaction expressed by the volunteer probation counselor and probationer about their relationship. It is interesting that probationers reported a higher level of satisfaction with the relationship than the volunteers. However, it is important to note that expressed satisfaction was not related to the actual success of probationers in terms of behaviour or follow-up (Mehaffey, 1973).

A Colorado study found no significant relationship between sex, age, race, occupation, education, or marital status and success of volunteers (Brewington, 1970). In Edmonton, attempts were made at the early stages of the volunteer program to screen those who applied, but at least one program official admitted that he saw no relationship between the screening and the success of the volunteers.

A recent Toronto study also showed no significant relationship between sex, age, birthplace, religion, occupation, marital status, duration of marriage and number of children, anticipated future changes, service or fraternal group affiliation, family's attitude, reason for volunteering, months of service, and age difference between volunteers and probationers (Pirs, 1975). This study included three groups of subjects: 128 volunteers, 271 volunteer-supervised probationers, and 300 randomly selected probation officer-supervised cases. Success for the probationer was defined as completion of the probation term without further charges and success for the volunteers as completing supervision of the probation term without further charges against the probationer.

Of the 128 volunteers, 60 percent were male and 40 percent female. The mean age of the males was 37 years and of the females 32 with a range of from 18 to 72 years for the whole sample. Most tended to be 25 to 39. Most were married (66 percent) while 23 percent were single and 6 percent were separated. The family's attitude toward their acting as volunteers was positive for 69 percent, and 76 percent had previous volunteer experience. The average number of months served as a volunteer was 26 with 53 percent serving more than two years and 28 percent more than three years.

Although the cases in the volunteer program and those supervised by regular probation officers were not randomly assigned, the study was able to make meaningful comparisons. The volunteers typically received cases of middle risk while probation officers tended to get a wide range of probationers. There were more females in the volunteer-supervised group, 28 percent compared with 20 percent for the probation officer-supervised group. The mean age was 22 years for volunteer-supervised subjects versus 27 years for probation officer-supervised subjects. Younger probationers tend generally to have a poorer success rate than older ones, and this was true in this study as well. Therefore, one would anticipate that the bias would be against the volunteers.

Although most of the characteristics of the volunteers turned out to be insignificant, certain findings are revealing. Women employed in the home tended to be significantly more successful than most other categories of volunteers.

In many volunteer programs, there is a frantic search for young males. Frequently, a volunteer agency is deluged with inquiries from young females. At least our experience with college students at the University of Alberta is that the females outnumber the male applicants considerably. This Toronto study suggests that communities might well utilize this enthusiastic female population more effectively.

Another surprising finding was that previous volunteer experience of any kind had a negative effect on success. Those who had either one or two previous experiences were significantly less successful than those with no previous experience. It is possible that experienced volunteers were given more difficult cases than the less experienced ones. Pirs also speculates that volunteers who have had too much volunteer experience become "burnt out" and are no longer as effective. This raises questions about staff as well. Do staff become "burnt out"? An additional finding, that there was a slight decrease in success with an increased volunteer caseload, is compatible with the "burning out" notion. Again, one must be careful, since successful volunteers may receive more difficult cases at a later time.

Comparing the two groups of probationers, Pirs found the probationers with volunteers had an 85 percent success rate and those with regular probation officers had a 75 percent success rate. It should be noted that the volunteers were working with younger probationers who usually have a higher failure rate on probation. However, the volunteers were more successful than the probation officers in all age categories (Pirs, 1975: Table 3). With younger offenders, age 16 to 21, the female probationers with volunteers had an 87 percent success rate while the males with volunteers had a 73 percent success rate. With regular probation officers the rate for females was 78 percent and males 68 percent. Since young females are sometimes viewed as more "difficult," the good performance of the volunteers in this area shows particular promise (Pirs, 1975: Table 6).

In general female probationers were more successful than male probationers, significantly so in the volunteer-supervised group and just short of significance in the probation officer-supervised group. This study led Pirs to the following conclusion:

> It is becoming increasingly clear that volunteers, while they might not perform better, do not appear to perform less effectively than trained professionals. Their prime advantage may be the amplification of time—more time spent with probationers, and in so doing allowing probation officers more time to supervise probationers as well (1975:3).

Although much of our information involves adults or young offenders aged 16 to 21, it provides guidelines for work with juveniles as well. One important difference is that volunteers with juveniles frequently must deal also with parents. At least one study suggests that volunteers are successful at establishing rapport with parents (Gandy *et al.*, 1975). Therefore, even though the evidence is not particularly rigorous, the use of volunteers holds promise.

Contrary evidence showing no improvement with volunteers

Unfortunately, but not surprisingly, there is also evidence demonstrating the lack of impact of volunteers working with juvenile probationers. Robert Berger and his colleagues assessed three different types of volunteer programs in a Michigan juvenile court (Berger *et al*, 1975). Volunteers served as probation officers, scholastic tutors or group counselors and each program was evaluated on the basis of reducing delinquency as measured by self-reported statements or contacts with the juvenile justice system. Each of the three strategies seemed temporarily to increase delinquency; however, in the long run, there seemed to be no difference between those who received volunteer services and those who did not. Berger and his colleagues recommended community programs over the volunteer efforts.

One aspect of volunteer programs which is difficult to assess is the understanding gained by the larger society. To what extent does this volunteer experience make the average citizen more supportive of changing procedures with regard to offenders? To what extent will these experiences increase the insightfulness of the general population and make it increasingly possible to make changes in the criminal justice system? Aside from the possible impact on offenders, volunteer programs may be a promising device for preparing society for change.

At the 1974 Canadian Congress of Criminology in Regina, John Hogarth suggested that victims of crimes sometimes become supportive of the delinquent after a period of interaction. Hogarth described a case of a man who was robbed by a juvenile and felt strongly that the boy should be punished severely. As time went on, the man asked why there were no "big brothers" around who might provide guidance for such boys. The man finally agreed to perform the role of big brother himself and went on to become an advocate on the boy's behalf.

The Use of Detached Gang Workers

Students of delinquency tend to assume that delinquency is most often a "group" activity. Hence, the gang has been viewed as a key element of delinquency. Malcolm Klein has pointed out the problems of this assumption (1969: Chapters 3 and 4); but despite theoretical weaknesses, gang delinquency has been a major concern of both scholars and policy makers. In the 1950's and 1960's gang delinquency was seen as a major issue, and a number of communities initiated projects designed to deal with groups of delinquent or potentially delinquent boys.

Some of the most important studies of gangs were done in Chicago, and *The Gang* by Frederic Thrasher, published in 1927, still stands as one of the more useful sources of information on group dynamics among young males in lower class settings. Later work by Clifford Shaw and Henry McKay provided the foundation for contributions by Solomon Kobrin and others at the Institute for Juvenile Research in Chicago.

While it may be inappropriate to describe the Chicago Area Project as the originator of the use of gang workers, these community-based programs experimented with a variety of outreach activities that later influenced detached worker programs. The goal of the Chicago Area Project was the development of indigenous leadership and neighbourhood organization (Kobrin, 1959).

The major thrust for "reaching out" to fighting gangs took place in New York city in the 1950's (New York City Youth Board, 1960). Although much advice for practitioners of street work came out of these activities, there was no clear strategy or evaluation which permitted conclusions on the effectiveness of this approach. In the 1960's the Mobilization for Youth Program was the most massive and expensive attempt to prevent delinquency ever launched in North America. A host of programs was utilized and many were directed at juvenile gangs. Again, there is no specific evaluation which would provide guidelines for future gang worker programs.

Walter B. Miller is well known to students of delinquency because of his ideas concerning "focal concerns" which characterize the lower class subculture (1957). Miller carefully documented the Roxbury Project, a gang worker project which involved seven workers (five men and two women) who maintained contact with approximately four hundred youngsters comprising the membership of twenty-one street gangs (1962). Seven of these gangs, totaling 205 members, were examined intensively. The workers succeeded in establishing and maintaining relationships and were also able to change the informal group relationships into a more formal type of club or athletic team. The reorganized groups engaged in a number of activities, such as athletic contests, dances and fund-raising dinners. Athletic teams moved from cellar positions to championships in city athletic leagues. One group grossed close to one thousand dollars at a fund-raising dance. The project also tried to open up access to schools and employment and the gang workers acted as go-betweens for the youngsters in a variety of other situations. They arranged for lawyers to appear in court, interceded with judges, probation officers and others. They spoke with directors of settlement houses and other institutions that would not have admitted the gang members under normal conditions. In other words, the gang workers were successful in achieving their more immediate goals. There is little doubt that the gang workers gained the respect of the youngsters. In fact, termination of a gang worker's services had to be undertaken with care so that the youngsters would not feel deserted.

Did the project bring about a decrease in delinquent behaviour? Fourteen behaviour categories were selected for analysis. These included theft, assault, drinking, etc. Without going into statistical details, several aspects of the final evaluation can be summarized. During the period of worker contact there was no significant reduction in the relative frequency of these actions. Similarly, there was no significant decrease in the frequency of statute violations during the period of worker contact. In addition, members of the gangs appeared in court most frequently during the period when the gang workers were providing their services. The patterns of court appearances and other indicators were remarkably similar for both project and control groups. The obvious conclusion is that the project had "negligible impact" in terms of changing delinquent behaviour.

Hans Mattick, Nathan Caplan and Gerald Suttles developed a program with the Chicago Boys Clubs between 1960 and 1966 in cooperation with the Institute for Social Research of the University of Michigan. The research and evaluation component of this project made up approximately 40 percent of the budget and illustrates the hypothesis that "the more sophisticated the evaluation, the greater the likelihood of finding evidence of failure."

The Chicago Youth Development Project utilized more community organization and involved more gang members than the Roxbury Project. It also used feedback procedures which enabled those involved to modify the approach of the program while it developed (Mattick and Caplan, 1965). As in the Roxbury Project, the gang workers were successful in their immediate goals. Employment opportunities were developed, effective worker-youth relationships were established, and various groups of youngsters became more capable of dealing with the larger community. As in the Roxbury Project, delinquency did not decrease. In fact, there was some indication that the boys who were served most intensively by gang workers tended to increase their delinquency. Caplan notes that:

> The subjects seem to have a special affinity for accepting help and a special disaffinity for "success" in terms of those behaviours which the program ideally wished to produce. Their behaviour arouses the suspicion that they possess the potential capability for demonstrating the desired behaviour changes were they inclined to do so. . . . The implication is that the subjects failed by choice; their behaviour, although not identical, seems similar in many ways to the behaviour of the Borstal boy described in the *Loneliness of the Long Distance Runner* by Sillitoe . . .
>
> It may be true that the subjects were either unaccustomed or disinclined to success, but it must be kept in mind that the forces fatal to success may have more to do with incompatible ideologies than an over-determined response to deeply imbedded personality dynamics (Caplan, 1968: 85).

Caplan points out that some of the boys seemed to be moving in the direction of behavioural change and then "backslid" as they came closer to nondelinquent objectives. The presence of a conforming adult who succeeds in interacting with gang members is simply not enough to overcome the many other factors which lead to delinquency. However, one of the advantages of carefully researched studies like the Chicago Youth Development Project is that they do more than just attempt to assess success or failure: they attempt to understand the dynamics of the situation. The paper by Caplan (1968) looks at those dynamics from a social-psychological perspective. Another byproduct of the project was Suttles' insightful study (1968) of the social order of the slum.

The Group Guidance and the Ladino Hills projects were completed in the Los Angeles area under the sponsorship of the Youth Studies Center at the University of Southern California. The Group Guidance Project involved four black gang "clusters" (sixteen subgroups) with total female and male membership of approximately eight hundred (Klein, 1971: Chapter 2). Emphasis was laid on group programming, such as weekly club meetings, outings, sports and other special activities, remedial reading, tutoring projects, and parents' clubs. As in the case of previous gang worker programs, the group activities were quite successful. Efforts in employment, education and community organization were less successful. The program was also complicated by a bitter dispute between the action agency and local enforcement agencies. Such disputes are not rare and deserve study in and of themselves. The nature of the interaction between an action program and various organizations within the community can profoundly affect the outcome of such activities (Miller, Baum and McNeil, 1966; Schwartz, 1966).

Klein and his colleagues found that involvement in the project was clearly associated with a significant increase in delinquency among the gang members. This was found to be especially true in the most intensively served gangs and, as Miller found in the Roxbury Project, among younger gang members.

> The increase was primarily in those offences that are ordinarily committed with companions but *not* with offences more often committed by oneself. The evaluation suggested that the increase in offences was, at least in part, attributable to the high level of group programming and the gang recruitment to which this led (Klein, 1971: 50).

There is the possibility, then, that attempts to involve gangs in group activities may be self-defeating, at least in terms of delinquent behaviour. It should be noted that the Spring Street Project in Vancouver, which might be seen as an outgrowth of gang worker programs, emphasized a much more individual approach. Social workers tended to maintain contact with boys as individuals rather than as part of a gang.

Since intensive involvement in group services seemed to be related to increases in delinquency, Klein and his colleagues initiated an additional eighteen-month program in 1966 with a Mexican-American gang cluster of approximately 140 members. The Ladino Hills Project was designed to reduce gang cohesiveness by providing alternative activities and by deliberately avoiding group programming. A reduction in cohesiveness was achieved and the entry of new members into the gang decreased. The number of delinquent offences per member did not change during the project period, but the steady reduction in the size of the gang led to an overall reduction of 35 percent in the number of offences. Here again, "success" was minimal: although the gangs themselves were weakened, and thereby committed fewer gang delinquencies, the behaviour patterns of individuals did not change.

In the assessment of gang worker programs several points are worth noting. First, the efforts to launch programs and sustain them were clearly successful. Rapport with delinquent gangs was achieved. The failure to reduce delinquency cannot be explained by lack of program implementation, yet the conclusion that gang worker programs are not effective in the reduction of juvenile delinquency is unavoidable. At times gang workers may inadvertently contribute to delinquent behaviour. It is also important to note that the carefully evaluated programs give us reason to be very cautious; enthusiastic support for these outreach programs tends to be based on those programs where evaluation has been less stringent.

The projects described above again suggest that a heavy emphasis on evaluation in terms of "success" in reducing delinquency may not warrant the large investment of resources required. The most profitable findings coming out of these studies may be those which help us to understand the dynamics of gang delinquency, as illustrated by the work done by Klein on gang cohesiveness (1969a). Clearly, these structures which play such an important part in the lives of youngsters are still poorly understood. Some scholars have described the groups as antisocial with Hitler-type leaders (Yablonsky, 1962). More recent research casts doubt on Yablonsky's conclusions and suggests that there may be considerable variety in gang structures (Miller, 1969). One fruitful aspect of gang worker studies has been the increasing awareness of the diversity and function of juvenile gangs. For example, many gang complexes have senior, junior and midget divisions. Usually the "midgets" are from twelve to fourteen years old. Klein (1974) notes that in the Los Angeles area some groups have retained the name "midget" even though the boys are now in their late teens and twenties. In other words, some gangs seem to be stable and continuous structures. On the other hand, Mattick (1974) describes the gang structure as continually changing. Gangs disappear and new ones arise from year to year. Instead of assuming that gangs take only one form, it is more likely that we are dealing with groups with a variety of forms.

It is advisable to guard against the growth of cynicism which is a possible result of evaluations which find a lack of success in detached worker programs. It is important that youth service personnel remain flexible in their approach. For example, a worker with the Ottawa Youth Service Bureau learned that a youngster committed a theft. He approached the youth and "chewed him out." The next day the two of them met with the victim and the juvenile offered to make restitution. The case never went to court. It is impossible to evaluate the "success" of such an incident, but the initiative and concern shown by the worker are typical of those qualities that are essential to preserve, regardless of the absence of measurable improvement in delinquency prevention. In Ottawa, the Youth Services Bureau maintains a variety of programs. If things go badly in one sphere there is the chance to shift resources and disenchanted personnel to another.

While flexibility does not automatically mean success, it may permit those working for organizations such as the Ottawa Youth Bureau to build on the knowledge they gain. It is also important to note that such flexibility would make evaluation even more difficult, since it would be impossible to maintain similar conditions over time. As argued earlier this is another reason why the evaluation of such programs, in terms of their "success" at preventing delinquency, may be ill-advised. Shifting goals and strategies may be much more crucial than evaluation at this stage of development.

Progress has been made since detached worker programs were at the height of their popularity in the fifties and sixties. Initial advocates of detached worker programs engaged in wishful thinking. For example, James Keech, who started the detached worker program in Ottawa, describes a group of boys who were involved in several burglaries.

> When asked why they had done these things, one boy remarked that it gave him a thrill to be able to sneak into a building and get out without being caught. The worker accidently stumbled onto what seemed to be a substitute for this in a barn at the supporting agency's camp. The group became so involved in playing a combination of hide-and-seek and tag in the hay that they did not want to leave, even to eat lunch. Hiding under hay, to avoid being caught, seemed to fulfill the same need for these young boys as illegally entering a building (Keech, 1962: 19).

Fifteen years later those who have been involved in a careful evaluation of detached worker programs would probably be less inclined to view these activities as substitute satisfactions for illegal activities.

Conclusion

Most of the delinquency prevention strategies reviewed here still receive enthusiastic support and are likely to continue to be used in the future. While they have critics as well, most of the above procedures will be recommended and implemented again in the future. Clearly, the optimists have been more vocal than the cynics in the past two decades, and vested interests will lead to some continuity with the past. Wishy-washy liberals can give only a small cheer for the optimists, but a cynical approach may lead to the loss of a few humanitarian gains; hence, stumbling ahead with humility seems to be a reasonable alternative.

The programs reviewed in the next three chapters are not necessarily unique compared to the ones discussed here; but the battle cries of the optimists and the cynics sound louder.

Chapter 10

Short-Term Behavioural Changes

I have on my table a violin string. It is free. I twist one end of it and it responds. It is free. But it is not free to do what a violin string is supposed to do—produce music. So I take it, fix it in my violin and tighten it until it is taut. Only then is it free to be a violin string.

—SIR RABINDRANATH TAGORE

Behaviour Modification

There are few delinquency prevention strategies which evoke more controversial reactions than behaviour modification. Advocates and opponents present their viewpoints with vigour. It is important, however, to take note of this strategy for a variety of reasons. Behaviour modification techniques are based on some of the more convincing work which has been done in the behavioural sciences. Behaviour modification practitioners have clearly demonstrated that they can change behaviour, at least in the short run. Whether one should change behaviour and what the long-term consequences and implications can be are moral rather than scientific questions that society will have to decide.

Brian Murphy, a psychologist with the Canadian Penitentiary Service in British Columbia, and Paul Gendreau, a psychologist with the Ontario Correctional Services, have both argued that desirable behavioural changes can be induced in correctional settings. Murphy states his basic premises as follows:

> Social systems, like humans, are positive feedback systems, which means that they can modify their future behaviour on the basis of past and present information about their present behaviour and its consequences. It is this feedback process which makes learning and change of behaviour possible. . . .
>
> Whether a person becomes and/or remains a delinquent or a nondelinquent is determined by the actions of the other systems in his environment and on his interpretations of these actions through his positive feedback mechanism. . . . For practical purposes the behaviour of a human being or any other feedback system is controlled to a very large extent by the other systems in his environment and to a very small extent independently by himself. (1973: 293-94).

These ideas have been applied to delinquency prevention programs in a variety of ways. One example is the token economy. A youngster sent to an institution utilizing the token economy learns that there are rewards for a variety of activities: five cents a day for getting up and dressed at a certain time, ten cents for cleaning up his room each day, fifteen cents if he attends a mathematics class, etc. The money (or tokens) accumulated can be spent in the local "store" or to purchase privileges. Naturally, there is considerable debate over the link between making people conform to specific behavioural patterns within an institutional setting and changing more complex behavioural patterns in the larger society. The proponents of behaviour modification would argue that these techniques can be used to modify complex social interaction in a variety of situations. To illustrate the potential of this method, it might be interesting to see just how the staff members of a correctional institution were initiated into the token economy.

Paul Zelhart, a psychologist at the University of Alberta, collaborated with other psychologists to initiate a token economy in the correctional system in the state of Arkansas (Marr, Lilliston and Zelhart, 1974). These psychologists were faced with the problem of how to teach token economy principles to staff who might be hostile to the program. They decided to use a token economy to teach the token economy. Prison personnel first met with the psychologists in a motel. A small minority was actively opposed to the activities and attended because they were told to do so. The majority had a "wait and see" attitude but tended to be cynical. The goal was to produce acceptance of the token economy in five days.

The personnel were assigned to rooms with limited facilities. For example, there was no plug in the bathtub. They were handed a "reinforcement menu" along with the explanation that they could earn tokens in the sessions to begin the following morning and that the tokens could be used for buying items from the menu. For example, a plug for the bathtub cost one token, a more pleasant room with a shower and colour T.V. cost twelve tokens; permission to leave their rooms after 7 P.M. cost twelve tokens for the entire evening and three for one hour or less.

The following morning the sessions began with lectures, discussions and demonstrations to convey principles of the token economy. The prison personnel were reinforced (given tokens) when they were on time, took notes, asked worthwhile questions, and responded in a way that indicated positive attitudes toward the program. Specific behaviours were reinforced differentially depending on the individual and the situation. One quiet individual was given tokens for nodding his head in agreement at the beginning stages. Later he was reinforced when he spoke in complete sentences to the entire group.

> Those few participants who were intially positive toward the token economy maintained their favourable attitudes and were initially the hardest workers in the institute. Both those who were negatively disposed and those who were suspicious but more open showed the same type of predictable behaviour: an initial period of increased hostility and resistance followed by a gradually increased acceptance. By the end of the institute, *every one* of the prison personnel was expressing favourable attitudes toward the token economy (Marr, Lilliston and Zelhart, 1974: 443).

It is important to note that the favourable expressions occurred far in excess of the requirements of the reinforcement menu. The token economy clearly had the power to make the subjects behave in ways they were not initially inclined. For example, one of the prison guards originally thought the program was "a pile of shit."

> He had attained about 23 tokens toward a room (12), purchase of freedom for the night (12), and ashtray hours the next day. In front of this man's peers, a staff member held up a token and asked if he thought the system was useless. The man hesitated, looked at the token, and said no, at which time he was given the token. Asked if he thought it had possible uses in his prison, he said yes, received a token, amidst the laughter of the other participants, and then listed a few of the possible applications in modifying behaviour of the inmates, for which he received some more tokens. Later, at the conclusion of the institute, this man was strongly in favour of the token economy, attributing his own about-face to his own experiences (Marr, Lilliston and Zelhart, 1974: 443).

This illustration points out the need to reinforce at appropriate stages. The subject is not simply rewarded for accomplishing certain predetermined tasks, but is reinforced for attitudes and subtle changes in behaviour at different stages. If one could successfully change the attitudes and behaviour of prison personnel in five days, it seems that the possibility of influencing the behaviour patterns of juveniles, under some circumstances, does exist.

The reader might argue that delinquency is not the product of individual behaviour, but of a social milieu and the selective response of a society to delinquency. We do not need complete agreement on the causes of delinquency as long as we acknowledge that the behaviour of individuals is a contributing factor. Even if one viewed behaviour as being the primary factor in only a small percentage of cases, one can still see that behavioural modification techniques might be successfully employed on selected groups. Some delinquents might receive better social treatment if they smiled more or were better groomed. While this may not decrease delinquency, these goals may be worthwhile in themselves. Naturally, decisions as to how individuals should be selected for "treatment" is an issue. There is also the danger that behaviour modification techniques can be abused (Chorover, 1973).

One way in which the token economy might be helpful is in modifying patterns which tend to interfere with long-range goals. For example, if a potentially capable youngster were encountering problems because of low academic achievement, techniques which would help him increase academic skills and open future educational opportunities could have a long-range impact. True, delinquents may not wish to volunteer for behaviour modification programs and the morality of forcing treatment on anyone is questionable. Nevertheless, for some troublesome and troubled people, such as sex offenders, behaviour modification might be a definite boom. The issue becomes moral rather than technical.

At the Kennedy Youth Center in Kentucky items of litter were subtly marked and placed with other trash scattered about the grounds. Residents collected the trash and deposited it at a central location where they were rewarded for each piece of marked litter found (Hayes, Johnston and Cone, 1973). This strategy resulted in the reduction of litter. The reader may well argue that this has nothing to do with delinquency, but it does illustrate how order might be maintained with minimum stress in an institution. Such an accomplishment should not be ignored. Efforts to maintain order frequently defeat attempts to offer constructive programs at juvenile institutions.

The long-range impact of behaviour modification

Is there any clear evidence that behaviour modification has a long-range impact on delinquency? The California Youth Center Project launched a four-year program utilizing behaviour modification and transactional analysis to rehabilitate delinquents. Approximately nine hundred juveniles were involved. The subjects experienced positive attitudinal and behavioural changes and left the institution feeling more optimistic and confident, and less anxious, aggressive, hostile and withdrawn (Jesness, 1974). Both behavioural modification and transactional analysis appeared equally effective.

After two years, the post-release arrest records showed that only 23 percent of the juveniles had records clear of arrest and it seemed that many without arrest records had been and would, in the future be involved in illegal behaviour. Like many sophisticated studies the findings are complex, but the researchers concluded that the program had little impact on the offenders' lives.

Another criticism of behaviour modification centres around research that shows that extrinsic rewards, awards that are expected, can, in the long run, decrease interest in a particular activity. (Lepper and Greene, 1975; Lepper, Greene and Nisbett, 1973). This research shows that children who were told they would get a prize for drawing pictures engaged in this activity less often during the next two weeks than children who were not rewarded. The argument is that the children who were not given prizes received intrinsic reward from the drawing itself. It is this type of reward which may lead to basic changes in behaviour patterns. In other words, one may temporarily change behaviour, but if rewards do not continue, perhaps the behaviour that brought the reward will cease as well.

However, the same researchers note that token economy programs may be used to develop initial interest in an activity. Therefore, they do not argue for the abandonment of extrinsic rewards, but rather if one wishes to foster an interest in activities, one should use the minimum amount of pressure and reward. William Notz of the University of Manitoba notes that the relationship between intrinsic and extrinsic motivation is still unclear (Notz, 1975). Clearly, findings in this area will be relevant to behaviour modification programs in the future.

Ross and McKay (1976) worked with a behaviour modification program in Ontario which led to some inconsistent conclusions. Although the strategy seemed to be effective in terms of institutional adjustment, it led to an increase in recidivism and more post-institutional antisocial behaviour. However, the researchers learned that some of the girls in their study became familiar with reinforcement therapy and were using these techniques on their peers. They were conducting a treatment program of their own. Accordingly, Ross and McKay developed a new program: peer therapist training. Girls were given specific training in the principles of positive reinforcement and were encouraged to modify the behaviour of their peers. The strategy provided an effective means of mobilizing peer group pressure as a therapeutic force towards positive social behaviour. In contrast, many authoritarian treatment programs make adolescents feel coerced into changing their behaviour. In this program the girls saw themselves as responsible for changes. This self-attribution and group pressure seem essential for the persistence of behavioural change.

Programs such as the one described by Ross and McKay may be more successful because the psychologists who direct them tend to remain sensitive to criticism and new findings; many of their colleagues are suspicious of behaviour modification. Counselors and psychiatrists, on the other hand, seem less sensitive to criticism, possibly because they work in more institutionalized situations where there is less willingness to assess whether their activities are having a beneficial impact on their clients. The milieu surrounding behaviour modification makes it harder for practices to become entrenched, as they have in some aspects of psychiatry and counseling.

Differential Treatment According to Individual Characteristics

For many years it has been said that treatment should be tailored to the individual. It has also been claimed that action programs would benefit by responding differentially to certain types of groups. Those involved with the detached worker program in Ottawa, for example, have argued that different strategies are appropriate for nuisance groups, chronic delinquent groups and passively delinquent groups (Keech, 1962). The problem is to develop meaningful typologies which can be applied in practical situations. We will focus on the work by Marguerite Q. Warren and draw heavily from a chapter in her forthcoming book (1977).

Warren's basic argument is that an important factor behind the confusing findings arising out of intervention programs is that there has been a masking or concealing effect when all treated individuals are lumped together. Beneficial effects and detrimental effects of the same intervention program on different individuals tend to cancel each other out. Therefore, the question is not whether behaviour modification is effective in treating juvenile offenders, but rather for which offenders is behaviour modification the most useful. Warren notes a number of programs which displayed differential findings, such as a study of survival training in primitive areas in Massachusetts which seemed to be effective for those delinquents who were "reacting to an adolescent growth crisis" but was not effective for more immature and emotionally disturbed boys (Kelly and Baer, 1971).

The development of interpersonal maturity

Naturally, a rationale or theory is necessary for categorizing juveniles. Warren advocates the theory referred to as the Development of Interpersonal Maturity (Sullivan, Grant and Grant, 1957). She has applied this scheme to the correctional system in a number of ways (Warren, 1971). It should be noted that this theory is not a theory of delinquency but rather a general theory of personality development. It suggests that psychological development in all individuals can be meaningfully described in terms of seven successive levels of interpersonal maturity. Each stage is defined by a crucial interpersonal problem which must be solved before further progress can occur. Individuals may become fixed at a particular level. No assumption is made that delinquents fall at any particular stage, but rather that they, like others, will be found at a number of points along the continuum. It is not that delinquents are "immature" but knowing a delinquent's maturity level would help us to understand the meaning of his behaviour as well as the nature of intervention strategies required.

This theory served as the basis for a number of intervention studies in California. The community treatment programs discussed in Chapter 8 are one application. In addition to utilizing the interpersonal-level (I-level) theory, these studies began to define subtypes within the I-level (Warren, 1969). Empirical data suggested that the subtype categories within I-levels responded differently to their perception of the world. For example, I-2 delinquents (aggressive and passive asocials) seemed to respond in two major ways, I-3 delinquents (immature conformists, conformists and manipulators) in three different ways, and I-4's (acting-out neurotics, anxious neurotics, situation emotion reactors, and cultural identifiers) in four different ways. The theory argues that movement from the I-4 to I-5 level generally does not take place until middle or late adolescence. Therefore, the applicability of this scheme to delinquency prevention programs will be determined primarily by the effectiveness of the categorization of these lower levels of interpersonal maturity.

The subtypes of levels I-2, I-3, and I-4 generate nine categories. Only three of these categories constituted 88 percent of the juvenile offender population in the community treatment project described in Chapter 8 (Palmer, 1974). They were called passive conformists, power-oriented and neurotic. The first two were at the I-3 level of interpersonal development and the third was at the I-4 level of development. The neurotic category included two original subtypes identified as acting-out neurotic and anxious neurotic. Although one must be aware that findings from these intervention projects are frequently inconsistent, it is worth recalling some general outcomes: boys classified as neurotic (53 percent of the population) performed much better in the intensive community program than in the traditional program. Boys in the power-oriented group (21 percent) performed worse in the community program than in the traditional program. Boys in the passive conformist group (15 percent) performed somewhat better in the community program. For girls the differences were inconsistent. Warren would argue that the impact of intervention programs is not so much negative as complex.

What are the implications of this strategy? One logical step is to inquire into the possibility of moving children from one I-level to the next. Warren feels that this is possible. In terms of intervention strategy, there is some suggestion that more aggressive I-2 children require some restraint and that a behaviour modification program is appropriate. In the case of more passive I-2 children a protective-style group home with an intensive community-based program may be appropriate. Although it is not clear whether an increase in I-level takes place for the aggressive I-2's, there seems to be growth for the passive children along the I-level continuum. There is little reason to believe that punishment will help these passive children to mature.

At the I-3 level the weaker passive-conformists and the tougher power-oriented individuals respond differently. Again, the passive children show considerable progress to the next I-level in a community-based program. They also do well as far as delinquency is concerned during the contact period; however, the success rate does not hold up beyond agency contact.

Many who are cynical of intervention programs emphasize this failure to produce enduring change, but even a postponement of delinquent involvement for a year or two during adolescence should be seen as a positive achievement.

A Winnipeg study randomly assigned sixteen juveniles to each of three treatment groups (Barkwell, 1976). In one they were given I-level ratings and assigned to the probation officer whose characteristics best fitted the youngster's need. In the alternate treatment groups youngsters were assigned without I-level assessment. Both groups were with parole officers with medium-intensity caseloads (30 to 40 clients). The third group, or surveillance group, was assigned to officers with caseloads of 60 or more.

Changes in self-concept were tested and then retested after six months. Delinquency was measured after one year. The improvement in self-concept was significantly greater for the I-level group than the two control groups ($p<.025$). Similarly, delinquency reduction scores of the I-level group were significantly higher than those of the control groups ($p<.01$). School and work attendance also improved for the I-level group, who had a mean of 17.1 days of attendance per month compared with 12.1 and 9.9 for the alternate and surveillance group. This difference was also statistically significant ($p<.025$).

True, someone like Paul Lerman has not reviewed these data in the manner that he has examined the California Community Treatment Project (1975), so it is possible that many weaknesses are still concealed, but for the time being, this small study is an excellent illustration of one of those rare programs that demonstrated success.

Let us now turn to the practical question of whether this knowledge could be implemented. If one were able to record an I-level score for every juvenile entering our criminal justice system, would it be a useful tool? Even if one assumed that the utilization of such knowledge for treatment purposes is in its infancy, it might be particularly valuable for analyzing data, following the detailed record keeping strategy recommended in Chapter 5. In the study discussed earlier which used volunteers (Pirs, 1975), some way of matching clients according to an interpersonal maturity scale would have added another dimension to that evaluation. Similarly, if such data had been available to Lambert and Madden in their study of the Vanier Centre (1974) they might have been valuable. In other words, even if there is considerable debate over the application of this particular I-level scheme, it would make excellent sense to add such a variable to our data inventory if we ever succeed in establishing a systematic data gathering procedure for juveniles passing through our juvenile courts in Canada. Eventually, the analysis of such data might actually lead to some meaningful improvements in our treatment programs.

A major rub comes, however, at the diagnostic stage. The typology developed by Warren and her colleagues is not easy to apply. Could we make progress with a simpler scheme? Would information from school records give us clues that would permit researchers with modest skills to classify children in a manner similar to the I-level? It is possible that even a crude classification scheme would be useful. Who knows, we might even find a category of individuals who responded well to individual counseling, thereby taking advantage of our present most popular ineffective intervention technique.

Chapter 11

Conventional Approaches—Forestry Camps, Training Programs, Probation and Parole

The desire to take medicine is perhaps the greatest feature which distinguishes man from animals. . . .
—WILLIAM OSLER

Getting Into the Woods

Many of us feel there is something inherently desirable about getting delinquent boys to participate in a rugged outdoor life. British Columbia has been particularly active in establishing outdoor programs. Although one could easily argue that such activities are worthwile in themselves, as could be said about any number of recreational activities, there seems to be little evidence that they have any influence on future delinquent behaviour. A series of careful studies by the California Youth Authority came to a familiar conclusion. Parole violation rates for those who had been assigend to forestry camps were similar to the rates of those who were assigned to institutions (Seckel, 1974a).

However, several aspects of the California studies are worth noting (Seckel, 1974). The two California forestry camps reflected clear differences in goal orientation. One emphasized direct training and controlled guidance. The other emphasized a more permissive, therapeutic approach. In general the boys assigned to the permissive/therapeutic camp expressed more favourable attitudes toward the staff and the program. However, neither camp produced evidence of success on questionnaires or parole violations. One might assume that a camp milieu would be more conducive to rehabilitative procedures that would in turn have long-run benefits. Despite the reasonableness of this assumption the evidence does not support it.

On the positive side, the cost of maintaining a youngster in a camp is less than in an institution. Furthermore, some of these camps perform useful and necessary work in firefighting and forestry conservation. The setting is probably healthful and one might argue that it is desirable for young Canadians to learn outdoor skills. There is a danger though that work in the woods may be abused. The employment of juveniles in road gangs and farm work has occasionally exploited them for cheap labour. In adult prisons there has been a reaction against activities such as making licence plates. The argument has been made that these programs were not designed specifically for rehabilitation and therefore should be abandoned. With the growing awareness that rehabilitation programs have been disappointing, it might be worthwhile to reconsider some work activities with reasonable levels of pay for juveniles and adult inmates. Working in the woods may not turn out to be therapeutic, but a real job does not seem like a bad idea.

The client's viewpoint

One drawback to the foresty camps may be the way they are viewed by the client. Many middle class persons view the outdoors quite differently than others from a different cultural background. We noticed this on a camping trip with ten "acting out hostile boys." One morning we found ourselves standing before a beautiful alpine lake surrounded by an evergreen forest just a bit below timberline. For the two adults the scenery was enchanting, but a boy standing nearby sneered and said, "Trees. Nothin' but trees. God I'm sick of seeing trees." He had been bored for several days. It is difficult to view these programs through the eyes of the client.

Although training youth to use minibikes may not seem related to outdoor training, the logic is similar. The philosophy expressed by this project described in the February 1975 *Liaison*, the monthly newsletter for the criminal justice system in Canada, reflects a "keep them busy" approach to delinquency.

> The only realistic approach to the mounting problem of delinquency . . . is massive and dedicated community involvement in programs such as . . . "Project Mini-Moto." . . . The major factor contributing to the alienation of youth from community and society in general is the absence of challenging and constructive opportunities for involvement. . . . The motor bike will, hopefully, become an integration factor, . . . To an alienated youngster, . . . grown-ups and grown-up institutions are immediately suspect. The old ways of battling delinquency have become obsolete. Most youth agencies and projects simply don't attract the youngsters who could best benefit from their programs.

While one should not automatically assume that such a project will have little impact on delinquency, it would be surprising if this particular activity turns out to be unique. The crucial aspect of projects like Mini-Moto is whether or not they lead to real integration in the community, or simply keep juveniles busy.

Rather than leave the reader with the impression that involving juveniles in various outdoor activities is irrelevant to delinquency, I will try to put these ideas into some meaningful framework. Many delinquent youth seem to be alienated from the community. If some of these activities give juveniles a *genuine* stake in society, a decrease in delinquency might result. Many of these activities, however, are divorced from the mainstream of social life. Camping, hiking and riding motorbikes might be fun, but do they lead to responsible adulthood? Meaningful employment, on the other hand, seems to be related to a decrease in crime.

In the final chapter, I will argue that only basic changes in society which will absorb juveniles into meaningful work, training, or education leading to genuine job opportunities, will have a significant impact on delinquency. These changes seem unlikely, because modern Western society increasingly excludes juveniles from productive participation in such roles. Many excuses are given about how youth are undependable, not trained, etc., but history shows that these excuses are rationalizations. When their labour has been needed in the past, whether it was to oil machinery in a factory, to act as shepherds, or to carry guns, children have been absorbed into the economic structure. Today they are simply not needed.

These ideas will be developed in more detail later, but it might be reasonable to judge most delinquency prevention programs in terms of their ability to give juveniles responsible roles to play in society. "Getting them into the woods" is part of the "keep them busy" mentality. This is not the same as meaningful involvement in a world that is at least partially of their own making. This may be the major failing in these programs and also those which "give them a trade," or "teach them to think."

Vocational and Educational Programs

Vocational programs have been part of conventional institutions for many years. When careful assessments are made of such programs and the performance of trainees is compared with that of other groups not previously defined there seems to be little difference between trainees and inmates who do not receive such training. Again the California system has generated a significant portion of this research. Similar findings resulted from evaluations of vocational training in a men's penitentiary in the state of Washington and also in the Draper Correctional Center in Alabama (Greenberg, 1977).

As with other programs, controlled experiments are rare; but one extensive program was conducted by the federal government in the United States which emphasized vocational training after release from prison (Fulton, 1969). In general, the disappointing results suggest that the controls did slightly better than those who received assistance, but the differences were small and not statistically significant. Greenberg (1977) reports that an after-release Minnesota study showed just the opposite result: the training group did somewhat better, but the difference was not statistically significant and disappeared when the program ended (Ericson and Moberg, 1968).

These two vocational programs in post-release settings typify the findings of a wide range of vocational programs in or out of institutions—they just do not seem to have much impact on future crime or delinquency (Martinson, 1974b; Greenberg, 1977). While there are occasional glimpses of better performance which might be related to vocational training, the differences tend to be very small if not nonexistent.

Of course, training and educational programs should not be neglected, but we should view them as having possible merit in their own right rather than as cures for delinquency. In Canada, a few training programs have been part of a behavioural modification perspective (Parlett and Ayers, 1971; Murphy, 1972).

Brian Murphy, with the Canadian Penitentiary Service, is an advocate of using training programs in our correctional institutions. His experience with the Matsqui and other institutions in British Columbia has led to a number of observations regarding training programs.

> It is important for the analyst to be aware of two particular difficulties bearing upon establishing new quantitative and qualitative behaviour for delinquent subjects. Firstly, some of the delinquent types of behaviour engaged in by subjects will have been highly beneficial experiences. This will often, for example, be true of stealing, trafficking, and other forms of illegal employment and of opiate use. It will probably be impossible to replace these kinds of behaviour with other behaviour unless the replacement can be made to provide a greater net benefit. Secondly, delinquents will be competing for nondelinquent rewards with nondelinquents who may be appreciably more knowledgeable and skilled than they are at taking possession of the requisite opportunities. Unless the delinquent subjects succeed in obtaining legitimate rewards through legitimate behaviour against the stiff competition, they will continue their previously rewarding delinquent behaviour. In order to succeed in obtaining legitimate rewards against the stiff, established competition, and to make legitimate means more attractive than illegitimate means of obtaining reward, the delinquent subjects may have to be better prepared than the competition in most, if not all, respects. Where this cannot be done, it may be necessary to artificially provide higher levels of reward for some time (Murphy, Shinyei, Murphy and Irons, 1973: 301).

Even if one succeeds in changing behaviour inside an institution, Murphy notes the need for a circle of friends who will encourage legal employment and actively reward the search for such employment. One can see that this could be an extremely difficult task. Murphy and his colleagues note:

> Although clinical conditioning procedures may facilitate establishing or extinguishing behaviour, such behaviour changes will seldom endure long unless net benefit consequent upon that behaviour is maintained at appropriate levels. . . .

> Similary, newly established behaviour will be quickly extinguished unless positive net benefit is realized most of the time when it is engaged in (1973:303).

While Murphy is a strong advocate of behaviour modification principles and their application to training within a correctional setting, his own comments point to areas of difficulty—difficulties of such magnitude that it is possible that these comprehensive programs are unlikely to succeed even if resistance on moral grounds were overcome. From a practical point of view, it is likely that behaviour modification will make its very modest contribution in a piecemeal manner; for example, with educational programs which provide specific skills.

One type of program which initially seemed to have promise for young offenders involved computer programming. In some situations inmates who learned computer skills were involved on research projects and were later hired by the research division of the correctional service. It is distinctly possible that this training was a step toward other opportunities, and that for these unique individuals, this program could be seen as successful. However, Greenberg (1977) reports that an IBM training program for young offenders at Rikers Island yielded surprising findings. The recidivism rate for the trainees was 48 percent compared with 66 percent of the untrained control group for one year after release. When program dropouts were included, however, the recidivism rate for the training group rose to 58 percent and at the end of the second year had reached 92 percent (Sullivan and Mandell, 1967).

Training programs sometimes play a large role in institutions for youthful female offenders. In one California institution women prisoners received training in ceramics, cosmetology, vocational sewing, laundry, housekeeping, and nursing (Spencer and Berecochea, 1971). When compared with those who did not receive training but whose institutional work assignments were related to the areas where training was offered, the trainees had the same rates of return to prison within one year of release.

It has been argued that parolees do not get jobs in their trades because their technical training is inadequate or that inmates become involved in vocational training solely in order to obtain early parole dates. However, Dickover, Painter and Maynard (1970) concluded that this notion requires revision. In some areas such as welding and auto mechanics, there was a reasonable amount of transfer of skills from the vocational training. In areas such as refrigeration, air conditioning and masonry there was little transfer.

Dickover and his colleagues learned that the parole agents were not greatly involved in the placement of vocational trainees in jobs. This may be in contrast to the Canadian system. At least Waller (1974) reports that Canadian parole officers collaborated to a higher degree with the

Department of Manpower in placing inmates on jobs. Employers indicated that the principle problems they had with parolees were absenteeism and problems associated with alcohol or drugs. There is reason to believe that actual vocational skill is a relatively minor factor in terms of encouraging or discouraging crime. Evidently, many unskilled people have little problem avoiding criminal involvement. While vocational training in a juvenile correctional system can be justified for a number of reasons, it seems to have a negligible impact on future crime rates.

Recently a number of experimental college education programs for prisoners (Project Newgate) have been instituted, but there is little evidence that these programs reduce recidivism (Baker *et al*, 1973). Two of the programs attempted to establish control groups but failed, illustrating the difficulties described in Chapters 3 and 4. Several programs also noted that there was hostility toward college education programs for criminals, because a staff member can barely afford a college education for his family or for himself. As a result, the Warden at the Rockview prison in Pennsylvania has made efforts to provide free education courses for staff, for academic credit or for pay increases.

Several of the Newgate projects gave rise to considerable local political debate and some police harassment. In three projects there were power struggles between prison bureaucracies and the program staff. Such struggles usually occur at the initial stages of programs such as Newgate. After training programs are well established in prisons, however, Dan Glaser's survey of many United States federal institutions (1969:66) suggests that an important side effect was that work supervisors established better relations with inmates than most other staff members. In other words, programs can alter institutions even if they do not significantly change inmates. Again, understanding the dynamics of these changes may be more crucial than studying the recidivism rates of inmates.

A study in British Columbia which was similar to the Newgate program offered college instruction but was able to make comparisons with a control group (Parlett and Ayers, 1971). The initial findings appeared to be quite positive, but as time passed the research staff members discovered problems that made comparisons difficult. When the star pupil of the program made it to the "eight most wanted men in Canada" list, however, it was clear that the education was not automatically used in the manner intended. Some of the insights gained from these British Columbia projects may prove more useful than evidence concerning outcomes.

The final study to be discussed in this chapter is based on a full-time work program for boys at the Kawartha Lakes Training School in Ontario and a part-time volunteer program for girls at Pine Ridge (Ontario, 1975). Without control groups, comparisons are difficult. But of the 85 cases analyzed at both three months and six months after release in the community, 14 percent were either returned to training school or had been charged with a criminal offence. Those who were either working or attending school were considered positive outcomes and they constituted 52 percent of the group. Trying to assess long-term impact was difficult because the files covered intervals of one to 17 months. But for 48 cases which reported events more than six months after graduation, 33 percent were working or attending school, 42 percent were considered marginal (AWOL, out of school and work), and 19 percent were back in training school or charged with a criminal offence.

While the data will make more sense with future comparisons, the study noted that it was difficult for the boys to adapt from the supervised program to work or school in the community even though they seemed to have acquired specific skills. The girls were in a work-study program involving unpaid volunteer work. While the girls seemed to show greater progress in terms of personal growth and acquisition of interpersonal skills than the boys, they would have preferred to have been paid. With the advent of coeducational training schools in Ontario this discriminatory practice is likely to cease.

Probation and Parole Services

Many juveniles who go to court end up with a probation officer and never go to a training school. Parole, on the other hand, is an early release from an institution. Although parole services generally involve adults and more experienced criminals, the logic of supervising people in the community is similar. Therefore, I am assuming that the research presented here applies to both probation or parole.

Earlier I argued that incarceration tended to have a negative impact on juveniles. Logically, then, one would argue for probation as an alternative. We must ask, however, if probation has any positive factors to recommend it, or is it simply a way of avoiding prison? Similarly, is parole simply worthwhile as a device for reducing prison sentences or does it have other benefits? The study by Waller *Men Released From Prison* (1974) tends to support previous findings in the United States: parole does not seem to make much of a difference when compared with straight release without supervision. However, Waller did learn that crime rates during the period of supervision tended to be lower. This is consistent with the findings of Fisher and Erickson (1973). Therefore, one could argue that postponing criminal involvement until the end of the parole period could be seen as a worthwhile, though temporary, gain. Waller also produced the interesting finding that a man's desire to go on parole was a better predictor of reduced criminal involvement than the decision on the part of the parole board to grant parole. Parole is not an automatic process in Canada as it is in some jurisdictions in the United States.

In Quebec André Bourdon (1966) compared 247 men released on parole with 105 men released at the end of sentence without parole supervision. Although these two groups were not comparable, Bourdon controlled for many of the variables related to parole success. He concluded that the higher success rate for those on parole compared with those with straight releases was largely a function of the selection process which leads to those most likely to succeed in being selected for parole. When supervised and unsupervised releases with similar characteristics were compared, the failure rates were similar.

Some argue that parole officers would be more effective if their caseloads were reduced. A California study compared small (15-man), medium (30-man), and large (80-man or more) caseloads. There was some indication that those with small and medium caseloads performed significantly better than those with large caseloads (Havel, 1965). Unfortunately, later studies on caseload size have produced inconsistent findings.

A study in Massachusetts compared the effects of small caseloads of boys (25) with large caseloads (75). At the end of six months there was no difference in recidivism (Schwitzgebel and Baer, 1967). A more recent California study compared caseloads of 36 with control groups carrying 72 cases (Davis, 1974). In the first cohort the experimental group seemed to do much better than the controls at six, twelve, and eighteen months. In the second cohort the smaller experimental group did slightly worse than the controls at six months, twelve months, and eighteen months. Obviously, the findings are either difficult to interpret or support a growing suspicion that the unique aspects of each situation make consistent findings improbable.

Rather than simply saying that parole accomplishes little, it is more appropriate to ask whether or not there are differences between types of clients, types of parole programs and settings, and types of parole officers. Not surprisingly, an early focus of parole research was on the type of client. It is also not surprising that there has been relatively little attention given to the type of officer. The tradition of looking at "them" rather than at "us" is deeply imbedded.

In addition to studying caseload size, Joan Havel (1965) argued that different types of parole officers combined with different types of clients might produce different results. The parolees in her study were classified as low maturity and high maturity. Agents were classified as those representing an "external" approach, primarily concerned with factors external to the parolee and trying to give the parolee help meeting everyday problems by structuring the parole situation. Other agents were classified as representing the "internal" approach, focusing more on what is happening inside the parolee and encouraging him to look inside himself instead of blaming the environment for his problems. It was anticipated that low maturity parolees would do better with external agents and high maturity parolees would do better with internal agents. The findings did not indicate that such interaction occurred.

While matching certain types of parole officers with parolees has not led to any great breakthroughs, there have been some interesting findings. In one California study involving juveniles, parole officers who were described as relationship/self-expression-oriented were compared with others who were surveillance/self-control-oriented (Palmer, 1973b). Youths usually viewed the relationship/self-expression-oriented parole officers as counselors or friends who placed considerable emphasis on family rather than peer relationships. Such agents interacted especially well with youths who were communicative and alert, impulsive and anxious,or verbally hostile and offensive. While the surveillance/self-control-oriented workers were least effective with those who were verbally hostile and defensive, they seemed to be most effective with anxious and moderately dependent youths.

It should be noted that the sophisticated type of design initiated by Joan Havel influenced other studies, but there were a number of problems which arose to interfere with a clear evaluation. For example, parole officers in different geographical areas seem to reflect different policies and different cultural milieux (Takagi, 1969). In addition, low status parole officers tended to recommend that parole be revoked more frequently than those higher in the organizational hierarchy (Robison and Takagi, 1968). A Minnesota study comparing different degrees of supervision suggested that more intensive supervision in smaller caseloads may have increased the chances that parole would be revoked for minor offences. We have seen earlier in Chapter 4 that involvement in a program can also produce the opposite effect and that closer contact with a social worker could lead to a greater tolerance for minor offences (Lerman, 1968).

To assess the effectiveness of parole, we must again rely on studies of adults, because of the lack of data on juvenile parole. However, some inferences can be made. The data suggest that increased supervision does lead to a decrease in official violations. The research does not make clear, however, whether this is because of a genuine decrease in delinquent behaviour or because parole officers have successfully intervened in the criminal justice process. Even if the second line of reasoning is correct, perhaps it should be viewed positively. While smaller caseloads do not automatically lead to more extensive contact between parolees and agents, there seems to be a slight indication that smaller caseloads do reduce delinquent behaviour.

While matching certain types of parole officers with certain types of clients does seem to be promising, it should be noted that procedures for classifying individuals are difficult to develop. For that reason, if resources are limited, it may be more profitable to look at different *conditions* of parole rather than the *personalities* of the people involved. For example, countries like Belgium have developed systems of semi-detention and weekend restraint. The recent changes in the National Parole Board system in Canada give one reason to believe that experiments with different conditions of parole will be forthcoming. Admittedly, experiences with adult offenders may have little bearing on juvenile probation and parole, but at present we know of no studies in Canada which focus directly on juveniles. Even though parole should not be seen as a cure, some comments by Irvin Waller are appropriate to end this chapter:

> There is plenty of room for innovation because, in terms of reducing the probability of rearrest and improving social functioning, it would be hard to find anything less effective than the present system. Presuming that rational, and hopefully effective, alternatives might exist, one could begin experimentation by spending at least $5,000 per inmate, a figure not out of line with the Solicitor General's cost quotes of $10,000 per inmate and $500 per parolee excluding the cost of prison construction. In the end, much of the innovation may simply be in reducing *cost* (1974: 207).

Chapter 12

Less Conventional Approaches to Delinquency

In skating over thin ice, our safety is in our speed.
—RALPH WALDO EMERSON

These past four chapters have discussed the conventional activities and programs currently being used in juvenile delinquency prevention. We will now examine some of the more unusual tactics that have been employed in this field.

Corrective Surgery

The surgical work done by Dr. Edward Lewison at the Oakalla Prison Farm, near Vancouver has extended over a twenty-year period and has involved nine hundred subjects. The surgery is primarily the correction of facial deformities. In some cases this surgery was purely cosmetic; in others there were functional deformities (Lewison, 1974). Prospective candidates for plastic surgery at Oakalla were interviewed by the medical doctor or a social worker. An attempt was made to analyse the possible impact of the surgery. Some individuals were felt to be unsuitable candidates.

> The individual who attributes all or most of his problems to his physical deformity frequently uses it as a crutch on which to rest his own sense of failure. Sudden withdrawal of this crutch may leave the individual without defences against his inadequacy and may plunge him into deep depression (Lewison, 1974: 45).

Lewison argues that such cases are rare. A second group of inmates who were not given corrective surgery were those who displayed severe psychoses.

Immediately following the surgery, beneficial psychological changes were noted. Subjects were more inclined to cooperate with those in authority and to participate in prison activities. Formerly hostile and aloof individuals became polite, even gracious in their manner. Many developed an eagerness to learn a trade and to qualify for transfer to a vocational rehabilitation centre.

Dr. Lewison was aware that he had been selective in his choice of candidates for surgery, and that some may have been less recidivist than average even without surgery. The initial studies suggested that 42 percent of those who received surgery returned to prison compared with 70 percent of the general inmate population. To carry out a more objective study, two hundred inmates seeking plastic surgery were interviewed. From this group, one hundred candidates were selected on an alternative basis. Sixty of the candidates selected came from Oakalla, which contained more chronic offenders and had no vocational program. This group was to be compared with 60 who received no surgery. Similarly, there were 40 subjects from the Haney Correctional Institute, which did have vocational services and contained inmates considered better prospects for rehabilitation. These 40 cases would be compared with 40 others from Haney who did not receive surgery. A follow-up study of the recidivism rate showed a 53 percent failure rate for those who received surgery at the Oakalla Prison Farm and over 75 percent for those who did not. At the Haney Correctional Institution the failure rate was 42 percent for those who received surgery and 57 percent for those who did not.

There will be many who will scoff at these findings and others who will object to them on a variety of grounds. Naturally, the "Hawthorn Effect" might have been present: having someone take an interest in the inmates could have changed their behaviour. On the other hand, the results of this study compare favourably with various other attempts to change criminal behaviour.

Originally, narcotics addicts were not considered good candidates for surgery because of their high recidivism rate. However, a controlled experiment was finally launched in which 24 narcotic offenders received surgery and were compared with 24 addicts in a control group. At the end of one year, 54 percent of those who had received surgery had returned to prison while for those who received no surgery the figure was 83 percent. Two years later, 87 percent of those who received surgery had returned to prison compared with 91 percent in the control group.

Dr. Lewison argues that while active addicts may benefit very little from corrective surgery, the burned-out addict may be helped by cosmetic surgery. An example was Mary, age 32. She was serving 18 months for drug possession, vagrancy and theft. She had had 22 previous convictions. Parental guidance had been lacking and her schooling was cut short to help support the family. She married when she was 22 and although both she and her husband spent much of their married life in jail, the marriage had been relatively stable. Mary had suffered an injury to her nose and face in an accident which had left a nasal deformity. Pleased with the results of surgery, she showed a marked improvement in her behaviour. After discharge she joined her husband and has not been in trouble with the law for four years and, as far as it is known, has not reverted to drug addiction.

Perhaps we should look at corrective surgery as only one example of a larger possible pattern. There are many ways to make people more attractive physically or socially. Admittedly, many present programs attempt to improve the social skills of delinquents. However, the motivation behind many of these programs is to make the subjects "good" rather than attractive. Would it not be more reasonable to use a variety of techniques that might simply improve appearances and skills?

Foster Homes

Frequently social workers find themselves investigating a family environment that appears to be extremely detrimental to the raising of children. One alternative to an unhealthy family situation is to place the child in a foster home. Attempts are made to find foster parents who will create a better environment for the child in order to improve his chances to develop into a normal adult.

Obviously, it is very difficult to assess the impact of foster homes. There is little data that compare children placed in foster homes with children who remained with their natural families. Furthermore, following the careers of such children into adulthood is rarely done. Therefore, one phase of the Cambridge-Somerville Youth Study is of particular interest. This long-term, intensive counseling program was actively involved for many years in the lives of potentially delinquent boys and their families. Nineteen of these boys were placed in foster homes in early adolescence. Choosing from the remaining sample in the study, the researchers selected nineteen boys whose early environments closely resembled the "natural families" of the boys who were later placed in foster homes (McCord, McCord and Thurber, 1960). Each of the boys in the control group was individually matched with the boys placed in foster homes on the basis of the following factors: presence or absence of a natural father in the home, deviance or non-deviance of the father, emotional attitude of the father toward the son, disciplinary techniques of the father, deviance or non-deviance of the mother, emotional attitude of the mother toward the son, and disciplinary techniques of the mother.

Other studies have shown that each of these factors is strongly related to adult deviance. Trained counselors visited the families an average of once a week over the five-year period, and thus more detailed information was available on these families than in most research projects. The situation, then, is one where we have two groups of "inadequate" families. In half of them boys were placed in foster homes and in the other half they were left with their natural "inadequate" families.

When the boys grew to adulthood their histories were traced to see if they had become criminal, alcoholic, or otherwise mentally unbalanced. The researchers had hypothesized that the foster home boys would have a lower rate of adult deviance than the matched controls. The results indicated the opposite. Of the nineteen boys in the control group, eight had criminal records as adults. Of the nineteen who had been placed in foster homes, fifteen had criminal records as adults.

The researchers reasoned that boys removed from their families might interpret this separation as "rejection" by the families. Other research in the Cambridge-Somerville Study showed that parental rejection was strongly associated with adult criminology. Therefore, the researchers examined those eight cases placed in foster homes where the natural fathers lived at home. Seven of these eight boys became criminals while only two of the eight boys who remained with their "inadequate" families became criminals. The conclusion of the researchers was that boys removed from homes where both natural parents are present will be more inclined to interpret the removal as rejection than boys in homes where only the mother is present.

While this sample is admittedly small, it is one of the few studies which has both extensive data, careful matching, and a long-term follow-up. It forces us to question the assumption that a child would be better off being removed from an "inadequate" family environment. Instead we must recognize that there could exist psychological supports in even the worst of families that cannot be duplicated even in a "healthy" foster home situation.

We should not confuse the implications of this study of foster homes with the question of adoption. A child permanently removed from an inadequate home at an early age and adopted by a supportive family has a far better chance to make a successful adjustment and develop into a normal adult. One principle is underlined by a number of studies: the family is still the major factor in producing healthily socialized individuals. Any assistance that can be given to a problem family that enables it to keep its members together is likely to be more beneficial than breaking the family up. In Holland and some other northern European countries, there has been a systematic attempt to provide continuous support to those families that are in distress, although there is constant debate over what sorts of activities best assist these families.

Changing the Schools

Many programs have been launched in various school systems to cope with children who have behaviour and academic problems. A study launched in Kansas City utilized techniques that make sense to most social scientists or educators (Ahlstrom and Havighurst, 1971). The experimental and control subjects in this study came from low status junior high schools and were considered to be the most maladjusted boys in these schools. The experimental program consisted of small classes and included a work program in which the boys were paid for their labour while they developed work habits and occupational skills. Individual tutoring in academic areas was provided. The work training began as supervised projects, moved into genuine part-time jobs, and finally the boys were employed in full-time jobs. It would be difficult to ask for a more sensible strategy; however, the results were disappointing. By age eighteen or nineteen, 68 percent of the boys in the experimental group had police records. Only 12 percent had completed high school and those who did were at the bottom of the class. The control sample performed at about the same level.

There were some unanticipated negative effects of the program. The experimental classrooms were more "relaxed" than regular classrooms and there was more fighting and other objectionable behaviour upsetting to teachers and administrators. In addition, the boys felt stigmatized by being part of the program. Even the teachers working in the program felt they had been assigned to work with the "failures."

It is possible that this type of negative consequence could have been avoided by a slightly different strategy. As the reader may recall from Chapter 3, the teaching machine testing program with Opportunities for Youth attempted to create an environment where the boys saw the activity as a meaningful task. It may be advisable to avoid segregating "problem" children and thereby identifying them as such. Perhaps it would be more effective to apply programs of this nature to the total population of a school instead of working with a selected segment? Although the well-adjusted children might profit more than those considered to be problems, this strategy might be a more realistic way of reaching the target population. In other words, specific educational and training programs for problem children may not be rewarding, but that does not imply that general attempts to improve the quality of teaching and to provide work opportunities as part of school experience are not valuable in themselves.

One interesting aspect of the Ahlstrom and Havighurst study is that the boys whose parents refused to consent to their participating in the experimental program did better than those who took part. It is not clear why this was so. Were these parents more advantaged and therefore more willing to oppose the wishes of administrators? Did the parents' refusal mean that they refused to accept the idea that their child was maladjusted?

There are basically two views of the school system vis-à-vis delinquency. The first states that the problem lies with the juvenile and that it is the school's role to help or change those children who are deviant. The second view is that the school system is responsible for producing the delinquents. William Amos has reviewed a number of delinquency prevention programs in the schools (Amos and Wellford, 1967: Chapter 7). Although aware of many deficiencies in the schools, he feels that many of the criticisms have been unfair. Most of his suggestions for delinquency prevention programs in the schools were a product of the attitudes of the late sixties: individual instruction, guidance counselors who "related" to the community, etc. After the disappointing results that have appeared in recent findings, it is possible that Amos would be less optimistic about many of the conventional suggestions that he makes in his chapter on delinquency prevention in the schools.

Taking advantage of some of these recent findings, Polk and Schafer (1972) argue that the educational system itself is a direct cause of delinquency. The emphasis on success stigmatizes individuals who fail and may later turn to delinquency to counteract their low status and self-image.

A similar theme is pursued by Delbert Elliot and Harwin Voss (1974). In a series of studies they present evidence that boys, but not necessarily girls, face status frustration in the schools. Hence, delinquency involvement was higher while boys were in school than after they left school. This was particularly true among dropout youths from lower class backgrounds. Of course there is the possibility that having a job was a factor in the reduction of delinquency. These data were gathered in Southern California in the early 1960's when jobs for youth were more available than in the late 1970's. However, there are other data that support the hypothesis that the school setting is particularly stressful for certain segments of the young male population. For example, Kelly and Pink (1973) note that a decreasing level of school attendance was a strong predictor of adolescent rebellion and delinquency.

The Shotgun Approach

One of the characteristics of evaluators of delinquency prevention programs is that they like to assess the impact of distinct factors or separate variables, such as the impact of classroom size, or individual counseling, or a gang worker program. The evaluation of a program or system as a whole meets resistance because it is argued that there would be no way of measuring which variables were the most meaningful. True, a program attempting many things at once is difficult, if not impossible to evaluate. Again, a striving for scientific purity may lead researchers to focus on trivial variables. Could it be that variety, flexibility, and constant change are the characteristics that contribute to the success of a delinquency prevention program? Should constant change be treated as a scientific variable?

Earlier we described the Hawthorn Effect, the tendency of people to respond favourably when someone pays attention to them. Many programs seem to go through an initial period of vigour and then gradually subside. Is it possible to build the Hawthorn Effect into delinquency prevention programs? Conventional evaluation would be almost impossible. However, if we are willing to sacrifice clear evaluations, a program dedicated to change, flexibility, and multiple approaches might be a worthwhile experiment. The 1966 Reduction of Delinquency through Expansion of Opportunity project (RODEO) would probably not be flattered by being considered a "shotgun" approach. The project clearly set out specific strategies and goals and was certainly not directing its activities in a haphazard manner, but the characteristic of the RODEO project which was most significant was its multi-faceted approach.

The RODEO project assumed that "chronic delinquency in poverty areas is often a result of alienation from the educational and opportunity systems of the larger community" (Los Angeles County Probation Department, 1966). Therefore, the reduction of delinquency could be achieved by working with schools, employers, training facilities, and other agencies to expand a boy's capabilities and find opportunities for him in the larger community. In addition, the RODEO proposal spelt out a variety of strategies for intervening between a boy and the larger community. Actually, the techniques used by the RODEO project were not new, although they were innovative in a number of ways. For example, indigenous nonprofessionals had direct responsibility for working with specific boys and families. The program involved individual guidance, family-centred conferences, and guided group interaction. To respond more specifically to the academic needs of juveniles, tutoring was provided and there were also back-to-school workshops for the parents, with the hope that a more positive attitude toward school would develop. The neighbourhood youth core participants paid boys an hourly wage to work as on-the-job trainees in various public and private agencies (Rushen and Hunter, 1970).

A five-year study from 1967 to 1971 provided an evaluation (De La Paz, 1974). A total of 195 minors were involved in the evaluation, 120 in the RODEO experimental group, 43 in the "in-camp" control group, and 32 in the "in-community" control group. While the evaluation summary states that the boys were assigned randomly to the three different groups and that there were not significant differences in the background characteristics of the three groups, it is not clear why some boys were sent to the in-camp group, which was usually for more serious delinquents, and why others were sent to the in-community group.

At any rate the three groups seemed to be comparable and the boys in each had accumulated impressive delinquency records. The RODEO group had favourable probation terminations in 70 percent of its cases compared with 58 percent for the in-camp group and 59 percent for the in-community group. During the follow up period, which averaged thirty-seven months, the proportion of favourable terminations with no arrest records dropped to : RODEO—19.3 percent; in-camp—12.0 percent; in-community—15.8 percent. As one can see, the RODEO project seemed to be the most successful, but it is important to note that less than one-fifth of the boys managed to avoid arrest again in a three-year period. Notice also, that we are speaking only of those who were *favourably* terminated from juvenile probation status. Of those who were favourably terminated, did the RODEO project delay arrest? After eighteen months

71.1 percent of the RODEO boys had experienced their first police contact, compared with 84 percent of the in-camp boys and 84.2 percent of the in-community boys. How many were *not* sent back to jail? RODEO—25 percent; in-camp—16 percent; in-community—21 percent.

There were some changing patterns in the delinquent activities between the period of 32 months before and 37 months after the program. The proportion of property offences decreased after the programs: RODEO—from 67.5 percent to 47 percent; in-community—63.1 percent to 36.8 percent; in-camp—remained at 56 percent. On the other hand, the proportion of offences against persons increased except for the in-camp group: RODEO—from 7.2 percent to 20.5 percent; in-community—from 15.8 percent to 26.3 percent; in-camp—from 24.0 percent to 16.0 percent. It is also interesting to note that the mean maximum sentence for each felony offence was longer for the RODEO group and the in-camp group but decreased somewhat for the in-community group.

When we look back at the results of the RODEO project as described above, it is important to make two observations. First, the gains seem to be slight and erratic. Secondly, the types of error described in Chapter 4 by Lerman could easily have influenced this project. However, since most training school programs (or in-camp programs) are very expensive, alternative strategies which show even modest gains might be worthwhile. A constantly changing, multi-faceted approach may be frustrating to those who are determined to make assessments, but it may also create enthusiasm and flexibility and increase the possibility of a favourable impact.

Are We Expecting Too Much?

Stuart Adams has been involved in evaluation research for many years. He argues that given the apparent lack of rigour in correctional evaluation research and the apparent low percentage of positive findings, it would be worthwhile making comparisons with other disciplines. High-technology industries might be seen as an area where a high return is expected on the investment of time and energy in research. A former president of Du Pont estimated that no more than one in twenty of Du Pont's research projects eventually paid off. In other industries failure rates seem to be correspondingly high. Most of the effort spent in research does not lead to commercial success. During three decades of intensive medical research, there has been little improvement in the life expectancy of adults and no discoveries of cures for many major diseases that afflict Western mankind (Adams, 1975: 10). In other words, perhaps we are making unreasonable demands on correctional research.

Adams also attempts to summarize the reviews of research that have been done to date. He acknowledges the high number of failures but notes that the gains slightly outweigh the losses. He also argues that treatment seems to be more effective for juveniles than for adults.

Whom should the public believe? Perhaps society has been unreasonably demanding. Instead of comparing present-day humane programs with the vengeful, punitive treatments of the past, researchers compare one innovative program with a more conventional one, forgetting that the "conventional" program may have improved considerably over the years. While training schools tend to have a negative influence on juveniles, a more humane attitude has developed in these training schools. Many of these changes have taken place gradually without the benefit of careful evaluations or theoretical rationales. Probably society has become a bit more humane, a bit more sensitive, and perhaps even a bit wiser. It is difficult to evaluate these subtle changes in a scientific way. On the other hand, self-deception would be unwise. Research directed at the dynamics of delinquency prevention programs, and on the basic assumptions underlying these programs would be more rewarding than assessing the impact of treatment on recidivism rates. It is promising to note that researchers are moving in this direction but as long as the primary pressure is to show whether a project is "good" or "bad," it will be difficult to make significant progress.

Chapter 13

Increasing the Odds in the Society As a Whole

Last night I invented a new pleasure, and as I was giving it the first trial an angel and a devil came rushing toward my house. They met at the door and fought with each other over my newly-created pleasure; the one crying, "It's a sin!"—the other, "It's a virtue!"

—KAHLIL GIBRAN

Chapters 8 through 12 reviewed some of the attempts to modify delinquency. If we compare these experiments with those done in most scientific laboratories, the results are not surprising. In most labs, the majority of experiments fail and the gains made in each specific attempt are usually very small. Efforts at delinquency prevention seem to follow a similar pattern, but the failures take longer and create more stress. There is no indication of dramatic improvements on the horizon. However, we might be able to increase the likelihood of launching effective programs if we can see that delinquency is tied in to other aspects of our society. The suggestions that follow assume that fairly fundamental changes would be necessary to make a meaningful impact on delinquency—changes that society would probably resist.

Large-Scale Changes That Could Influence Delinquency

There is a tendency to treat juvenile delinquency as a disease that can be cured when instead it should be thought of as an enduring characteristic of modern social life. Juvenile delinquency rates would be lower in a society with less geographical and social mobility. Similarily, a society with very strict legal restrictions on behaviour would likely have less delinquency. For most Canadians, however, mobility and tolerance for a variety of behaviours are essential to our view of a healthy and free society. It is naive to think we can gain in one area without paying a price somewhere else. If a wide range of attitudes and behavioural preferences were restricted, the likelihood of developing those patterns which lead to more acceptable behaviours would decrease. Obviously, no society could tolerate unlimited variety, but how much variety can be eliminated before the capacity of a society to adjust and endure suffers?

The court systems, the schools and other institutions which deal with social control tend to restrict the range of behavioural activities. While this is understandable, society must ask itself how much is gained when the range of behavioural preferences is severely restricted. Instead of expanding our definitions of juvenile delinquency and insisting that various agencies become involved in dealing with delinquency, we might consider moving in the opposite direction. What is the *least* we could do? What would the consequences be if we accepted a wider range of behavioural patterns?

The use of marijuana provides an excellent illustration. Our society tolerates more dangerous drugs like alcohol and tobacco while not allowing marijuana, which according to present evidence must be classified as relatively harmless. Argument on behalf of a more tolerant approach to marijuana should not be seen as an encouragement of drug use, but rather as an illustration of an area where tolerance might have more positive long-range consequences than the present criminalization of marijuana users.

Our punitive attitude toward juvenile delinquency is disguised under the heading, "doing it for their own good." For example, promiscuous fifteen-year-old girls are put in jail, but promiscuous fifteen-year-old boys are not. What would be the implications of providing contraceptive information at an early age and allowing sexual activities to be private concerns? Would society benefit if it insisted that all under-age girls working as prostitutes register with social insurance, belong to a union, and enjoy the benefits available to most working persons? In addition, these girls could be offered apprenticeship programs in industry, other training programs, or scholarships. If we were to view the services provided by juvenile prostitutes as being no less socially damaging than the services offered by those who work in the liquor industry, by the advertising industry which encourages the purchase of large automobiles, or by lobbyists who work on behalf of industries which pollute our environment, then it would be easier to incorporate juvenile prostitutes into the legitimate occupational structure.

Does it take much imagination to extend our tolerance to other services that have been available to society for a long time and will continue to be available in the future? In other words, bringing marginal people involved in questionable activities into the mainstream of society may in fact give them a greater stake in the health of that society. It is difficult to compare the morality of the manufacturer of cigarettes with the morality of those who rent their bodies. How do we weigh the damage to society of lung cancer, alcoholism or gonorrhea? We already show great tolerance for certain types of deviant behaviour. It is expected that clerks will steal from stores, dock workers will steal from cargoes, professors will steal stationery from universities, and people will cheat on their income tax. Obviously, people in power "get away" with more than those without power. Since juveniles lack power and have little stake in society, we should anticipate a high incidence of deviance.

Bringing juveniles back

Many people would consider a strategy of tolerance irresponsible, but is it responsible to persist in punishing juveniles for trivial offences while ignoring more damaging behaviour on the part of influential adults? Is it not possible that the criminal prosecution of juveniles is in fact damaging the capacity of society to "work through" the problem of delinquency? It has been demonstrated that our formal control mechanisms have had little impact on juvenile theft and vandalism. Have we carefully examined the *informal* mechanisms which seem to influence vandalism? If juveniles shared the responsibility of building and maintaining the buildings in which they studied, possibly they would protect that property more than they do now. At the present time, most Western societies tend to exclude juveniles from constructive roles in society.

During periods of high unemployment, youths have a high rate of delinquency as do those who come from underprivileged backgounds and ethnic minorities. Rather than attempting to control delinquency by formal mechanisms, we should be asking what sort of incentives for acceptable behaviour could be created. A society which limits the entrance of young people into the labour force and establishes rules that are different for juveniles and adults does not encourage the young to share responsibility for the quality of life in that society.

It is interesting to note that the peak age for delinquency in England is fourteen years while in Canada and the United States it is sixteen years. The incidence of male delinquency drops considerably among employed juveniles. How could society integrate young people at an earlier age than it does presently? Should we not insist that the time to continue educational activities is when one is thirty or forty?

Obviously, unemployed youth are part of a larger societal problem. Instead of replacing humans with machines, a labour-intensive economy should be encouraged (Gans, 1976). While automation of dirty and tedious jobs may be beneficial to society, "working supplies the crucial feeling of being a useful member of society, and that feeling is indispensable to self-respect and emotional well being" (Gans, 1976: 1). Unemployment influences the quality of family life and mental health, the political and economic sphere and also crime and delinquency.

In addition, the way labour is utilized by the economy not only influences crime but may have a direct impact on the way society responds to those who commit crimes. One historical approach notes that when labour was scarce, for example, when the British colonies were being established in America and Australia, the prevailing philosophy was not to waste labour by sentencing criminals to prison or to execution but instead to send them to work in penal colonies abroad (Rusche and Kirchheimer, 1939). There were labour shortages in the eighteenth century in certain parts of the world, but the picture changed in the first part of the nineteenth century in Europe. After the Napoleonic Wars, soldiers returned home to compete with other labourers. Crime increased, and the demand for harsher treatment of criminals became widespread. In the first half of the nineteenth century, England, France, Switzerland, Bavaria, and Prussia saw the high frequency of crime as resulting from weaknesses in legislation and court practices. Punishments for criminal acts became harsher during this period.

If history repeats itself, periods of high unemployment may lead to potentially productive labour wasting away in jail and further rationalizations for keeping young people out of the job market. Simple suggestions regarding juvenile delinquency prevention should be regarded with suspicion, but creating satisfying jobs for everyone in society, including children, may be one obvious way to reduce delinquency.

A counterforce to some of these factors involving unemployment may be found in the changing age distribution in North America (Mohr, 1976). Children are becoming scarcer, as many unemployed teachers can testify. The reverse baby boom will soon be reaching adolescence, and the adult world may not work as hard keeping this energetic but troublesome group ghettoized in what has been labelled the "youth culture." There is some debate over the causes of the youth culture. Did youth create it, or was it imposed on them? It is possible that the adult world has been happy to use a variety of distractions to keep young people from competing for adult roles.

In Chapter 8, I argued for community-based corrections programs as opposed to institutional ones. These strategies probably should not be seen as either treatment or rehabilitation, but rather as the creation of situations that avoid making matters worse.

If a juvenile is kept in contact with the community, he is not automatically insulated from a delinquent subculture, nor is he necessarily in contact with those community elements which would lead to nondelinquency. Compared with institutional programs, however, a number of delinquency reducing mechanisms are potentially available. As we have already emphasized, one of the most important is employment. Admittedly, the work pattern for many juvenile delinquents is sporadic and not inclined to lead to a stable involvement in the work force. The work opportunities open to urban, lower-class youth are relatively unrewarding compared with the excitement and companionship of street life

(Short and Strodtbeck, 1965: 39-40, 222-227). Efforts to create the conditions of stable employment for these juveniles should be part of a strategy for maintaining community contact. In other words, an isolated community-based program will have little effect if juveniles do not gain access to opportunities in the larger community.

The task of maintaining community contact, then, must be the responsibility of society as a whole rather than one or two branches of government. A strong sense of community shared by juveniles is essential to the reduction of delinquency. In the early 1960's there was some hope that the Office of Economic Opportunity would be able to make meaningful changes among the "hard core" poor in the U.S. The results of the program were disappointing, but the insights of Amos and Wellford are still valid today (1967:Ch. 13). Some urban areas are simply not communities and thus lack the mechanisms to help juveniles develop a stake in society. Canada may be in a slightly better situation than the United States in this respect. There has been more support for multiculturalism, at least officially, and the remnants of community life may be stronger in the working class areas and slums of Canadian cities.

In the 1920's in Vienna the socialist government of that city built housing complexes which had remarkably different social consequences than some of the housing projects built in places like Chicago during the same era. A genuine social cohesiveness seemed to develop; there was an interest in education; athletic and other activity groups were a part of the structure of the housing complexes; and generally there was a sense of identity. There was also political influence, because people living in these complexes tended to be working class members of the socialist party, which ruled the city of Vienna, and usually was a powerful minority at the national level. Perhaps the key here was genuine political influence. By comparison, enclaves of working class people in urban centres in North America have relatively little political clout.

There is considerable merit in trying to encourage a stable and integrated lower class culture (Gans, 1962; Hackler, 1961). By contrast the North American model encourages working class people to struggle to move up the socio-economic ladder and leave their roots behind. For example, the school system encourages everyone to strive toward college. When we think of a community, we think of a middle class community. When we talk of changing attitudes of juvenile delinquents, the goal is to supplant them with middle class values.

Do we tend automatically to define working class people as failures? A well-integrated lower class community, which provided its own rewards for involvement, would less likely be a breeding ground for delinquency. Such a community might have values that differ from middle class values without necessarily being inferior or harmful to society. Basically, many community-based programs favour involvement in a "constructive" community as defined by middle class values. We do not seriously consider the possibility of encouraging a non-criminal, lower class community. We approve of lower class communities in North America when populated by "quaint" ethnic groups, such as the Chinese communities in Toronto, Vancouver and San Francisco. But when the second or third generation lives in similar areas, we judge that they have failed. The sons and daughters, to be deemed successful, should have left the "ghetto."

To summarize, maintaining contacts with a viable and appreciative community is one way of reducing those acts which violate the norms of that community. At the present time we expect juveniles to identify with a middle class community which is foreign and in many respects inaccessible to them. As long as the only acceptable community is strange and aloof, it will not receive the loyalty and affection of juveniles and is more likely to be the target of their aggression and exploitation.

It is realistic to recognize that society will not be restructured simply to change the pattern of delinquency. However, delinquency is only one indicator of societal stress. If a number of social problems could be alleviated by a well-integrated working class structure, perhaps this goal should be an element in policy thinking. Such reforms would require political action. Some argue that Canada has never had a dynamic political system. Both major political parties are closely linked with corporate enterprise (Porter, 1965: Chapter 12). Unlike the United States, however, meaningful reform parties with socialist ideologies have attained power at the provincial level. Beginning with the C.C.F. in Saskatchewan which evolved into the New Democratic Party, this political element has had a strong impact in British Columbia, Saskatchewan and Manitoba. A viable socialist political party which unified the working classes and provided them with the political influence that would enable them to demand their share of the benefits of the system could be a more effective way of dealing with certain types of social concerns than our present system, which pretends that opportunity is equally open to all. Would a well integrated working class, with political clout, provide an identity for many delinquency prone youth? However, the acceptance of a stable and cohesive working class is unlikely in North America because it would undermine the values of upward mobility and ever-increasing productivity that are essential to the present socio-economic system.

Increasing family support

There is a great deal of agreement on the importance of the quality of family life to adolescent behaviour. To argue that our society needs to devote resources to maintaining and improving the quality of family life is neither new or controversial. Canada has a family allowance plan which automatically pays benefits to all mothers. There is no means test or any other criteria to classify recipients as being in a lower social position. In other words, there is direct, though admittedly modest, financial support given to all families in Canada.

In the United States, there seems to be different pattern. After a family falls apart, various agencies spring to its aid, and the process may lead to a family having to go through the degrading process of identifying itself as "a family in trouble." There is some hazard in identifying a family as "a problem" before providing extensive help. If all families were seen as worthy of preventative maintenance, we might reap a better return for our investment. In Canada, we have no grounds to be smug about our social service, but there seem to be more widespread precedents for basic social services compared to the United States.

There is a whole complex of social services related to the quality of family life. Child care services may be crucial to maintain a one-parent family. Workmen's Compensation programs that support workers while they recuperate from an injury are illustrations of services that indirectly influence the quality of family life. Some people complain about providing such services free to people who can afford to pay for them. Wedded to a free enterprise philosophy, they would rather risk the suffering of borderline cases than help someone unnecessarily. However there is no way of making necessary services in society available to everyone who needs them without making those services universal. Some will decry the decline of the "rugged individualism that has made this country great" or the "threat of creeping socialism," but one of the positive characteristics of Western society has been a trend toward providing certain basic services to everyone in that society as a right not a privilege. Indirectly, these services relieve certain pressures that are factors in delinquency.

Suggestions for Small-Scale Projects to Decrease Delinquency

In the above section we have discussed large-scale societal support programs. Such programs do not lend themselves to piecemeal approaches but require a commitment to principles. I will now turn to suggestions for individual small-scale projects that could be just as valid approaches to the delinquency problem as large, all-encompassing programs which give the impression they are carefully thought out and coordinated.

Providing child shelters

It has been noted that our society has a proclivity to "help" juveniles do those things which we feel would be good for them. Rarely do we try to create situations where a juvenile would be relatively free to work through his or her own problems. Sometimes, juveniles find themselves in a strained family situation and would like to leave temporarily. One of the services a community might offer to juveniles is a temporary shelter, a place juveniles could come to with no questions asked. Obviously, such a place could not be completely free of rules or restraints. Sympathetic staff should be present to listen to those who want to talk about their situation; however, a counselor does not have to spring into action and get something done. There may be some merit in letting the juvenile initiate necessary steps with a staff member providing consultation and occasionally expediting matters. For example, a juvenile may wish to contact his home and let them know where he is. On the other hand, he may not. Suppose an irate parent wants to come down and remove the juvenile forcibly? This could be a touchy situation, but there are a variety of ways of providing a juvenile with "protection."

While staying in a shelter for a few days, a juvenile could continue attending school and maintain other social contacts. Most cases of family stress are temporary and usually children do not intend to stay away from home, nor are they so alienated from their parents that the emotional ties are completely ruptured. A cooling-off period may permit a juvenile to return home without having been exposed to other community situations which could have increased the likelihood of delinquency.

These shelters could be attached to some other sort of institution, a YMCA, a community centre, etc. The important point is that action be initiated primarily by the juvenile and that there is available a counselor or some other adult who is ready with suggestions, alternatives, and the ability to expedite a strategy worked out by the youngster. At the present time, our mechanisms for child care tend to swallow up a child and transfer the decisions to professionals who supposedly know what to do. A strategy of cooperation instead of control is suggested here. Obviously, the mechanics of such a strategy would vary tremendously from community to community. The reader should note that my choice of a child shelter is primarily an illustration of a principle: providing help that leaves the main choices in the hands of the client.

Utilizing "gatekeepers" to society

It is common for neighbourhoods populated by delinquent gangs to have a hangout in a store managed by an individual who is opposed to illegal behaviour. Frequently, such individuals have a fairly close attachment to the boys and girls in the neighbourhood. In one neighbourhood of "Mid-City" a gang called the Bandits hung out at Ben's Variety Store (Miller, 1969). Ben was the owner and sole employee of the variety store, which was the physical and psychic centre of the Bandit gang. Ben had been there for years and looked on the whole of the Bandit neighbourhood as his personal fiefdom and responsibility. He knew everybody and was concerned with everybody. He sold groceries, extended credit, put on bandaids, and advised the world in general, and the Bandits in particular, on a variety of issues. He was a bachelor and had adopted the neighbourhood as his extended family and the two hundred adolescents who hung out on the corner as his sons and daughters. Ben watched their adventures and misadventures with indignation, disgust and sympathy. He voiced strong opinions on many issues, including the behaviour of the younger generation.

While constantly criticizing the delinquent behaviour of the Bandits and predicting that they would end up in serious trouble, he was also supportive of them in times of need. One boy had just quit his job, saying that the pay was poor and the supervisor was bossy. But the boy did not want to tell his mother for a while because it would upset her. Ben was concerned. While giving a lecture about staying with a job, he also gave the boy money to give to his mother so she wouldn't know that he had quit.

Although the Bandits stole extensively from the surrounding community, they never stole from Ben. While the Bandits considered it their right to make trouble in and around the store, they were indignant at the temerity of "outside" kids daring to consider Ben's a target of illegal activity.

The role played by Ben in his community is not rare. There seem to be a number of "gatekeepers" to conventional society who live, work and interact in a milieu where delinquency is common. While openly opposed to criminal behaviour themselves, they maintain social ties and emotional bonds with delinquent youngsters. Theories of delinquency neglect the importance of these informal community leaders who often fill the role of professional social workers (Riviera and Short, 1967).

The question is: could these "gatekeepers" to conventional society become a bridge which would enable delinquents to make an easier transition to mainstream society? Supposing Ben were allowed to hand out five college scholarships each year? Would it be wise if the welfare worker checked with Ben before cutting off an allowance?

It is worth noting that society invests heavily in social workers who have to learn how to develop rapport with delinquents, psychologists how to empathize with their clients, and probation officers how to provide guidance for juveniles under their supervision. Most of these professionals have little success opening up the gates to conventional society. Making use of people like Ben might be no more successful, but it would be a far less expensive and wasteful way of utilizing community resources in the prevention of delinquency.

The New Technology: Slave or Master?

There is little doubt that technology is changing our world dramatically. It is not always possible to predict the consequences of such changes and how they might influence delinquent behaviour. Social control agencies are already utilizing this technology rather effectively. We might ask ourselves if this technology could be utilized in more imaginative ways. Let us examine a situation which may be a potential source of conflict between juveniles and police. One technology of interest is recording of the human voice to make "voice prints" that can identify people in a manner similar to the use of fingerprints.

Let us imagine that a policeman is walking a beat and sees a long-haired young man standing on a street corner. The policeman suspects that the young man may be engaged in selling heroin. He walks by and says hello. The young man answers, "Hello." The policeman is wearing a concealed microphone which picks up the voice of the young man, relays it by radio to a central computer, which checks the "voice print" with the voice prints of all those who have been picked up for heroin trading in the past year. Finding that there is no record of involvement in heroin trade, the computer sends back a message to the policeman which says, "Looks like this is just another man with long hair."

One may see this as a terrible misuse of technology to help Big Brother keep watch on us; but there is another aspect to the question. Could we use the same technology to avoid misunderstandings and unnecessary conflict? Let us look at the way stereotyping helps all of us, including police, do our jobs.

As part of social life, all of us are utilizing certain clues and characteristics to put people in categories. At times this system will lead to errors, but rather than being an undesirable mechanism, it saves much time and energy and will be with us forever. In addition, the notion that stereotypes are inaccurate is questionable (Mackie, 1973). If the policeman confronting the young man is provided with correct information as soon as possible, a problem might be avoided. Many of our problems arise when police act inappropriately. In a world where social control agencies operate in the midst of strangers, devices that would help people assess each other accurately could be helpful.

In the area of credit, a centralized information storage system works efficiently to expedite the cashing of cheques, etc. For example, when a person in a strange city finds himself short of money, he can go to a bank and get cash if he provides the bank with the information necessary to check his reliability as a borrower. Many would agree that the technology that expedites this process is advantageous, while others regard it as an invasion of privacy. However, we sometimes forget that even with a low level of technology, various agencies are continually going through the process of sorting and classifying people into good and bad credit risks, those who are potentially dangerous, allergic to certain drugs, etc. It is somewhat naive to think the process will change.It is also interesting that many people feel more comfortable if the technology is inaccurate, fearing that perfection would lead to universal social control. Yet surely procedures that would minimize the errors that occur between agencies of social control and their clients would have more advantages than disadvantages. Keeping a file of voice prints, gathered unobtrusively, obviously raises a number of ethical questions, but the potential gains resulting from using technology to decrease error should be taken into account.

We might extend this logic a bit further. In small, cohesive communities, everyone knows everyone else and therefore they are all in a position to exert social control. Such a society has an advantage in terms of preventing certain types of deviant behaviour. Of course there is also the disadvantage of individual freedom and social variety being severely limited. Is there some way to achieve a balance between the freedom possible in large urban settings and the benefits which accrue from informal social control devices which make it difficult to deviate in socially harmful ways? As an RCMP officer from a rural area commented, "When you see Mabel's car go by and it isn't Mabel behind the wheel, you get suspicious."

Let us turn to another illustration which might be more relevant to juvenile delinquency. A junior high teacher had a class made up of students who were slower than average readers. One day a new student came to class. Her parents were migrant farmers and she arrived in the community in the middle of the term. Since the counselor had no other school records, and since Maria had moved frequently with her Mexican parents, she was placed in a slow class. In a very short time it became clear that Maria was in fact intellectually above average. The teacher was faced with a dilemma: Maria liked the other students in the class very much and they liked her in return. Which was more important, the psychological security of friends, or the intellectual stimulation of a more challenging class? Before the term ended, Maria's parents had to leave the community to follow the crops. In frustration all the teacher could do was to give Maria a letter, asking her to give it to her next school counselor. In that letter the teacher tried to point out that this Spanish-speaking child with an irregular school pattern was neither illiterate nor lacking intelligence. However, mild-mannered Maria probably would not push this letter under the nose of the first counselor she would see and insist that she be assessed more appropriately. In this situation *accurate* information would be preferable to reliance on stereotypes.

School systems and their record keeping are not unlike many other agencies which interact with children in terms of categorical and stereotyped thinking. While it may not be possible to react to everyone as an individual, technology could at least improve the accuracy of the information which forms the basis of that agency's response to the individual child. In other words, our bureaucracies and other complexities of modern life may be hardest on those individuals who come from the disadvantaged portion of society. Assuming that these bureaucracies will continue, is it not possible that one of the most highly developed technological areas available to us, communications, could not be utilized more effectively to correct some of the damaging aspects of this system?

The Mass Media

While we are on the topic of technology, let us focus on the mass media. The evidence about the impact of television violence on the behaviour of youngsters is not clear at present, but there may be little merit in the vast amount of violence which prevades our mass media. In the present wave of police programs, rarely can we sit through a half an hour without seeing a policeman shoot someone. If a child is considering a career as a policeman, what sort of image does he have? Is this the sort of image we wish to have of our policemen? Juveniles learn to anticipate that a confrontation with a police officer will mean looking down the wrong end of .38 Special.

Basically, television seems intent on convincing children that policemen are violent people who constantly interact with violent citizens. If a child has any inclinations toward violence, this is obviously the career for him. In fact, the police spend much of their time assisting people. Of course showing policemen in a helping role would not make an exciting TV program.

Some laboratory experiments suggest that children learn aggression from film-mediated models and then perform this behaviour under suitable circumstances (Bandura, 1965). Others have argued that television can only feed the malignant impulses that already exist in some children (Schramm, Lyle and Parker, 1961). Hartnagel, Teevan and McIntyre (1975) showed that adolescents didn't seem to be directly influenced by TV violence as much as younger children, but suggest some indirect effects.

> Adolescents may be less susceptible to the influence of televised violence than are younger children. Alternatively, by the time of adolescence children may have already been exposed to a large quantity of violent television content and have acquired from such an exposure a repertoire of violent attitudes and behaviours. The main socializing effects of exposure to television violence may have already occurred by adolescence. . . . Television may make viewers so accustomed to violence that they define it as normal. Violent television content may also generate the attitude that violent means for resolving disputes are acceptable, or at least effective (348-349).

It should be noted that while the public complains rather loudly when bad guys use violence in the comics or on the screen, violence is tolerated when good guys clobber bad guys. In the real world, the distinction between good guys and bad guys is not so clear. Is it possible that observing many role models for violence, even if performed by good guys, creates a potential for violence in general? Minimizing violence in our mass media might not have a direct impact on the increasing violence which may have reached its peak during the late sixties; however, one could argue that a society which finds violence so fascinating is also a society that can anticipate its wider use by people in all walks of life, be they policemen, robbers, hockey players, drunken husbands, or juveniles. There is abundant evidence that we model our behaviour after others. Therefore it is not surprising to find that dramatic crimes are contagious. The publicity given to "skyjacking" seemed to lead to more incidents of this sort. Kidnap attempts have become epidemic in certain countries. Assassination attempts on public figures breed other such attempts. Under these conditions one could argue that the technology which has led to almost immediate communication of violent events has also made a contribution to violent juvenile crime.

If we are genuinely concerned about juvenile delinquency we should consider changes in the focus of our mass media. True, there may be objections to manipulating these media and the gains may not be very consequential; but since any progress in this area will be modest, changes in this direction are worth considering.

Chapter 14

Increasing the Odds in the Juvenile Justice System

The best we can hope for is to discover the costs of certain kinds of actions—of the controllers as well as the controlled—and the conditions under which such knowledge will enter into evaluation and policy formation.

—EDWIN LEMERT

Making the Role of Coercion Explicit

Those working within the juvenile system frequently deny that their activities contain any punitive motives. This is unrealistic. Instead we should recognize that parents, schools and agencies have and use a variety of coercive tools. Society takes action to prevent delinquency because its behaviour pattern causes problem for *us*. Perhaps this should be made more clear: we should say to delinquents, "It is not *your* welfare that is paramount in our minds but *our* well-being. Your behaviour is annoying and we will make it painful for you if you persist." Such reasoning makes sense to most juveniles.

Recommending physical punishment for delinquent behaviour is not the best way to maintain one's reputation as a "bleeding heart." However, let us tell the story of Johnny, who failed the sixth grade twice and entered the seventh grade with many strikes against him. Johnny was considered a problem by a number of people. His prognosis was poor, and his mother had trouble controlling him. Like many children with problems in school, Johnny was slightly above average in intelligence and had a pleasant personality, but his talents were not directed toward those activities which traditionally lead to success. In the classroom he demonstrated his ingenuity by the many imaginative ways in which he disrupted lessons. Johnny's antics came to dominate every class and his teachers were unsuccessful in competing for the attention of the other students.

Johnny's academic performance was poor and his disruptive behaviour became famous throughout the school. Johnny's math teacher seemed to get along with him better than most of his teachers and he tried to intervene to help Johnny. However, Johnny's parents did not respond to his invitations to discuss Johnny's behaviour and although

Johnny developed a friendly relationship with his math teacher, no other progress was made. One day Johnny stole a book from the library. The math teacher heard of it and brought Johnny before the principal. Johnny was suspended until his parents would come to the school.

The problem was to work out some sort of strategy that would have meaning. Johnny was clearly intellectually capable. During those rare occasions when he paid attention in class or prepared his homework, Johnny participated effectively in classroom activities. Therefore, the math teacher reasoned, if Johnny would simply prepare his homework, he would be more likely to take part in class in a positive manner. When the parents appeared, they admitted having difficulties with Johnny and agreed to go along with any suggestions the school made. The math teacher offered Johnny a "contract." The contract stated that Johnny would agree to do all his homework and other school work. That was *all*.

The contract said nothing about disruptive behaviour, "being good," or anything related. Johnny was simply to do his school work. The contract was made out in multiple copies and duly signed by Johnny, his math teacher, his parents, the vice-principal and the principal. Everyone seemed to be satisfied with the contract, including Johnny.

To monitor this process, Johnny would first check with his English and history teacher, who would give him a short note to take to his math and science teacher. If his work was completed, he could go home as usual. If not, he would have to sit down and complete it in the math teacher's classroom. If he failed to do this, he would have to go to the vice-principal the next day, who would call Johnny's father, who would then come to the school and administer one swat with a paddle. If the father could not be reached or wished to delegate the authority to the vice-principal, the swat would be administered by the vice-principal. These conditions were all in the contract.

Shortly afterwards, Johnny arrived after school in the math teacher's class saying that his bicycle had a flat tire and he just *had* to catch the bus. The math teacher invited Johnny to have a seat and start on his lessons. The math teacher would call Johnny's mother and tell her that he would be late that evening. Another time Johnny arrived after school with a limp. "I'll never be able to walk on this sprained ankle." The math teacher responded, "Have a seat, Johnny. I'll find a stick for you that will serve as a crutch." Johnny was imaginative, but the math teacher was adamant. Both Johnny and the math teacher were able to see the humour in the situation and their relationship remained positive. In addition, Johnny was performing much better in the classroom and increasingly finished homework at home in advance.

One day Johnny did not appear in his math classroom after school. He went home without having checked with the math teacher. The next day the math teacher asked him when was a good time to fulfill his contract.

There was no anger, no recriminations. The vice-principal called the father who predictably delegated the task to the vice-principal. The math teacher asked Johnny if he had remembered to wear his heaviest pair of pants and both teacher and student seemed to be on good terms when they visited the vice-principal. The vice-principal was a cheerful man and as the three of them reread the contract, it was clear what had to be done; but the contract did not say whether Johnny was to receive an "easy" swat or a "hard" one. After a brief discussion the math teacher recommended an easy one. Both Johnny and the vice-principal agreed.

Johnny never found out what the "hard" swat was like. He never again failed to check with the math teacher after class and he soon found it was much easier to do his work on schedule so that he rarely had to stay after school. His scholastic performance improved dramatically and he became an eager participant in classroom activities. He was still a clown, but his humour frequently contributed to the lesson instead of detracting from it. He even became genuinely enthusiastic about some of his subjects and ended the school year for the first time with excellent grades. His rapport with both students and teachers had improved considerably.

Johnny's case may have been exceptional, and certainly many factors were involved in addition to a swat with a paddle. The point is, that some enforcement mechanism was needed to achieve the other goals. It would be desirable if enforcement mechanisms could operate in such a manner that they do not destroy the positive features of human relations. Frequently, in school systems where physical punishment is forbidden, students are scolded, preached to, and threatened with all sorts of punishments which never materialize. Society does not hesitate to use psychological devices to coerce children to obey, but for some reason we consider physical punishment more vicious.

The indiscriminate beating of children is obviously not recommended; however, if certain borderlines can be clearly drawn and enforced by a painful stimulus, such as a swat with a paddle, there may be greater freedom *within* those limits. For example, Johnny never feared physical punishment in the classroom and his relationships with his teachers and the vice-principal were much better after his "easy" swat than before. Thoughtfully administered physical punishment could play a positive role in controlling certain forms of deviance.

My earlier plea for tolerance does not imply that we should tolerate all forms of juvenile misconduct. Since society will continue to use various techniques for demanding conformity, it should select those which are maximally effective and minimally damaging. In school, if punishment could be administered with humour, with the feeling that a juvenile has paid his debt, and with personal acceptance on the part of a teacher, it could be a more effective deterrent than the unfulfilled threats and sometimes personal insults that are presently being used.

Physical punishment should naturally be used with care. Much of our present trend away from corporal punishment is based on the assumption that it is somehow more hurtful than the psychological bruises we currently administer to children while deceiving ourselves that we are helping them. Perhaps it would be healthier if we recognized that our concern is not primarily in "helping" but rather in getting juveniles to conform to societal rules. Johnny would not likely have been convinced if his teachers had tried to persuade him that they were trying to help him, but he could understand that, if he did not change his behaviour to suit his teachers' needs, he would suffer pain. If we made it clear to juveniles that the main reason we wish them to conform is for *our* benefit rather than theirs, more honest and effective communication would probably result.

As a word of caution, it must be remembered that problem children differ considerably. For certain types, physical punishment could be a mistake. In their study of the classification system for placing wards in training schools in Ontario, Lambert and Birkenmayer (1972) suggest that there are at least two categories of individuals. Those in the first category have lived in reasonably stable environments and do not show evidence of serious emotional disturbance prior to admission. They tend to have scholastic problems and have committed a delinquent act serious enough to lead to placement in a training school. The second category consists of those with emotional problems or who come from an unstable and hostile family environment.

For those who fall into the first category, structured settings with firm limits may be useful and the moderate use of physical punishment may be superior to other methods of "setting firm limits." On the other hand, physical punishment should be used more cautiously with those in the second category. It need not be avoided completely, because it is possible that mild physical punishment, which encompasses forgiveness, acceptance, and even a certain amount of humour, could have a positive therapeutic role. It is important, however, to be aware that punishment by itself is not therapy. Its use has to be assessed carefully in terms of accomplishing other goals.

How is physical punishment viewed by those processed by the justice system? Richard Ericson's study (1975) of an English detention centre revealed that the boys felt physical punishment to be much more just than other disciplinary measures. In general, boys in this institution felt the courts were unjust and many of the procedures of the detention centre humiliated them and were unfair. They also distinguished between staff members who were fair and unfair. Those who followed the rules (which were seen as pointless and unjust) by the book and took away a few days remission of sentence for violations were seen as unfair. However, those who gave the boys a "thumping" for violations but did not take away their "good time" were seen as fair. In general, those staff members who minimized social distance between themselves and the boys, avoided humiliating them, and occasionally did them favours were also likely to "thump" boys who got out of line. This method of maintaining discipline by the "good screws" was seen as just while formally prescribed disciplinary measures were seen as unjust. "Bad screws" also thumped boys and some were considered sadistic, but these staff members were condemned for their inconsistency and inappropriate responses rather than for the thumping itself.

Whose view of justice should prevail? Later we will discuss some of the newer trends toward a justice model rather than a treatment model for juveniles. If justice is to make sense, it has to be viewed through the eyes of its recipients. The categorical rejection of the use of punishment may be our hang-up, not theirs.

Punishment to reduce the impact of non-conformity

Jackson Toby has noted that the punishment of offenders sustains the morale of conformists.

> A student who studies hard and gets a lower grade on a quiz than students who cheat may become cynical about the principle of honest effort on examinations. One socially significant consequence of punishing non-conformists is that punishment may reduce the potentially disruptive effect of their non-conformity . . .
>
> Punishment is not mere vindictiveness. Without punishment "upright people" might be demoralized by the defiance of the collective conscience. If unpunished deviance tends to demoralize the conformist, punishment is a means of repairing "the wounds made upon collective sentiment" . . . One who resists temptation . . . would like to feel that these self-imposed abnegations have some meaning. When he sees others defy rules without untoward consequences, he needs some reassurance that his sacrifices were made in a good cause (1971: 501-502).

If rehabilitation programs had proven their effectiveness, we could dispense with this argument more easily; but most programs have little impact. Therefore, more attention to "justice" may provide its own reward.

The Use of Deterrents in General

The recent debate on capital punishment has tended to confuse the arguments surrounding the use of deterrents. The evidence related to capital punishment shows that it is an ineffective deterrent to violent crimes, but nevertheless it would be a mistake to believe that some criminal acts cannot be deterred. The question is, under what conditions will deterrents be effective? If punishment is fast and certain, the behaviour is more likely to disappear. When one puts a hand on a hot stove, one is "punished" rapidly and certainly. However, our criminal justice system works contrary to this rule. Punishment is usually slow and the likelihood of being punished for a specific crime is often small.

William Chambliss (1967) divides acts into *instrumental* and *expressive* behaviour. Instrumental acts are performed to achieve a specific goal. Expressive acts may express an emotion or act out a role. If the act is instrumental, for example, parking illegally or cheating on income tax, punishment is likely to be effective. On the other hand a woman who stabs her husband in response to continual beatings administered while he is drunk might be acting expressively. The threat of punishment is unlikely to be an effective deterrent.

Chambliss also argues that those with a *high degree of commitment* to crime as a way of life will be more difficult to deter than those who are less committed. Therefore, instrumental deviance by people with a low commitment to crime as a way of life may be deterred by the threat of punishment. The wife who is considering poisoning her husband for his life insurance, an instrumental act by a person with low commitment to criminal behaviour, might be easily deterred. However, many drug addicts whose behaviour may be expressive and impulsive, and who have a high commitment to a life of crime may not be deterred by the threat of punishment.

Chambliss argues that our society tends to punish most severely those persons and crimes that are least deterable and punishes least severely those persons and crimes that are most deterable. It would be worthwhile to extend this logic to the treatment of juveniles. Middle class youths who only occasionally steal for a little spare change might be seen as instrumental types with a low commitment. For such people, deterrence might work. On the other hand, boys in a slum area whose status in the eyes of their peers is determined by their daring exploits might not be easily deterred.

There are other variables which should be considered in developing a typology of acts which vary in their susceptability to deterrence. Laurie Beveridge, in a seminar at the University of Alberta, suggested that whether or not a crime is *mala prohibita* or *mala in se* would also make a difference. Is the crime wrong because it intrudes upon the rights of others as *defined by law* or is it wrong in itself? Figure 14.1 presents a chart which utilizes the notion of commitment to conventional society, the nature of the act, and the type of law violation to generate a typology of offences. The middle column outlines whether punishment is typically certain or severe for each type of offence. The right-hand column attempts to judge the effectiveness of punishment. While it might be difficult to find the empirical evidence which would complete the chart accurately, it is worthwhile discussing the utility of such a framework. For example, we have placed the skid row drunk in a category where the punishment tends typically to be certain. Probably the severity of that punishment differs from community to community. Our rating of the punishment for these offenders as medium may in fact be misleading. If

Figure 14.1
A Typology for Assessing the Likelihood and Efficacy of Punishment

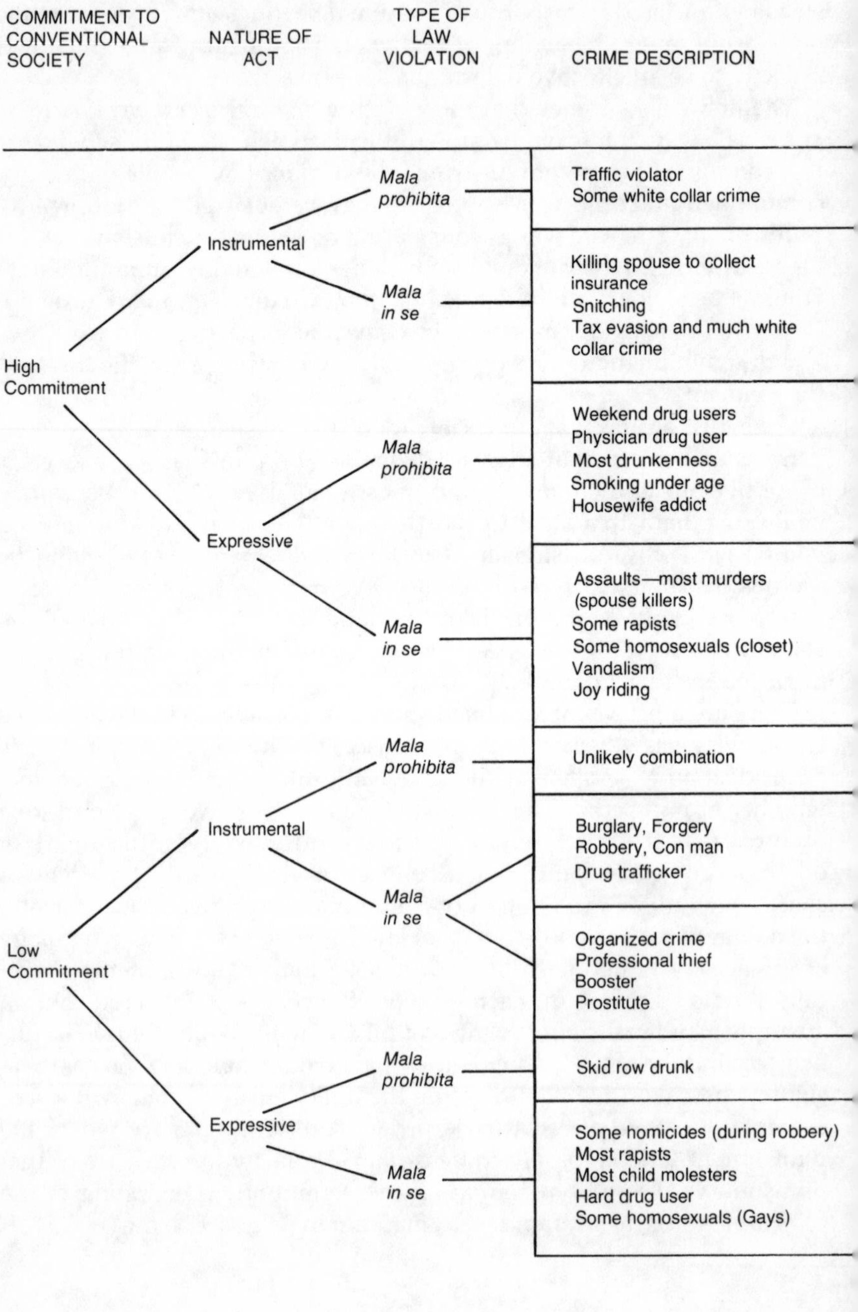

TYPICAL PUNISHMENT IS		EFFECTIVENESS IF PUNISHMENT WERE	
CERTAIN	SEVERE	CERTAIN	SEVERE
Med	Low	High	High
Very Low	Very Low	High	Med
High	High	High	High
Med-Low	Med-Low	High	Med
Low	Low	High	Med
Low	Med	Med-Low	Med-Low
Med-Low	Med	Med-High	Med
Low	Low	Med	Med-High
Low	Low	Med-Low	Med-High
Low	Low	Med	Med-High
High	High	Med-Low	Low
Med-High	High	Med-Low	Low
Low	Med	Med-High	Med-High
Low	Low	Med	Med
Med	Low	Med	Med
Not applicable		Not applicable	
High	Med-High	Med-High	Med-Low
Med	High	Med-High	Med-Low
Low	Med-Low	Med	Med-Low
Med-Low	Med	Med	Med-Low
Med-Low	Med	Med	Med-Low
Med-High	Med-Low	Med-Low	Med-Low
Very High	Med	Low	Low
Med-High	High	Med-Low	Med
Med-High	High	Med-Low	Low
Med-High	High	Med	Med
High	Med-High	Low	Low
Med-Low	Med	Low	Low

we look at the effectiveness of punishment, we could probably argue that even if punishment is certain for the skid row drunk, it is low in effectiveness. Similarly, severe punishment would probably be ineffective.

It is important to emphasize the arbitrary nature of this chart. There is nothing "true" about a classification scheme. Other variables might prove to be more rewarding. In addition, the way various behaviours have been classified could differ depending on who is making the decision. For example, we have homosexuals classified as *mala in se*. There may have been some agreement on such a decision thirty years ago, but today many would place homosexuality in another slot or more likely remove it from any scheme of criminality. It is important never to think of such schemes as more than tools. If a scheme helps to sort out our responses to different types of deviance, then it is a useful tool.

The categorization scheme offered in Figure 14.1 is probably less useful for juveniles than for adults. Instead of the variables used here, variables which are more meaningful for juvenile behaviour are needed. For example, the two categories of offenders described by Lambert and Birkenmayer (1972), those from stable environments and those from unstable environments, would be logical variables to use. The point, however, should be clear. Examination of the combinations of situations, personalities, and other factors involved in delinquency is required to determine empirically whether various types of deterrents make sense. If punishment is being used in situations where it is least effective and not being used in areas where it might be beneficial, perhaps a shift in policy is needed.

Let us close this brief discussion on deterrence by simply noting that certain characteristics of sanctions need to be taken into account. These would include: the certainty and severity of the sanction, the speed with which the sanction is applied, and the status of the sanctioner. The last point implies that it makes a difference who does the sanctioning.

Actually, the situation may be much more complicated. For example, the probability of punishment may actually be less crucial than the *perception* of probability. Jensen (1969) found that adolescents who believed there was a high probability of punishment for delinquent offences tended to be less delinquent. Waldo and Chiricos (1972) found a similar pattern among college students for both marijuana use and theft. This was particularly true of marijuana use. They concluded that deterrence was more effective with respect to crimes that lack wide moral support. For behaviour that is more commonly considered immoral, informal sanctions or control by internal inhibitions are already operating, and deterrents may play a smaller role. This would be compatible with the finding that parking violators can be deterred more effectively than murderers. There are many informal sanctions against murder. If these fail, additional formal sanctions may not be effective.

To apply this logic to juveniles, one might argue that juveniles who see nothing wrong with occasional stealing would be deterred more effectively by punishment than those who commit more serious acts. Do delinquents and non-delinquents have differential perceptions of arrest and conviction? Claster (1967) found no significant differences between delinquents and non-delinquents in their knowledge of their probability of arrest and conviction; however, delinquents who thought they might commit various crimes perceived the probability of personal arrest to be lower than did the non-delinquents who thought they might also commit such crimes.

The renewed interest in deterrence will probably lead to meaningful explanations in the future, but presently there are only a few hints. Most deterrents will probably have a limited impact on serious crimes and on those acts where the probability of arrest is slight. The few serious acts of delinquency probably take place under conditions where a variety of informal sanctions have already failed. It is unlikely that additional formal sanctions will help. But most juvenile delinquency involves relatively minor offences, and in most of these situations the likelihood of arrest is very small. In other areas of behaviour, such as the detection of and punishment for cheating in the classroom, deterrents clearly seem to work (Tittle and Rowe, 1973). It seems that increased knowledge on the effectiveness of punishment will not influence policy as long as society continues to favour those in privileged positions who might be susceptible to punishment.

For the typical lower class juvenile offender, sanctions are generally uncertain. Usually they are not severe although juveniles sometimes get long sentences under the guise of treatment. Punishment usually takes place some time after the event and is administered by people who may or may not have credibility in the eyes of the juvenile. Although certain punishment could deter some delinquency and may make a contribution to justice, it is unlikely that punishment *per se* will deter in the majority of situations.

The Adminstration of Juvenile Justice

There has been a recent movement in North America to pay more attention to the rights of children. One aspect of this controversy concerns juvenile court legislation. A series of articles by Michael Valpy in the Toronto *Globe and Mail* in May 1973 reflects some of these concerns. The cliche, "in the best interests of the child," has evidently provided flexibility in the juvenile court, but the rights of the child have sometimes been ignored and some cases have been judged in a way that appears arbitrary by the standards of the adult criminal justice system. Let us ask whether or not more formal procedures in juvenile court would have positive returns.

From the standpoint of the adult world, to spend relatively little time proving the guilt or innocence of a child in juvenile court may make sense. Our Juvenile Delinquents Act of 1929 expressed the mood of its time. Delinquents should be seen as in need of care rather than in need of punishment. For many decades now the focus has been not on what delinquents have done but how they can be rehabilitated. From the standpoint of the *juvenile,* however, the notion of justice may be very important. A fair trial may in fact be a contributing factor to the effectiveness of any further procedures.

In Austria, for example, every juvenile *must* be defended by a lawyer (for adults a lawyer is optional). The Austrian state attorney is not quite the same as our prosecuting attorney because he sometimes brings out facts on behalf of the defendant as well. However, the courtroom procedure is formal and after the presentation of the case, the two judges plus the two lay judges and the court scribe leave the room to deliberate before returning to announce the verdict. In over 90 percent of the cases the child is judged guilty. In some cases one could argue that the defence was not particularly thorough, and it is quite possible that some sort of recommended program for the child was worked out before the trial began (Hackler, 1975), but from the point of view of the juvenile, it is clear that a genuine trial has been held.

Relatively little research has been done to see whether the person processed by the criminal justice system really understands what is happening. For example, a young Indian served time in an institution in the Northwest Territories. After being released he told his friends that everyone treated him very nicely and he was well fed and housed. However, he complained that no one had paid him yet!

A basic aspect of our criminal justice system is that the person being punished cannot "benefit" from the experience unless he understands the reasons for that punishment. This applies to juveniles as well and viewing the system as one which punishes rather than helps would be closer to reality and would make more sense to most juveniles. There has been a tendency to talk to a juvenile about his family, his relationships with siblings, etc., but relatively little time is spent talking about the crime that was committed. It is no wonder that repeating offenders show little evidence of a sense of responsibility for the criminal acts they have committed.

Even if punishment were swifter and more often administered, the rehabilitative aspects of a sentence in a juvenile court should not be ignored. Perhaps a juvenile should be required to pay for damages or perform work for a victim. A contract of restitution could be used.

At the present time, a juvenile comes into a system that is both powerful and extremely lenient. Most juveniles are under the influence of informal mechanisms which make serious delinquency rare. But another category of juvenile offender is influenced by criminogenic factors. Not only does he lack adequate role models for conforming behaviour, but peer pressures and other factors are supportive of delinquent behaviour. Such a juvenile sees the juvenile court and the police as part of a system to be opposed and manipulated. Although these experiences may be negative for a few individuals, and may criminalize them, many experienced delinquents adapt to the system with relatively little strain. Again, these are juveniles who are not necessarily emotionally disturbed, but who have been socialized in a different manner. For such individuals, normal socio-dynamic factors are operating. A system which, *from their perspective,* is comprehensible, fair and predictable, might have positive impact.

One concern is that the rule of law would permit shrewder juveniles to escape punishment. Should this be a major concern? A characteristic of the adult court system is that the odds are supposed to be on the side of the defendant. For some reason the same standard does not apply to the juvenile. Juveniles are forced to accept "treatment" regardless of their guilt or innocence. Unfortunately, there is little evidence that the treatment received does any good or that a youth who somehow avoids the system is worse off.

If a higher percentage of juveniles were "acquitted," there is no evidence that the results would be less effective than finding a child guilty, lecturing him, threatening him if he does not shape up, and then assigning him to a probation officer. For those who were found guilty, punishment could lead to more respect for the system.

Another alternative to the traditional juvenile justice system has been attempted in East Palo Alto, California, a community with a high delinquency rate. The program has a panel of six young people ranging in age from sixteen to twenty-nine. Panel members talk informally with young people accused of crimes and discuss what can be done. A youth who is dissatisfied with a panel decision is free to disregard it, but in nineteen months not one of the 157 youths who came before the panel objected to the decision made on his behalf.

If juvenile delinquents lack faith in the juvenile justice system, such panels of peers might have merit. At present society systematically excludes certain groups from responsible roles. Making the system appear fair to those involved, and combining this with mechanisms which make it painful when someone fails to meet reasonable demands, may have some advantages over the present situation.

To summarize, although the power of the juvenile justice system tends to be used benevolently, the clients of the system rarely appreciate this benevolence. Lessening the power of the system through the introduction of procedures used in adult courts, while increasing the likelihood of modest punishment if one is found guilty, might permit the system to operate more in keeping with basic principles of human behaviour.

Suspendees, restrainees, and isolatees

A few people who have been highly critical of the treatment approach in corrections have suggested some interesting alternatives. Wilks and Martinson (1976) talk about three categories of offenders, according to whether the offenders need a warning, restraint or isolation. Wilks and Martinson suggest that if a person were convicted, he would receive a fixed sentence to custody, but this would almost always be suspended unless there were some indication that the person could not be deterred. A *suspendee* would not report to a probation officer or submit to any treatment. He simply would have to avoid conviction for another offense. If convicted while a suspendee, he would have to serve a sentence as a *restrainee* or as an *isolate*. Restrainees require more than the threat of law alone to deter them from illegal behaviour. Like suspendees, restrainees would not be required to report to probation officers or receive treatment, but they would be placed under surveillance. The restraining agent would have no direct contact with the restrainee, would not be known to the restrainee, and would have no police powers. The sole purpose of the restraining agent would be to observe the restrainee and call the police if he observes the restrainee committing a crime. To guard against corruption, agents would be periodically shifted to different restrainees. The restraining agents could be para-professionals, for example, ex-offenders, unemployed teenagers and housewives. Wilks and Martinson suggest that this does not have to be an expensive proposition because most people lead a highly scheduled existence and a random pattern of surveillance would suffice. An important feature of this strategy is that the fate of the individual is in his own hands. The third category of isolate is not new. It simply implies segregation, and the assumption is that incarceration is punishment.

Would this strategy make sense for juveniles? Almost always, first offenders in juvenile court are returned home. Threats of future punishment are made, but they are usually vague rather than specific. Wilks and Martinson simply suggest that the threat be made specific. During periods of suspension or restraint, a juvenile would naturally have access to a counselor or any other child welfare services, but there would be no confusion between the justice and the welfare system. Taking part in any program with welfare would not prevent punishment. Punishment would be avoided only by not committing crimes. Similarly, welfare staff would have no power to influence punishment.

Wilks and Martinson offer isolation only as the third stage. However, one could consider other forms of punishment, such as shoveling snow or possibly one swat with a paddle. However, the third stage is not treatment—it is clearly punishment. In the case of juveniles, one could apply this logic without using severe punishment, but the punishment *must* be administered if criminal acts are committed and the isolate stage is used.

Such a model is clearly legalistic. It denies completely the use of various treatment programs. It argues that the courts should not sentence people to treatment. Let us pursue the idea of putting the choice of treatment even further into the hands of clients. Assume for a moment that a juvenile placed in isolation or under restraint might be given vouchers for various services.

The use of vouchers for various services

Juveniles who are forced into treatment programs may respond negatively. A juvenile or adult prisoner who participates in a specific program with the belief that it will increase the likelihood of early release may have a greater interest in manipulating the release process than a sincere desire to change. Greenberg (1973) has suggested that a voucher system might be one way of increasing the effectiveness of some of the services already in existence. For example, a juvenile placed in a training school might receive vouchers worth one thousand dollars. This "money" could be spent for psychiatric services, counseling, vocational training, education classes, books, magazines, musical instruments, arts and crafts supplies, or athletic equipment. The residents would be able to pool their funds if they wished to purchase services that are too "expensive" for a single client. The juveniles would have complete freedom to purchase whatever they wanted, regardless of whether administrators considered their choices to be unsuitable.

At present, administrators and staff of training schools have little or no vested interest in the popularity of their programs. They can continue to provide whatever services they feel are appropriate as long as they meet the requirements of the institution. Theoretically, the voucher system would enable the clients to "fire" those professionals who were less competent and unable or unwilling to provide satisfactory goods and services. This would be a genuine incentive for treatment staff to make their programs appealing to their charges.

The relationship between treatment personnel and clients might also change. At the present time treatment staff are part of the "prison administration" In a setting where treatment personnel see themselves as having more in common with administrators than with the clients, and the clients share this assessment, the conditions for effective treatment may not exist. Under the voucher system those counselors who are seen as unfair, aloof, or ineffective by the clients would be in trouble. The clients could terminate their employment simply by withholding vouchers.

Admittedly, many influential forces in the delinquency field would find the above suggestions unacceptable, but some sort of modified scheme might be seen more favourably. Job security for treatment personnel could be guaranteed while still providing flexibility depending on the demands of the clients. One could even manipulate the prices being paid for services. If the psychiatrist was not popular, his services might be offered for fifty cents an hour. The price of athletic and musical equipment could be high. However, it may be dangerous to move too far from realistic costs: a juvenile may not respect the services of a fifty cent per hour psychiatrist.

A voucher system might be expanded outside a training institution. Could a juvenile purchase a probation officer? A volunteer? Tuition in an auto mechanics course? Actually, a voucher system should be seen as only one of many imaginative attempts to make basic changes in a poorly functioning system. These wild schemes would probably not be dramatically successful, but certainly little would be lost if such experiments were attempted. Yet it is unlikely that the systems presently processing juveniles are willing to become so imaginative, flexible and adventurous.

Individualization versus uniformity of sentencing

Since this book is primarily concerned with juveniles, it may seem inappropriate to focus heavily on sentencing. Many would argue that early intervention is necessary to prevent delinquency. The problem is that earlier intervention techniques have not been effective (Wolfgang, Figlio and Sellin, 1972). Although the dividends to be had by concentrating on sentencing practices will undoubtedly be small, it may be one of the areas where public policy can in fact bring about change.

Before attempting to make recommendations regarding the sentencing of juveniles, we must face the problem of individualization versus uniformity of sentencing. A system which focuses primarily on justice would argue that uniform punishments should be assigned for given misdeeds. The twentieth century has seen the growth of sentences "tailored to the individual" with the hope that this strategy will rehabilitate the offender. This principle has also been applied to juveniles.

Lynn McDonald of Dalhousie University provides a perceptive discussion of these two sentencing approaches (1969). She notes that the individualized approach draws its greatest supporters from people who are typically the most attuned to injustice and abuse (1969: 12). Despite the damage done by some treatment, the advocates *mean* well, but in fact the individual sentencing approach may result in punishing the weak and least responsible more than those who are strong and more responsible.

Reduced responsibility for a criminal act provides some justification for punishing the offender less. A man with many personal problems may be seen as less responsible than a person under less stress. The weaker man might deserve less punishment than the stronger, but McDonald points out that the present version of individualization of sentence reverses the pattern. "The same characteristics that make a man seem less to blame for his behaviour also makes him a worse prospect for training" (1969: 14). Instead of focusing on the question of responsibility, the focus could shift to the probability of future criminal acts. The clever, middle class juvenile who gets caught may be seen as highly responsible, but he is also a good risk in the future. Individualization of treatment would argue that society gains little by treating such people harshly. Individualization in terms of responsibility and ability, on the other hand, would argue that the middle class juvenile should be treated more severely. In practice, the juvenile or young adult who has received the short end of the stick most of his life receives more "treatment" even though it is increasingly difficult to distinguish treatment from punishment. The individualization principle leads to the most severe penalties being imposed on the weakest members of society.

With uniform sentencing a juvenile court judge would have to sentence the mayor's son to the same punishment as a child who has been a ward of the welfare department. One implication of such sentencing patterns might be that the powerful people in society would favour more modest punishments. In fact, that may have happened in the case of marijuana violations. As more middle and upper class youths received harsh penalties, there was resistance to the severity of the punishment. Punishing the strong may be an effective way of being sure that the laws are carefully reviewed. By contrast, punishing or treating the weak does not lead to public scrutiny. There is no similar force for correcting abuses where a rehabilitation philosophy is maintained. This mentality assumes the offender is sick and needs treatment. The advice of the sick is not usually sought or accepted. Hence a justice model creates pressures for external review. A treatment model creates a pattern where unjust practices can be more easily hidden from the public view.

McDonald (1969) notes that although retribution and uniformity of punishment can be cruel, the scale of punishments in a uniform scheme can be legislated more easily. By contrast, a treatment approach, along with individualized treatment, often contains punitive elements that are not visible to the public and difficult to control. McDonald closes her paper with an attempt to assess the consequences of a shift to retribution from rehabilitation. Under retribution those who would be punished the most severely would be the most blameworthy morally—the sinners; under rehabilitation the most severely punished would be those most difficult to treat—the nonconformists or misfits. Extending this logic to juveniles, as one emphasizes rehabilitation for children who need help, middle class children typically escape treatment (or punishment). On the other hand children from lower class families, especially those that seem inadequate in a variety of ways, would be more subject to court intervention. This process could lead to a further lowering of status of such problem families.

Uniform sentencing would emphasize various forms of punishment rather than treatment. While this may not automatically have an impact on delinquency *per se,* society might become much more interested in its training schools if middle class parents knew their delinquent children were just as likely to be sentenced to them as lower class youths. If the police, probation officer, and courtroom process did not emphasize the differences in the inadequacy of various families but instead focused upon the delinquent act, the inequalities between social classes might decrease. Social services to families would still be available but they would not be delivered under the guise of rehabilitation programs for juvenile delinquents.

How to translate some of these ideas into a coherent sentencing policy? Since rehabilitation programs have been minimally effective, they should be used much more cautiously in the future. In the meantime, a serious look should be taken at the effectiveness of mild punishment. Mild punishment used more frequently and over a wider strata of juveniles may be more consistent with justice than some of our present techniques.

The efficacy of short periods of incarceration

At the present time, we attempt to make training schools relatively pleasant places. Is this a reasonable strategy? The assumption is that boys who go to such places are very tough, consider the experience a joke, and gain status among their peers from their stay. This assumption was questioned when Baum and Wheeler found that the initial experience for most of these boys was quite unpleasant (1966). They missed their homes, their mothers' cooking, and saw their new colleagues as potentially dangerous. Over time boys do adjust to the training school, develop loyalties to other delinquents, share knowledge about criminal enterprise, and develop attitudes and norms that are consistent with their present situation (Ericson, 1975). In other words, does the potential punitive effect of incarceration become lost because juveniles eventually adapt to the environment of their incarceration?

An alternative strategy might be to make sure that the first few days in any institution are as unpleasant as possible, without being cruel. The more they miss their families and friends on the outside, the better. If released after a few days and returned home immediately, would there be any deterrent effect? It is difficult to say, but we do know that longer terms of incarceration tend to have a negative influence on future behaviour.

In a study of adult inmates Wheeler (1961) learned that attitudes toward the conventional world seemed to take the form of a U-shaped curve over time. Many prisoners entered the institution aware that they had done wrong and wishing to pay their debt to society. Basically, their attitudes were prosocial. With time they began to identify increasingly with the inmate subculture and develop more antisocial attitudes. Shortly before release, prosocial attitudes began to reappear. This phenomenon seemed to exist independent of the length of sentence. Richard Ericson (1975) discovered a similar shift in attitudes for boys in an English detention centre as they neared the time of release after a four-month incarceration. The implication is that the time between admission and release was unconstructive and if this period were to be shortened the same pattern would exist. In general, evidence from British and American studies suggest that longer institutional sentences seem to be no more effective in preventing delinquency than shorter ones (Hood and Sparks, 1970: 190). The argument that a child must stay in a training school long enough to "improve" has not been supported with factual evidence.

The use of short-term imprisonment as shock treatment for juveniles should be seen as very experimental. While it may be a reasonable alternative to a longer stay in a training school, the evidence is not available to justify frequent use of this strategy at this time (Friday and Petersen, 1973).

The use of fines

Some would argue that it is very difficult to be fair when imposing fines. Obviously there are a number of facets to the question of imposing fines, but some English studies suggest that fines are more effective than probation, imprisonment, outright discharge, and a variety of treatment programs (Hood and Sparks, 1970: Tables 6:2 and 6:3). Clearly, in our society, fines are considered to be a form of punishment. How about a choice between a fine and a swat with a paddle? Some may prefer the more heroic choice.

To summarize, our sentencing structure for delinquency is just as inadequate as other parts of the juvenile justice system. The administration of clear forms of punishment for those found guilty of delinquency is a strategy that merits serious consideration. There is no indication that much is gained by making such punishment prolonged or particularly intense. In fact, one could argue that the sooner the punishment takes place and the sooner it is finished, the better. Since society is concerned with developing and preserving a humane system, it is clear that sanctions should be only as painful or as restrictive as is necessary to achieve a defined social purpose. It is difficult to see how a policy of this sort, if kept public, could lead to serious abuse. Perhaps a few middle class juveniles would be over-sanctioned in terms of future delinquent involvement. The damage done to privileged individuals would probably be slight, but might be a fair tradeoff for the sense of justice which might develop in some lower class juveniles.

Chapter 15

The Uncertain Future

Oh wad some power the giftie gie us
To see oursels as others see us?
It wad frae monie a blunder free us,
An' foolish notion.

—ROBERT BURNS

What Sort of Knowledge Is Most Helpful?

Theoreticians can rarely resist the impulse to close a discussion without expressing the need for more research, and a number of other ritualistic phrases. We will try to disguise this procedure by suggesting that certain types of knowledge may be more useful than other types for meddling in the lives of others. Before we can ask ourselves what sort of knowledge is needed, it would be wise to look at the type of knowledge we already have.

What Type of Knowledge Do We Have?

Malcolm Klein (1973) suggests that there are three categories of assumed knowledge: clinical, theoretical and empirical.

Clinical knowledge evolves through an accumulation of personal experience. It becomes part of "gut-level" feelings about situations, is frequently anti-intellectual, and avoids abstract conceptualization. It may be "true" knowledge but it is also unverified and therefore untrustworthy. Different people can utilize their clinical knowledge to come to opposite conclusions. Klein argues that clinical knowledge has long-range value in its potential to provide insights, and hence can generate hypotheses which can be tested.

If a series of hypotheses can be linked together in a logical manner, theoretical knowledge develops. Obviously, Einstein's theory of relativity, Boyle's law, and a host of other well integrated theories enabled physicists, engineers and others to predict, control and modify the natural world dramatically. Alas, the major theories in delinquency might be seen as still struggling to be born.

There has been a tendency to expound popular theories rather than test them. When empirical tests have been made, the results have generally been disheartening. Not only are the structures of most theories of delinquency inadequate, when they occasionally do make clear statements about the real world, the evidence frequently does not support them.

The third category of assumed knowledge is empirical data. We must be cautious here because many of our "facts" are questionable due to inadequacies in research design, sloppy research procedures, etc. We do know that open institutions, half-way houses and residential treatment centres have yet to prove their value in rehabilitation, but they are no worse than standard institutional settings. Moreover, although ineffective, they are less expensive.

This logic brings us to community treatment projects which, as noted earlier, produce mixed findings. But possibly the most important empirical fact to come out of community treatment programs is not the impact on the offender but rather the *response of the community* to such activities. Klein (1973) illustrates the problem with a seminar he conducted with some architectural students. He gave the students some data on crime and recidivism rates and asked them to design an approach (not a facility) suitable for corrections. They came up with a modern, vocationally oriented, maximum security prison.

Next, he told them that recidivism rates for such institutions were very high. They went back to the drawing board and the result was an open institution. Again they were told of high recidivism rates for such institutions and to design an alternative which would take into account that rehabilitation needed some contact with home and neighbourhood. The new design was a residential treatment centre.

When Klein suggested that recidivism figures were still high in such cases, even though building and maintenance costs were lower, the architecture students were still unwilling to go along with a final suggestion that supervised treatment *in the community* would be the next strategy. That idea was not acceptable. This situation illustrates a major dilemma: the application of knowledge versus the demands of a public that wishes to keep certain problems at arm's length. To oversimplify, the facts suggest that juvenile delinquents cannot be rehabilitated outside of the community, but most people do not want them in their community. At the same time, many feel they should be rehabilitated.

In the field of delinquency prevention, our clinical knowledge conflicts with reality, our theoretical knowledge is woefully inadequate, and our empirical data are overwhelmingly negative in terms of providing positive suggestions. While other disciplines can justifiably claim that "someone should listen to us," scholars in the field of deviance have little to offer. Those of us who consider ourselves experts in the field continually criticize the simplistic solutions offered by the layman, but where does our specialized knowledge take us? At this stage our recommendations for prevention programs should not be given a great deal of weight. Perhaps we should also note another interesting characteristic of social science knowledge: those who have weak and inadequate theories are still frequently among the most vocal in terms of providing advice for social policy.

Are there certain selected categories of required knowledge that are more promising for the future? Klein describes four areas where there is great need for more knowledge. Action research might generate answers to some of these important questions.

1. As delinquency prevention programs move toward increasing levels of community treatment, they must concern themselves with levels of tolerance within the community for this type of activity.

> How do we assess their tolerance levels? How do we build up the tolerance thresholds? What kinds of offences and what kinds of offenders are more visible and which are more easily tolerated by the property owner, the parent, the police officer? What kinds of community settings are likely to exhibit predictable reactions? (1973: 44).

Despite the concern with these questions we are still limited to clinical knowledge in dealing with them. We need to have theoretical and empirical knowledge now, in order to avoid endlessly repeating our past mistakes.

2. How does one incorporate successful aspects of a program into a regular program? How does one eliminate or modify negative aspects of programs?

Careful research reports tend to end up in that graveyard of evaluations, the administrator's filing cabinet. They rarely lead to change. In fact, one disclosure of the ineffectiveness of a work-study program led to its expansion by agency administrators (Longstreth, Shanley and Rice, 1964). Klein argues that researchers and practitioners need to participate in joint research ventures on the organizational and political contextual factors related to program experimentation and the utilization of research findings. We need empirical evidence on the advantages of in-house versus non-in-house research.

3. Collaboration between researchers and practitioners tends to get blocked by differences in values, language, experience, and by honest misunderstandings. Therefore, we need to do research on the collaborative process itself. The resulting knowledge should be incorporated into the training of both researchers and practitioners.

4. Community agencies, police, court officials, and correctional agencies act as if they had separate societal mandates. It makes little sense to assess the effectiveness of one element within the larger criminal justice system and assume that it somehow is not influenced by the total system. Therefore we need a total systems analysis of the criminal justice system that can trace the impact of changes made in one part of the system. Effectiveness can only be tested if we know what is happening in the other component parts of the system.

As long as we seek the cure for crime in the family, neuroses, the ghetto, etc., we will overlook political issues that affect society's response to delinquent behaviour. Klein concludes that we must organize our research questions around the nature of the problem, not the nature of our several professions.

Researchers, scholars, politicians, and people in positions to influence public policy tend to assess delinquency from a single perspective and exclude all others. This makes it difficult to question assumptions and be open to a range of alternatives. For example, the common approach to delinquency prevention has focused on the problems within the juvenile. This perspective often blinds us to other factors which may be more important. Sometimes, this view is broadened slightly to include the family, but there is still little recognition that the dynamic workings of our welfare system, schools, and courts may be contributing factors to delinquency.

There are others who take the opposite view. Crime or delinquency is a "status" or a characteristic assigned by society to certain individuals. This perspective in its extremity ignores the reality that individual children are different. Even if we assume that many situations influence individual behaviour that are outside the control of the individual, we find that some individual characteristics must be taken into account if we are to understand delinquent behaviour and develop intelligent policies.

Of course one may study a single causal factor for scientific purposes. One may wish to focus on an individual characteristic such as extroversion-introversion or on the class structure of society to see how much utility such factors have in explaining crime or delinquency. Unfortunately some academics become wedded to the factors they are studying and credit them with greater influence than they deserve. Although it is impossible for everyone to be completely objective, it is necessary to recognize that psychiatrists will favour certain variables, sociologists others, and people working in welfare and court systems will have their points of view as well.

The Utilization of Basic Principles of Behaviour

Explanations of delinquency, and policies designed to change it, should be compatible with basic principles governing human behaviour. This statement may appear indisputably obvious, but for some reason many of our strategies seem to treat delinquency as if it were an unique entity totally unrelated to normal behaviour. To illustrate, our behaviour is moulded by the opinions of people we like. We sometimes do silly things in order to please our friends. We also refrain from doing things we would like to do and things we believe are correct because we are afraid that such behaviour might be disapproved of by our friends. One might prefer not to smoke marijuana (or drink alcohol, or commit adultery, or commit daring acts of theft) but being with friends who give status for these acts naturally tends to increase the likelihood that such behaviour will take place.

Such behaviour might be explained by cognitive dissonance, a theory dealing with individuals.

Cognitive dissonance

There are many basic principles of human behaviour that might be utilized effectively in the delinquency issue. For example, the cognitive dissonance theory argues that people will attempt to reduce "strain" in their social systems (Festinger, 1957). A boy who commits delinquent acts because of pressure from his peer group may find it difficult to maintain the belief that such delinquent acts are wrong. Once committed to these activities through group pressure, it may be easier to rationalize his behaviour as appropriate. Such a rationalization permits the reduction of emotional strain. If we were able to understand the strains which exist in adolescent social situations, perhaps we could predict behaviour more effectively. Furthermore, we might be able to introduce new strains into the system which could only be resolved by nondelinquent behaviour.

Since delinquency prevention requires an understanding of the way components of the criminal justice interact, it behooves us to look at theories that look at groups as well as individuals.

Group interaction

In his presidential address to the Society for the Study of Social Problems, Edwin Lemert (1974) suggested that it might be profitable to view societal reaction to deviance as group interaction. He reviews some of the deficiencies of the labelling approach, radical criticisms, and older conceptions of symbolic interaction. In trying to understand how procedures for defining deviance arise, he argues that the results cannot be viewed as the creation of any one group. Rather, the emergence of a new morality, and also programs that reflect such attitudes, could be profitably viewed as the interaction of groups. The judges, court workers, and police are not a single entity; they are representatives of the many groups which somehow must coordinate activities toward a common goal. The psychologically oriented theories of George Herbert Mead suggest "taking the role of the other" to discover what is in the minds of those creating changes, but this process does not take into account the interests and claims of various groups that must decide on the amount of time and energy they will expend, or other values that must be sacrificed in order to reach certain goals. Compromises and expeditious behaviour typify most group interaction. The juvenile justice system would appear to be an appropriate focus for such an orientation.

The willingness to intervene

The community in which juveniles live will play a role both in the definition of deviance and the way in which the society responds. In a study of two thousand households in Edmonton, attempts were made to determine differences in neighbourhoods that might influence delinquency (Hackler, Ho and Urquhart-Ross, 1974). It was hypothesized that in those neighbourhoods where there was a great deal of cohesiveness among residents, a communication network develops which is related to lower rates of delinquency. This cohesiveness would also lead to a greater inclination to respond to delinquency informally and take action within the community rather than involving the police.

The findings were confusing. The ideas received support among those neighbourhoods that were low in social mobility but were not supported when those neighbourhoods with high social mobility were tested as a group. In other words, the dynamics which might lead a community to respond vigorously to potential deviance may differ according to the type of neighbourhood. A stable neighbourhood might function according to the pattern described here, but in other types of neighbourhoods, different factors might be more important. The point is that there are few studies that attempt to understand how neighbourhoods respond to deviance and how this might influence official responses to delinquency. If the community plays a major role in delinquency prevention, studies of community cohesiveness and related variables are necessary.

We have been restricted in our thinking by treating delinquency and its prevention as if they were something special. However, general theories of behaviour may be more useful. We have briefly noted some ideas at the individual, group and community level. Students of social policy must be aware that specialized theories of delinquency may be less adequate than theories that bring together a wider portion of the social spectrum.

Awareness of fads versus the accumulation of compatible knowledge

It seems that fads are a normal part of human behaviour. However, it might be profitable to recognize that fads influence our explanations of delinquency and our response to it. While it may be difficult for those in policy-making positions to resist some fads, it might be wiser not to build long-term programs based on their popularity. A look at some past fads might be revealing. In his book, *The Manufacture of Madness,* Thomas Szasz tells us that in 1885 in Paris hysteria was treated by the surgical removal of the ovary. In London and Vienna it was treated by the surgical removal of the clitoris. In Heidelberg it was treated by the cauterization of the clitoris. In 1905, Bernard Sachs, prominent New York psychiatrist and author of *A Treatise on Nervous Disease of Children,* recommended treating masturbation in children with cauterization of the spine and genitals (1970: 293-4).

At the present time there is a great deal of emotional debate over psychiatric procedures, much of which is the result of conflicting fads within the profession. Faddism, therefore, should be treated as a serious factor when evaluating theories and programs. Some of these fads may make major contributions; however, weighing each new program against accumulated knowledge based on the scientific method would be a safer way to proceed in terms of long-range policy.

Am I being inconsistent in arguing for the utilization of scientific knowledge while being skeptical of the careful evaluation of experimental programs? In one sense, such experimental programs and their evaluation would be a major source of scientific knowledge. However, the tremendous resources demanded by such programs and their negative implications suggests that they provide only a small return. There are a variety of other knowledge-seeking procedures which are more profitable. To develop meaningful delinquency prevention programs, we need to tolerate a wide range of intellectual inquiry. Given time the better ideas prove themselves. While this process seems to be much slower in the social sciences than in the physical sciences, and particularly tardy in the field of crime and delinquency, the tendency is there. If each new fad can be measured against the yardstick of knowledge, policy issues will not be resolved, but more meaningful programs should result.

Who Benefits by Defining Delinquency?

To understand delinquency prevention we must also understand who benefits the most when delinquency is defined in certain ways and when it receives a great deal of public attention.

It is important to understand our own responses to "evil." We like to think in terms of "causes" of delinquency, since the notion of causation suggests there are cures. The search for causes and the identification of social problems takes political, social and economic routes. For example, the emergence of the "drug problem" is an excellent example of the political nature of problem identification and definition (Reasons, 1974). A number of scholars have examined the dynamics surrounding the evolution of the drug problem, identifying the "moral entrepreneurs" who initiated legislation and for years were able to sell a particular type of morality to most of the social control agencies in North America. Similar questions have not been asked of the "delinquency" problem. By focusing on "cures," we fail to realize that many people and agencies have a vested interest in the way delinquency is defined and treated.

Most social "problems" come and go (Berger, 1976). Divorce was seen as a social problem in earlier sociology texts. Today, divorce seems to be considered less of a social problem than it was at one time. Ecology was an issue that arose some years ago, then faded, only to return with renewed vigour in the last decade. Delinquency and crime currently have a high profile in the public's awareness.

We need to ask who began the agitation that led to the recognition of delinquency. What sort of interest groups will gain by elevating a certain form of human behaviour to the status of a "problem?" During the prohibition of alcohol in the United States, both organized criminals in the bootlegging business and groups like the Women's Christian Temperance Union were working to maintain prohibition. The bootleggers wished to maintain their profitable illegal business and the WCTU was simply against drinking. One might argue that when a variety of different interest groups is rewarded for the official recognition of a problem, the likelihood of discovering a "problem" increases.

Certain agencies also benefit if problems are defined in new ways. Tove Dahl (1974) describes how the Norwegian educational system and a number of other interest groups in the country found it to their advantage to create a Child Welfare Act. As in North America, the claim was made that these services were offered to help children. Dahl believes these new definitions of the problem were primarily for the benefit of the agencies and other institutions.

Has the creation of juvenile delinquency as a special social problem served the needs and interests of selected portions of the population who were in a position to implement the necessary legislation? In an insightful article, Blumer (1971) notes that social problems come into being through a process of collective definition. This process determines whether social problems arise, whether they become legitimated, and how they are taken into account in official social policy.

> Sociologists who seek to develop theories of social problems on the premise that social problems are lodged in some kind of objective social structure are misreading their world. To attribute social problems to presumed structural strains, upsets in the equilibrium of the social system, dysfunctions, breakdown of social norms, clash of social values, or deviations of social conformity, is to unwittingly transfer to a suppositious social structure what belongs to the process of collective definition (1971: 306).

While some scholars might take issue with Blumer, more questions need to be asked about how social problems come to be defined. The inability of certain groups to gain attention for what they believe to be problems is also an area of interest.

The interdependency of causes is another frustrating fact of the delinquency prevention system:

> . . . a system in which the roots of action are numerous, intertwined, and not uniformly entangled. Some roots are more closely bound to each other; some are stronger than others. It may be impossible, however, to disentangle one source of action from all

> others. In dense causal systems there are ramifications. Touching the system here effects it there, and there, and there. The despair of the would-be societal engineers is this fact, that in the social web one cannot "do just one thing." One cannot change a law, enforce it, ignore it, or enact any reform of our collective enterprise without starting a chain of effects, many of which are bound to be unforeseen and some of which are bound to be undesirable (Nettler, 1974: 250).

Although Nettler probably views delinquency from a different perspective than Blumer, both of these scholars raise issues that are traditionally neglected when well-meaning citizens attempt to "do something" about delinquency. As Blumer would suggest, the very motivation to do something needs to be explained. Are they really selecting the problem of delinquency because it is a burning issue to be solved? Why spend time and energy in this area when other areas of concern are neglected? Answers to such questions are not obvious, but the formation of action groups responding to perceived problems must be studied as a phenomenon in itself, in addition to those individuals or situations defined as the problem.

The typical citizens' committee on youth crime is interested in cures. This very orientation places certain limitations on the questions that will be asked. The type of persons who serve on such committees will be influenced by a number of political and personal factors. If a government wishes a certain credibility, high status persons and a few "experts" will be included. Depending on the political goals, the committee will include broad or narrow representation. The needs of these individual committee members as well as the needs of the groups they represent will influence the dynamics of the committee and the outcome. When a committee is finished studying the "problem," a report must be issued and recommendations made. Such recommendations will probably take the form of a list of changes to be made in our current social control procedures. The work of such committees should not be seen as worthless, but on the other hand, they probably have no consequential impact on delinquency. The "ripple effect" from such recommendations will depend on the influence the committee has on other policy making bodies. Such influence may also be irrelevant to the problem of delinquency. New legislation might serve various interest groups and the psychological needs of the society without serving juveniles. Attempts to see the larger dynamic process might encourage humbler recommendations rather than the arrogant ones that are now proposed so readily.

The reader has probably noted that this book did not try to cover everything about delinquency. For example, it spent little time describing various types of delinquency. It also spent little time discussing "causes" of delinquency. While these topics are important to the Canadian scene, they are not particularly *unique* to Canada. My concern was to focus on some of the ways society responds to delinquency. Again,

Canada may not be unique, but perhaps our smaller population compared with that of the United States makes the gap between the public, the researcher, and the policy-maker somewhat smaller. Therefore, it makes sense to discuss this aspect of the problem with the hope that Canadians can develop procedures that will not consist primarily of imitating the mistakes made elsewhere.

Bibliography

Adams, Stuart
1959 "Effectiveness of the Youth Authority Special Treatment Program: First Interim Report." Research Report No. 5. Sacramento: California Youth Authority (mimeo).

Adams, Stuart
1961a "Effectiveness of Interview Therapy with Older Youth Authority Wards: An Interim Evaluation of the PICO Project." Research Report No. 20. Sacramento: California Youth Authority (mimeo).

Adams, Stuart
1961b "Assessment of the Psychiatric Treatment Program, Phase I: Third Interim Report." Research Report No. 21. Sacramento: California Youth Authority.

Adams, Stuart
1967 "A cost approach to the assessment of gang rehabilitation techniques." Journal Research in Crime and Delinquency 4: 166-182.

Adams, Stuart
1974 Personal correspondence.

Adams, Stuart
1975 Evaluative Research in Corrections. US Department of Justice, National Institute of Law Enforcement and Criminal Justice.

Ahlstrom, Winton M. and Robert J. Havighurst
1971 400 Losers. San Francisco: Jossey-Bass.

Amos, William and Charles Wellford
1967 Delinquency Prevention: Theory and Practice. Englewood Cliffs, New Jersey: Prentice Hall.

Andrews, D. A., J. S. Wormith, D. J. Kennedy, and Wendy Daigle
1973 "The attitudinal effects of structured discussions and recreational association between young criminal offenders and undergraduate volunteers." Ministry of Correctional Services, Toronto.

Andrews, D. A., G. J. Young, S. Wormith, Carole Anne Searle, and Marina Kouri
1973 "The attitudinal effects of group discussions between young criminal offenders and community volunteers." Journal of Community Psychology 1: 417-422.

Baker, Keith, John Irwin, Steven Haberfeld, Margorie Seashore and Donald Leonard
1973 An Evaluation of New Gate and Other College Prison Education Programs. Report to the Office of Economic Opportunity.

Bandura, A.
1965 "Influence of models' reinforcement contingent upon the acquisition of imitative responses." Journal of Personality and Social Psychology 1: 589-95.

Barkwell, Lawrence
1976 "Differential treatment of juveniles on probation: an evaluation study." Canadian Journal of Criminology and Corrections 18: 363-378.

Baum, Martha and Stanton Wheeler
1966 "Becoming and inmate." in Stanton Wheeler (ed.) Controlling Delinquents. New York: Wiley.

Berger, Bennett
1976 Comments on Mel Kohn's paper at Social Problems meeting. San Francisco, August, 1975.

Berger, Robert, Joan Crowley, Martin Gold, John Gray, and Martha Arnold
1975 Experiment in a Juvenile Court: A Study of a Program of Volunteers Working with Juvenile Probationers. Ann Arbor: Institute for Juvenile Research.

Berleman, William C., James R. Seaberg, and Thomas W. Steinburn
1972 "The delinquency prevention experiment of the Seattle Atlantic Street Center." Social Service Review 46: 323-346.

Black, Donald J. and Albert J. Reiss, Jr.
1970 "Police control of juveniles." American Sociological Review 35: 63-77.

Blumer, Herbert
1971 "Social problems as collective behavior." Social Problems 18: 298-306.

Bottoms, A. E. and F. H. McClintock
1970 Unpublished paper cited at pp. 206-207 in Roger Hood and Richard Sparks, Key Issues in Criminology. New York: McGraw-Hill.

Bottoms, A. E. and F. H. McClintock
1973 Criminals Coming of Age: A Study of Institutional Adaptation in the Treatment of Adolescent Offenders. London: Heinemann.

Bourdon, André
1966 L'Influence de la libération conditionnelle sur la conduite future du délinquant: Analyse comparative de l'éffet sur le délinquant, d'une sortie sous libération conditionnelle et d'une sortie fin sentence. Unpublished MA thesis. Université de Montréal.

Brewington, Sue
1971 "Adult probation under volunteer supervision." District Court of El Paso County, Colorado Springs, Colorado.

Brown, P., P. Zelhart, and B. Schurr
1975 "Evaluating the effectiveness of re-education programs for convicted impaired drivers." In S. Israelstam and S. Lambert (eds.), Alcohol, Drugs, and Traffic Safety. Toronto: Addiction Research Foundation of Ontario.

(Canada) Commission of Inquiry into the Non-Medical Use of Drugs
1973 Final Report. Ottawa: Ministry of National Health and Welfare.

(Canada) Department of Justice
1965 Juvenile Delinquency in Canada. Report of the Committee on Juvenile Delinquency. Ottawa: Department of Justice.

(Canada) Department of the Solicitor General
1973a Report of the Task Force on Community-Based Residential Centres.

(Canada) Department of the Solicitor General
1973b The General Program for the Development of Psychiatric Services in Federal Correctional Services in Canada. Ottawa: Information Canada Ottawa: Solicitor General of Canada.

Canadian Committee on Corrections
1969 Towards Unity: Criminal Justice and Corrections. Ottawa: Solicitor General of Canada.

Caplan, Nathan
1968 "Treatment intervention and reciprocal interaction effects." Journal of Social Issues 24: 63-88.

Carlson, Kenneth A.
1973 "Some characteristics of recidivists in an Ontario institution for adult male first-incarcerates." Canadian Journal of Criminology and Corrections 15: 397-411.

Cassidy, R. Gordon, Elizabeth Cole, Carolyn Fuller, George Hopkinson, and Heather Milne
1974 Criminal Justice Process in Canada, 1963-1971. Statistics Division Report #4/74. Ministry of the Solicitor General and Secretariat of the Treasury Board (mimeo).

Cavior, N.
1972 "Facial attractiveness and juvenile delinquency." Paper presented at Eastern Psychological Association Convention.

Chambliss, William J.
1967 "Types of deviance and the effectiveness of legal sanctions." Wisconsin Law Review, Summer: 703-719.

Chambliss, William and Robert Seidman
1971 Law, Order, and Power. Reading, Massachusetts: Addison-Wesley.

Chapman, L. J. and J. P. Chapman
1967 "Genesis of popular but erroneous psychodiagnostic observation." Journal of Abnormal Psychology 72: 193-204.

Chorover, Stephan L.
1973 "Big brother and psychotechnology." Psychology Today 7: 43-54.

Claster, Daniel
1967 "Comparison of risk perception between delinquents and nondelinquents." Journal of Criminal Law, Criminology, and Police Science 58: 80-86.

Collie, J.
1972 Personal correspondence.

Cohen, H. L.
1968 "Educational therapy: the design of learning environments." In J. M. Shlien (ed.), Research in Psychotherapy. Washington, D.C.: American Psychological Association.

Commission on Obscenity and Pornography
1970 Report. New York: New York Times.

Cousineau, D. F. and J. E. Veevers
1972 "Incarceration as a response to crime: the utilization of Canadian prisons." Canadian Journal of Criminology and Corrections 14: 10-31.

Cressey, Donald R.
1958 "The nature and effectiveness of correctional techniques." Law and Contemporary Problems 23.

Dahl, Tove Stang
1974 "The emergence of the Norwegian Child Welfare Law." Scandinavian Studies in Criminology 5: 83-98.

Danet, B. N.
1964 "Prediction of mental illness in college students on the basis of 'Non-psychiatric' MMPI profiles." Journal of Consulting Psychology 68: 136-143.

Davies, D. I. and Kathleen Herman (eds.)
1971 Social Space: Canadian Perspectives. Toronto: New Press.

Davis, Carolyn
1974 "The parole research project." In Keith S. Griffiths and Gareth S. Ferdun (eds.), A Review of Accumulated Research. Sacramento: California Youth Authority.

De La Paz, Celso
1974 Impact Evaluation Summary, Reduction of Delinquency Through Expansion of Opportunity (RODEO), March 1967-December 1971. Report of the Los Angeles Probation Department.

Desroches, Fred
1973 "Regional psychiatric centres: a myopic view?" Canadian Journal of Criminology and Corrections 15: 200-218.

Deutscher, Irwin
1974 "Toward avoiding the goal-trap in evaluation research." Paper presented at annual meeting of the American Sociological Association in Montreal.

Deutscher, Irwin
1975 "Social theory and program evaluation: a metatheoretical note." Paper presented at annual meeting of the American Sociological Association in San Francisco, California.

Deutscher, Irwin
1976 "Public issues or private troubles: is evaluation research sociological?" Sociological Focus 9: 231-237.

Dickover, R. M., J. A. Painter, and V. E. Maynard
1970 A Study of Vocational Training in the California Department of Corrections. Research Report No. 40. Sacramento: Department of Corrections.

Doleschal, Eugene and I. Anttila
1971 Crime and Delinquency Research in Selected European Countries. Rockville, Maryland: National Institute of Mental Health.

Doleschal, Eugene and Nora Klapmuts
1973 "Toward a new criminology." Crime and Delinquency Literature 5: 607-626.

Elliot, Delbert S. and Harwin L. Voss
1974 Delinquency and Dropout. Lexington, Massachussets: Lexington Books.

Empey, LaMar
1967 Alternatives to Incarceration. Washington, D.C.: U.S. Department of Health, Education and Welfare, Office of Juvenile Delinquency and Youth Development.

Empey, LaMar
1976 Review of the Effectiveness of Correctional Treatment. Contemporary Sociology 5: 582-583.

Empey, LaMar, and Maynard Erickson
1972 The Provo Experiment. Lexington, Massachussets: Lexington Books.

Empey, LaMar T. and Steven G. Lubeck
1971 The Silverlake Experiment. Chicago: Aldine.

Erickson, Maynard L.
1973 "Group violations, socioeconomic status and official delinquency." Social Forces 52: 41-52.

Ericson, Richard C. and David O. Moberg
1968 The Rehabilitation of Parolees. Minneapolis: Minneapolis Rehabilitation Center.

Ericson, Richard V.
1973 "Turning the inside out: on limiting the use of imprisonment." John Howard Society of Ontario, Community Education Series 1, No. 3.

Ericson, Richard V.
1974 "Psychiatrists in prison: on admitting professional tinkers into a tinkers' paradise." Chitty's Law Journal 22: 29-33.

Ericson, Richard V.
1975 Young Offenders and Their Social Work. Westmead: Saxon House.

Evans, Robert Jr.
1973 Developing Policies for Public Security and Criminal Justice. Economic Council of Canada.

Eysenck, Hans J.
1961 Handbook of Abnormal Psychology. New York: Basic Books.

Festinger, Leon
1957 A Theory of Cognitive Dissonance. New York: Harper and Row.

Finlay, Doug and Dave Randall
1975 "Treating the 'untreatable' adolescent." Canada's Mental Health 23: 3-7.

Friday, Paul C. and David M. Petersen
1973 "Shock of imprisonment: short-term imprisonment as a treatment technique." Probation and Parole [no vol.] 33-41.

Fisher, Gene A. and Maynard L. Erickson
1973 "On assessing the effects of official reactions to juvenile delinquency." Journal of Research in Crime and Delinquency 10: 177-194.

Fogel, David
1975 We Are the Living Proof. Cincinatti, Ohio: Anderson Publishing Co.

Fulton, W. Scott
1969 A Future for Correctional Rehabilitation? Federal Offenders Rehabilitation Program, Final Report. Olympia, Washington: State of Washington.

Galvin, James, Kenneth Polk, Gerald Blake, and Garry Coventry
1977 "Diversion: positive alternatives or negative label?" Paper presented to Western Society of Criminology, in Las Vegas, February.

Gandy, John, Ruth Pitman, Margaret Strecker and Candace Yip
1975 "Parents' perceptions of the effect of volunteer probation officers on juvenile probationers." Canadian Journal of Criminology and Corrections 17: 5-20.

Gans, Herbert
1962 The Urban Villagers. New York: The Free Press.

Gans, Herbert
1976 "Jobs and services: toward a labor-intensive economy." Reprint from Center of Policy Research.

Giallombardo, Rose
1974 The Social World of Imprisoned Girls: A Comparative Study of Institutions for Juvenile Delinquents. New York: John Wiley.

Giffen, P. J.
1976 "Official rates of crime and delinquency." In W. T. McGrath (ed.), Crime and Its Treatment in Canada, 2nd Edition. Toronto: Macmillan of Canada.

Gill, Owen
1974 Whitegate: An Approved School in Transition. Liverpool: Liverpool University Press.

Gillis, Ronald
1973 "Types of human population density and social pathology." Paper presented to the Canadian Sociology and Anthropology Association, Kingston, May.

Glaser, Daniel
1969 The Effectiveness of a Prison and Parole System. Indianapolis: Bobbs-Merrill.

Glasser, William
1965 Reality Therapy. New York: Harper and Row.

Gove, Walter (ed.)
1975 The Labelling of Deviance: Evaluating a Perspective. New York: Wiley.

Gray, James
1972 Booze. Scarborough, Ontario: Signet.

Greenberg, David F.
1973 "A voucher system for corrections." Crime and Delinquency 2: 212-217.

Greenberg, David F.
1977 "The correctional effects of corrections: a survey of treatment evaluations," in David F. Greenberg (ed.) Corrections and Punishment: Structure, Function, and Process. Beverly Hills: Sage.

Grosman, Brian
1973 "The discretionary enforcement of law." Chitty's Law Journal 21.

Grygier, Tadeusz
1964 "The chronic petty offender: law enforcement or welfare problem?" Journal of Research in Crime and Delinquency 1: 155-170.

Guttman, Evelyn
1963 Effects of Short-Term Psychiatric Treatment on Boys in Two California Youth Authority Institutions. Research Report No. 36 Sacramento: California Youth Authority.

Hackler, James C.
1961 "The integration of a lower-class culture: some implications of a rigid class structure." Sociological Quarterly 3: 203-213.

Hackler, James
1966 "Boys, blisters, and behavior: the impact of a work program in an urban central area." Journal of Research in Crime and Delinquency 4: 155-164.

Hackler, James C.
1967 "Evaluation of delinquency prevention programs: ideals and compromises." Federal Probation 31: 22-26.

Hackler, James C.
1970 "Testing a causal model of delinquency." Sociological Quarterly 11: 511-522.

Hackler, James C.
1971 "A developmental theory of delinquency." Canadian Review of Sociology and Anthropology 8: 61-75.

Hackler, James C.
1975 "The flow of information in court: the juvenile court in Vienna as an illustration." Canadian Journal of Criminology and Corrections 17: 57-68.

Hackler, James C. and John Hagan
1975 "Work and teaching machines as delinquency prevention tools: a four year follow-up." Social Service Review 49: 92-106.

Hackler, James, Kwai-yiu Ho, and Carol Urquhart-Ross
1974 "The willingness to intervene: differing community characteristics." Social Problems 21: 328-344.

Hackler, James C. and Eric Linden
1970 "The response of adults to delinquency prevention programs: the race factor." Journal of Research in Crime and Delinquency 7: 31-45.

Hagan, John
1973 "Labelling and deviance: a case study in the 'sociology of the interesting' ". Social Problems 20: 447-458.

Hagan, John
1974 Criminal Justice in a Canadian Province. Unpublished Ph.D. dissertation, University of Alberta.

Hakeem, Michael
1958 "A critique of the psychiatric approach to crime and correction." Law and Contemporary Problems 23: 651-682.

Halleck, Seymour
1967 Psychiatry and the Dilemmas of Crime. New York: Harper and Row.

Hartnagel, Timothy F., James J. Teevan, and Jennie J. McIntyre
1975 "Television violence and violent behavior." Social Forces 51: 341-351.

Havel, Joan
1965 Special Intensive Parole Unit, Phase IV, Parole Outcome Study. Research Report No. 13. Sacramento: Department of Corrections.

Haynes, Steven C., V. Scott Johnson, and John D. Cone
1973 "The marked item technique: a practical procedure for litter control." Unpublished paper. Lexington, Kentucky: Kennedy Youth Center.

Heckbert, Doug
1976 Day Parole in Alberta: An Examination of Selected Benefits. Unpublished MA thesis. University of Alberta.

Hinsch, J., H. Leirer, and H. Steinert
1972 Ueber die resozialisierungsmassnahmen der Jugendgerichtsbarkeit und die Entwicklung jugendlicher Delinquenten. Vienna (mimeo).

Hirschi, Travis
1972 Review of The Silverlake Experiment. Social Forces 50: 529-31.

Hogarth, John
1971 Sentencing as a Human Process. Toronto: University of Toronto Press.

Hood, Roger and Richard Sparks
1970 Key Issues in Criminology. Toronto: McGraw-Hill.

Jacobs, Jane
1961 The Death and Life of Great American Cities. New York: Random House.

Jasinski, Jerzy
1966 "Delinquency generations in Poland." British Journal of Criminology 6: 170-182.

Jayewardene, C. H. S.
1973 "The death penalty and the safety of Canadian policemen." Canadian Journal of Criminology and Corrections 15: 356-366.

Jensen, Gary F.
1969 " 'Crime doesn't pay': correlates of a shared misunderstanding." Social Problems 17: 189-201.

Jesness, Carl F.
1974 Comparative Effectiveness of Behavior Modification and Transactional Analysis Programs for Delinquents. Report of the California Youth Authority, Sacramento.

Jew, Charles C., T. L. Clanon and Arthur L. Mattocks
1972 "The effectiveness of group psychotherapy in a correctional institution." American Journal of Psychiatry 129: 602-605.

Jones, Maxwell
1953 The Therapeutic Community. New York: Basic Books.

Juozapavicius, Gabija and Helen Wegessy
1974 A Study of the Probation Officers' Perceptions of the Use and Usefulness of Volunteers as Probation Officers in the Metropolitan Juvenile Court. Toronto: Ministry of Correctional Services.

Kassebaum, Gene, David Ward and Daniel Wilner
1971 Prison Treatment and Parole Survival. New York: Wiley.

Keech, J.
1962 Identifying and Controlling Delinquent Groups of Boys. The Laidlaw Foundation (brochure).

Kelly, Delos H. and William T. Pink
1973 "School commitment, youth rebellion, and delinquency." Criminology 10: 473-485.

Kelly, Francis J. and Daniel J. Baer
1971 "Physical challenge as a treatment for delinquency." Crime and Delinquency 17: 437-445.

Klein, John
1975 "Can we predict dangerousness?" A brief presented to the review board of the Calgary Police Commission on the December 20, 1974, shooting incident in the City of Calgary.

Klein, John
1976 "The dangerousness of dangerous offenders legislation: forensic folklore revisited." Canadian Journal of Criminology and Corrections 18: 109-122.

Klein, Malcolm W.
1969a "Gang cohesiveness, delinquency and a street worker program." Journal of Research in Crime and Delinquency 6: 135-166.

Klein, Malcolm W.
1969b "On the group context of delinquency." Sociology and Social Research 54: 63-71.

Klein, Malcolm W.
1971 Street Gangs and Street Workers. Englewood Cliffs N. J.: Prentice-Hall.

Klein, Malcolm, Solomon Kobrin, A. W. McEachern and Herbert Sigurdson
1971 "System rates: an approach to comprehensive criminal justice planning." Crime and Delinquency 17: 355-372.

Klein, Malcolm W.
1973 "Collaboration between practitioners and researchers: relevant knowledge in corrections." Federal Probation 37: 42-46.

Klein, Malcolm W.
1974 Personal correspondence.

Kobrin, Solomon
1959 "The Chicago area project—a 25-year assessment." Annals of the American Academy of Political and Social Science 322: 20-29.

Koenig, Daniel
1972 Review of The Silverlake Experiment. Sociology and Social Research 56: 396-397.

Kozol, Harry L., Richard J. Boucher and Ralph F. Garofalo
1972 "The diagnosis and treatment of dangerousness." Crime and Delinquency 18: 371-392.

Krause, Elliott A.
1966 "After the rehabilitation center." Social Problems 14: 197-206.

Krisberg, Barry
1975 Crime and Privilege: Toward a New Criminology. Englewood Cliffs, N.J.: Prentice Hall.

Lambert, Leah R. and Andrew C. Birkenmayer
1972 "An assessment of the classification system for placement of wards on training schools: II. Factors related to classification and community adjustment." Ministry of Correctional Services, Ontario.

Lambert, Leah R. and Patrick G. Madden
1974 The Vanier Centre for Women Research Report No. 1: an Examination of the Social Milieu. Ministry of Correctional Services, Ontario.

Lambert, Leah and Patrick Madden
1976 "The adult female offender: the road from institution to community life." Canadian Journal of Criminology and Corrections 18: 319-331.

LeBlanc, Marc
1973 "Théorie-recherche-pratique: une interaction à développer." Canadian Journal Of Criminology and Corrections 15: 13-24.

LeBlanc, Marc
1977 The Evaluation of Boscoville: A Comprehensive Research Model. Paper presented at the Seminar on Current Research in Criminal Justice in Canada, Canadian Association for the Advancement of Research in Crime and Criminal Justice. Calgary, July.

LeBlanc, Marc, Pier Angelo Achille, Maurice Cusson, and Jean Ducharme
1973 Evaluation de Boscoville. Research project prepared by the Groupe de recherche sur l'inadaptation juvenile, Université de Montréal.

LeDain, Gerald, Marie-Andrée Bertrand, Ian Campbell, Heinz Lehman, and Peter Stein
1972 Interim Report of the Commission of Inquiry into the Non-Medical Use of Drugs. Ottawa: Queen's Printer.

LeDain, Gerald, Marie-Andrée Bertrand, Ian Campbell, Heinz Lehman, and Peter Stein
1973 Final Report of the Commission of Inquiry into the Non-Medical Use of Drugs. Ottawa: Queen's Printer.

Lemert, Edwin M.
1971 Instead of Court: Diversion in Juvenile Justice. Rockville, Md.: National Institute of Mental Health.

Lepper, Mark and David Greene
1975 "Turning play into work: effects of adult surveillance and extrinsic rewards on children's intrinsic motivation." Journal of Personality and Social Psychology 31: 479-486.

Lepper, Mark, David Greene, and Richard Nisbett
1973 "Undermining children's intrinsic interest with extrinsic reward: a test of the 'overjustification' hypothesis." Journal of Personality and Social Psychology 28: 129-137.

Lerman, Paul
1968 "Evaluative studies of institutions for delinquents: implications for research and social policy." Social Work 13: 55-64.

Lerman, Paul
1971 "Child convicts." Trans-Action 8 (July-August).

Lerman, Paul
1975 Community Treatment and Social Control: A Critical Analysis of Juvenile Correctional Policy. Chicago, Illinois: University of Chicago Press.

Lewison, Edward
1974 "20 years of prison surgery: an evaluation." Canadian Journal of Otolaryngology 3: 42-50.

Lipton, Douglas, Robert Martinson, and Judith Wilks
1975 The Effectiveness of Correctional Treatment. New York: Praeger.

Logan, Charles H.
1972 "Evaluation research in crime and delinquency: a reappraisal." Journal of Criminal Law, Criminology, and Police Science 63: 378-387.

Longstreth, Langdon, Fred Stanley, and Roger E. Rice
1964 "Experimental evaluation of a high school program for potential dropouts." Journal of Educational Psychology 55: 228-236.

Los Angeles County Probation Department
1966 Reduction of Delinquency Through Expansion of Opportunity. A Proposal.

Mack, John A.
1956 Delinquency and the changing social pattern. Charles Russell Memorial Lecture. London.

Mackie, Marlene
1973 "Arriving at 'truth' by definition: the case of stereotype inaccuracy." Social Problems 20: 431-447.

Macnaughton-Smith, Peter
1976 Permission to Be Slightly Free. Ottawa: Law Reform Commission of Canada.

Magundkar, M. S. and Walter Saveland
1973 "Random-rounding to prevent statistical disclosures." Canadian Statistical Review.

Manitoba, Province of
1973 Manitoba Youth Centre Interim Program Outline.

Mann, W. E.
1967 Society Behind Bars. Toronto: [?].

Marks, Eli S., William Seltzer, and Karol J. Krotki
1975 Population Growth Estimation: A Handbook of Vital Statistics Measurement. Bridgeport, Connecticut: Population Council of New York and Key Book Service.

Marr, John N., Lawrence Lilliston, and Paul F. Zelhart
1974 "Using a token economy to teach the token economy." Professional Psychology (November): 440-445.

Martinson, Robert
1974a Personal correspondence.

Martinson, Robert
1974b "What works?—questions and answers about prison reform." The Public Interest 35: 22-54.

Martinson, Robert, Ted Palmer, and Stuart Adams
1976 Rehabilitation, Recidivism, and Research. Hackensack, New Jersey: National Council on Crime and Delinquency.

Mathews, Victor
1972 Socio-Legal Statistics in Alberta: A Review of their Availability and Statistics. Edmonton: Human Resources Research Council.

Mathiesen, Thomas
1974 The Politics of Abolition: Scandinavian Studies in Criminology. New York: Halsted Press.

Mattick, Hans W.
1974 Personal correspondence.

Mattick, Hans and Nathan Caplan
1962 The Chicago Youth Development Project. Chicago: Chicago Boys Clubs and Institute for Social Research, University of Michigan.

Mattick, Hans W. and Nathan S. Caplan
1964 The Chicago Youth Development Project. Ann Arbor: Institute for Social Research.

Mattick, Hans and Broderick Reischl
1975 Some Problems in the Evaluation of Criminal Justice Programs. Chicago: Center for Research in Criminal Justice, University of Illinois at Chicago Circle.

McClintock, F. H.
1961 Attendance Centres. London: Macmillan.

McCord, William and Joan McCord
1959 Origins of Crime. New York: Columbia University Press.

McCord, Joan, William McCord and Emily Thurber
1960 "The effects of foster home placement in the prevention of adult antisocial behavior." Social Service Review 34: 415-420.

McCord, Joan
1977 "Effects of client's age, sex of counselor, and rapport on the impact of treatment." Paper presented at the American Association of Psychiatric Services for Children, Washington, D.C.

McCorkle, Lloyd, Albert Elias and F. Lovel Bisby
1958 The Highfields Story. New York: Holt, Rinehart and Winston.

McDonald, Lynn
1969 "The principles of sentencing: a sociological critique." Unpublished paper.

McDonald, Lynn
1976 The Sociology of Law and Order. Montreal: Book Center.

McGrath, William T.
1976 "The juvenile and family courts." In W. T. McGrath (ed.), Crime and Its Treatment in Canada, 2nd Edition. Toronto: Macmillan of Canada.

McKee, J. A.
1971 "Learning rates and IQ's." Pacesetter 2: 27-31.

Mehaffey, T. D.
1973 "An introductory study to determine more effective matching of volunteer probation counsellors with probationers." University of Evansville, Indiana.

Merton, Robert K.
1938 "Social structure and anomie." American Sociological Review 3: 672-682.

Merton, Robert
1972 "Insiders and outsiders: a chapter in the sociology of knowledge." American Journal of Sociology 78: 9-47.

Meyer, Henry J., Edgar F. Borgatta and Wyatt C. Jones
1965 Girls at Vocational High. New York: Russel Sage Foundation.

Michelson, William
1970 Man and His Urban Environment. Don Mills: Addison-Wesley.

Miller, Walter B.
1958 "Lower class culture as a generating milieu of gang delinquency." Journal of Social Issues 14: 5-19.

Miller, Walter B.
1962 "The impact of a 'total-community' delinquency control project." Social Problems 10: 168-191.

Miller, Walter B.
1969 "White gangs." Trans-Action 6 (September): 11-26.

Miller, Walter B.
1974 "American youth gangs: past and present." in Abraham S. Blumberg (ed.), Current Perspectives on Criminal Behavior. New York: Alfred Knopf.

Miller, Walter B., Rainer C. Baum and Rosetta McNeil
1966 "Delinquency prevention and organizational relations." in Stanton Wheeler (ed.), Controlling Delinquents. New York: Wiley.

Mishel, W.
1968 Personality and Assessment. New York: Wiley.

Mohr, Hans
1976 Personal correspondence.

Moynihan, Daniel P.
1969 Maximum Feasible Misunderstanding. New York: Free Press.

Murphy, Brian C.
1972 A Quantitative Test of the Effectiveness of an Experimental Treatment Program for Delinquent Opiate Addicts. Research Centre Report 4. Ottawa: Solicitor General of Canada.

Murphy, Brian C.
1975 "Application of experimental, cost-benefit analysis to the evaluation of programmes to modify dangerous human behaviour." Unpublished paper.

Murphy, Brian and Martha Shinyei
1976 "Cons and straights: comparative free behaviour rates of 25 delinquents and 25 non-delinquents matched for age and legal occupation in British Columbia." Canadian Journal of Criminology and Corrections 18: 343-361.

Murphy, Brian, Martha J. Shinyei, Jeannette Murphy and Linda M. Irons
1973 British Columbia Federal Inmate Population Survey. Vancouver.

Murton, Thomas O.
1976 The Dilemma of Prison Reform. New York: Holt, Rinehart and Winston.

National Institute of Law Enforcement and Criminal Justice
1975 Volunteer Probation Counselor Program—An Exemplary Project. Summary from National Criminal Justice Reference Service.

Nettler, Gwynn
1970 Explanations. New York: McGraw-Hill.

Nettler, Gwynn
1972 "Knowing and doing." The American Sociologist 7: 3-7.

Nettler, Gwynn
1974 Explaining Crime. New York: McGraw-Hill.

Nettler, Gwynn
1976 Social Concerns. New York: McGraw-Hill.

New York City Youth Board
1960 Reaching the Fighting Gang. New York: New York City Youth Board.

Newman, Oscar
1972 Defensible Space. New York: Macmillan.

Notz, William
"Work motivation and the negative effects of extrinsic rewards." American Psychologist 30: 884-891.

Ohlin, Lloyd, Robert Coates and Alden Miller
1974 "Radical correctional reform: a case study of the Massachusetts Youth Correctional System." Harvard Educational Review 44: 74-111.

(Ontario) Planning and Research Branch
1975 Work-Study Programs in Two Ontario Training Schools. Toronto: Ministry of Correctional Services.

Oskamp, S.
1965 "Overconfidence in case-study judgments." Journal of Consulting Psychology 29: 261-265.

Outerbridge, William R.
1968 "The tyranny of treatment." Canadian Journal of Corrections 10: 378-387.

Outerbridge, William R.
1973 "Criminal justice in the seventies: in search of new perspectives on an old problem." Proceedings of the Canadian Congress of Criminology and Corrections 1973: Canadian Criminology and Corrections Association.

Palmer, Ted
1972 Differential Placement of Delinquents in Group Homes (Final Report). Sacramento: California Youth Authority and National Institute of Mental Health.

Palmer, Ted
1973a "The community treatment project in perspective: 1964-1973. Youth Authority Quarterly 26: 1-22.

Palmer, Ted
1973b "Matching worker and client in corrections." Social Work 18: 95-103.

Parlett, T. A. A.
1974 The Development of Attitudes and Morality in Adult Offenders. Unpublished Ph.D. Dissertation, University of Victoria, B.C.

Parlett, T. A. A.
1975 Personal correspondence.

Parlett, T. A. A. and J. D. Ayers
1971 "The modification of criminal personality through massed learning by programmed instruction." Canadian Journal of Criminology and Corrections 13: 155-165.

Pease, K., P. Durkin, I. Earnshaw, D. Payne and J. Thorpe
1975 Community Service Orders: A Home Office Research Unit Report. London, England: Her Majesty's Stationery Office.

Persons, Roy
1967 "Relationship between psychotherapy with institutionalized boys and subsequent community adjustment." Journal of Consulting Psychology 31: 137-

Peters, Dorothea
1973 Richter im Dienst der Macht: Zur gesellschaftlichen Verteilung der Kriminalitaet. Stuttgart: Enke Verlag.

Pirs, Susan
1975 "Assessment of the probation volunteer program in metropolitan Toronto." Ministry of Correctional Services, Ontario.

Pitman, R., M. Strecker and C. Yip
1973 "Parents' perceptions of the effect of volunteers on juvenile probationers: a replication." Ministry of Correctional Services, Ontario.

Platt, Anthony M.
1969 The Child Savers. Chicago: University of Chicago Press.

Polk, Kenneth and Walter Schafer (eds.)
1972 Schools and Delinquency. Englewood Cliffs N.J.: Prentice-Hall.

Porter, John
1965 The Vertical Mosaic. Toronto: University of Toronto Press.

Powers, Edwin and Helen Witmer
1951 An Experiment in the Prevention of Delinquency: The Cambridge-Sommerville Study. New York: Columbia University Press.

Quinney, Richard
1970 The Social Reality of Crime. Boston: Little, Brown.

Quinsey, Vernon and Bruce Sarbit
1975 "Behavioural changes associated with the introduction of a token economy in a maximum security psychiatric institution." Canadian Journal of Criminology and Corrections 17: 177-182.

Raphael, D.
1976 'Review of the sociology of law and order.' Encounter 47: 85-88.

Ratner, Robert
1974 Final Evaluation of the Spring Street Project (mimeo).

Reasons, Charles
1974 "The politics of drugs: an inquiry in the sociology of social problems." Sociological Quarterly 15: 381-404.

Riviera, Ramon J., and James F. Short, Jr.
1967 "Significant adults, caretakers, and structures of opportunity." Journal of Research in Crime and Delinquency 4: 76-97.

Robison, James
1969 It's Time to Stop Counting. The California Prison, Parole, and Probation System. Technical Supplement No. 2, A Special Report to the Assembly.

Robison, James
1973 "Correction Research." Federal Probation 37: 59-61.

Robison, James
1974 "Correctional research." Federal Probation 38: 58-59.

Robison, James and Richard Bass
1970 Intensive treatment program (a summary of the evaluation). 1970 Annual Research Review of the California Department of Corrections.

Robison, James and Gerald Smith
1971 "The effectiveness of correctional programs." Crime and Delinquency 17: 67-80.

Robison, James and Paul Takagi
1968 Case Decisions in a State Parole System. Research Report No. 31. Sacramento: Department of Corrections.

Roethlisberger, Fritz J. and William J. Dickson
1939 Management and the Worker. Cambridge: Harvard University Press.

Ross, Bob and H. Brian McKay
1976 "Adolescent therapists." Canada's Mental Health 24: 15-17.

Rubin, B.
1972 "Prediction of dangerousness in mentally ill criminals." Archives of General Psychiatry 27: 397.

Rusch, George and Otto Kirchheimer
1939 Punishment and Social Structure. New York: Columbia University Press.

Rushen, Ruth and E. Farley Hunter
1970 The RODEO Model. A Report of the County of Los Angeles Probation Department.

Salasin, Susan
1973 "Experimentation revisited: a conversation with Donald T. Campbell." Evaluation 1: 7-13.

Sarri, R. C. and E. Selo
1974 "Evaluation process and outcome in juvenile corrections and musings on a grim tale." In P. O. Davidson (ed.), Evaluation of Behavioral Programs in Community, Residential, and School Settings. Winnipeg: Research Press Co.

Scarpitti, Frank and Richard Stephenson
1966 "The use of the small group in the rehabilitation of delinquents." Federal Probation 30: no pages on reprint.

Schaefer, H. H. and P. L. Martin
1969 Behavioral Therapy. New York: McGraw-Hill.

Scheff, Thomas J.
1964 "The societal reaction to deviance: ascriptive elements in the psychiatric screening of mental patients in a midwestern state." Social Problems 11: 401-413.

Schramm, W. T., J. Lyle, and E. B. Parker
1961 Television in the Lives of Our Children. Stanford: Stanford University Press.

Schumacher, Ernst
1973 Small Is Beautiful: Economics as if People Mattered. New York: Harper and Row.

Schur, Edwin
1973 Radical Non-intervention: Rethinking the Delinquency Problem. Englewood Cliffs N.J.: Prentice Hall.

Schwartz, Herman
1972 "Prisoners' rights: some hopes and realities." in A Program for Prison Reform. Final Report of the Annual Chief Justice Earl Warren Conference on Advocacy in the United States. Roscoe-Pound-American Trial Lawyers Foundation, Cambridge.

Schwartz, Michael
1966 "The sociologist in an unsuccessful delinquency prevention planning project." in Arthur Shostak (ed.), Sociology in Action. Homewood, Illinois: Dorsey Press.

Schwitzgebel, Ralph K. and Daniel J. Baer
1967 "Intensive supervision by parole officers as a factor in recidivism reduction of male delinquents." Journal of Psychology 67: 75-82.

Scott, Robert A.
1967 "The selection of clients by social welfare agencies: the case of the blind." Social Problems 14: 248-257.

Seckel, Joachim P.
1965 Experiments in Group Counseling in Two Youth Authority Institutions, Research Report No. 46. Sacramento: California Youth Authority.

Seckel, Joachim P.
1974a "Forestry camp studies." in Keith S. Griffiths and Gareth S. Ferdun (eds.), A Review of Accumulated Research. Sacramento: California Youth Authority.

Seckel, Joachim P.
1974b "Individual and group counseling programs." in Keith S. Griffiths and Gareth S. Ferdun, (eds.), A Review of Accumulated Research. Sacramento: California Youth Authority.

Shaw, Clifford R. and Henry D. McKay
1942 Juvenile Delinquency and Urban Areas. Chicago: Chicago University Press.

Shoham, Shlomo and Moshe Sandberg
1964 "Suspended sentences in Israel: an evaluation of the preventive efficacy of prospective imprisonment." Crime and Delinquency 10: 74-83.

Shoham, Shlomo, Sarah Ben-David and Jonathan Smilansky
1971 "Rehabilitation treatment in institutions for juvenile delinquents in Israel." Abstracts on Criminology and Penology 11: 1-8 (Pages refer to reprint).

Short, James F. Jr. and Fred L. Strodtbeck
1965 Group Process and Gang Delinquency. Chicago: University of Chicago Press.

Simpson, Jon E. and Maurice D. Van Arsdol, Jr.
1967 "Residential history and educational status of delinquents and nondelinquents." Social Problems 15: 25-40.

Smart, R. G., D. Fejer and W. J. White
1973 "Medical use of drugs: trends in drug use among Metropolitan Toronto high school students." Addictions 20: 62-72.

Spender, Carol and John Berecochea
1971 Vocational Training at the California Institute for Women. Research Report No. 41. Sacramento: Department of Corrections.

Steadman, Henry
1972 "The psychiatrist as a conservative agent of social control." Social Problems 20: 263-271.

Steadman, Henry and Joseph Cocozza
1975 "We can't predict who is dangerous." Psychology Today 8 (January): 32-35.

Steadman, Henry and G. Keveles
1972 "The community adjustment of the Baxstrom patients: 1966-1970." American Journal of Psychiatry 129: 80-86.

Stoller, R. J. and R. H. Geertsma
1965 "The consistency of psychiatrists' clinical judgments." Journal of Nervous and Mental Disease 137: 58-66.

Stratton, John and Robert Terry
1968 Prevention of Delinquency: Problems and Programs. New York: Macmillan.

Street, David, Robert Vinter and Charles Perrow
1966 Organization for Treatment. New York: The Free Press.

Struening, Elmer and Marcia Guttentag
1975 Handbook of Evaluation Research (2 vols.). Beverly Hills, California: Sage.

Sullivan, Clyde E. and Wallace Mandell
1967 Restoration of Youth Through Training. New York: Wakoff Research Center.

Sullivan, C. E., M. Q. Grant and J. D. Grant
1957 "The development of interpersonal maturity: applications to delinquency." Psychiatry 20: 373-385.

Suttles, Gerald D.
1968 The Social Order of the Slum. Chicago: University of Chicago Press.

Szasz, Thomas S.
1970 The Manufacture of Madness. New York: Dell.

Taft, R.
1955 "The ability to judge people." Psychological Bulletin 52: 1-28.

Takagi, Paul T.
1969 "The effect of parole agents' judgments on recidivism rates." Psychiatry 32: 192-199.

Taylor, Ian, Paul Walton and Jock Young
1973 The New Criminology. London: Routledge and Kegan Paul.

Teilmann, Kathie, Malcolm Klein and Joseph Styles
1975 "The diversion explosion." Paper presented to Special Session on Diversion, Pacific Sociological Association, Victoria, B.C.

Termerlin, M. K.
1970 "Diagnostic bias in community mental health." Community Mental Health Journal 6: 110-117.

Thomson, G. M., Sherrie Barnhorst and Richard Barnhorst
1975 The Frontenac Diversion Programme. Kingston: Frontenac Family Court.

Thrasher, Frederic M.
1927 The Gang. Chicago: University of Chicago Press.

Tittle, Charles R. and Alan R. Rowe
1973 "Moral appeal, sanction threat, and deviance: an experimental test." Social Problems 20: 488-498.

Toby, Jackson
1965 "An evaluation of early identification and intensive treatment programs for predelinquents." Social Problems Vol. 13 160-175.

Toby, Jackson
1971 Contemporary Society. New York: Wiley.

Toby, Jackson
1974 "Is punishment necessary?" Journal of Criminal Law, Criminology and Police Science 55: 332-337.

Truax, Charles B., Donald G. Wargo and Leon D. Silver
1966 "Effects of group psychotherapy with high adequate empathy and nonpossessive warmth upon female institutionalized delinquents." Journal of Abnormal Psychology 71: 267

Ubell, Earl
1962 New York Herald Tribune. June 3.

Vinter, Robert, Theodore Newcomb and Rhea Kish (eds.)
1976 Time Out: A National Study of Juvenile Correctional Programs. Ann Arbor, Michigan: National Assessment of Juvenile Corrections.

Waldo, Gordon and Theodore Chiricos
1972 "Perceived penal sanction and self-reported criminality: a neglected approach to deterrence research." Social Problems 19: 522-540.

Waller, Irwin
1974 Men Released from Prison. Toronto: University of Toronto Press.

Waller, Irwin and Janet Chan
1974 "Prison use: a Canadian and international comparison." Criminal Law Quarterly 17: 47-71.

Walsh, Richard
1976 "Researcher-participant collaboration in corrections research: a case study." Canadian Journal of Criminology and Corrections 18: 387-400.

Warren, Marguerite Q.
1969 "The case for differential treatment of delinquents." The Annals of the American Academy of Political and Social Science 381: 47-59.

Warren, Marguerite Q.
1971 "Classification of offenders as an aid to efficient management and effective treatment." Journal of Criminal Law, Criminology, and Police Science 62: 239-258.

Warren, Marguerite Q.
1977 "Differential intervention with juvenile delinquents." Chapter from forthcoming book.

Weeks, H. Ashley
1958 Youthful Offenders at Highfields. Ann Arbor: University of Michigan Press.

Weidman, Donald R., John D. Waller, Dona MacNeil, Francine L. Tolson and Joseph S. Wholey
1975 Intensive Evaluation for Criminal Justice Planning Agencies. Washington, D.C.

Weiss, Carol H.
1970 "The politicization of evaluation research." Journal of Social Issues 26: 57-68.

Weiss, Carol H.
1973 "Where politics and evaluation research meet." Evaluation 1: 37-45.

Weiss, Robert S. and Martin Rein
1969 "The evaluation of broad-aim programs: a cautionary case and a moral." Annuals of the American Academy of Political and Social Science 385: 133-142.

Wenk, Ernst. A., James O. Robison, and Gerald W. Smith
1972 "Can violence be predicted?" Crime and Delinquency 18: 393-402.

Wheeler, Stanton
1961 "Socialization in correctional communities." American Sociological Review 26: 699-712.

Wheeler, Stanton, Edna Bonacich, Richard Cramer and Irving Zola
1966 "Agents of delinquency control." in Stanton Wheeler (ed.), Controlling Delinquents. New York: Wiley.

Whitehead, P. C. and R. G. Smart
1972 "Validity and reliability of self-reported drug use." Canadian Journal of Criminology and Corrections 14: 1-7.

Wilgosh, Lorraine
1973 "A study of group home placements as a possible correction of delinquent behaviour." Canadian Journal of Criminology and Corrections 15: 100-108.

Wilkins, Leslie T.
1960 Delinquent Generations. Home Office Research Unit Report #3 in Studies in the Causes of Delinquency and the Treatment of Offenders. London: Her Majesty's Stationery Office. Portions reprinted in Marvin E. Wolfgang, Leonard Savitz, and Norman Johnston (eds.), 1962, The Sociology of Crime and Delinquency. New York: Wiley.

Wilkins, Leslie
1969 Evaluation of Penal Measures. New York: Random House.

Wilks, Judith and Robert Martinson
1976 "Is the treatment of criminal offenders really necessary?" Federal Probation 40: 3-9.

Wilson, James Q.
1975 Thinking About Crime. New York: Basic Books.

Wolfgang, Marvin E., Robert M. Figlio and Thorsten Sellin
1972 Delinquency in a Birth Cohort. Chicago: University of Chicago Press.

Yablonsky, Lewis
1962 The Violent Gang. New York: Macmillan.

Yonge, Keith
1969 Personal statement by the president of the Canadian Psychiatric Association. Edmonton Journal. November 21.

Ziskin, J.
1969 Coping with Psychiatric and Psychological Testimony. Beverly Hills, California: Law and Psychology Press.

Zivan, Morton
1966 "Youth in trouble: a vocational approach." Final Report of a Research and Demonstration Project. Dobbs Ferry, N.Y., Children's Village (citation taken from Martinson, 1974).

Subject Index

Name Index